Parisian
HOME COOKING

Parisian

HOME COOKING

Conversations, Recipes,
and Tips from the Cooks
and Food Merchants
of Paris

MICHAEL ROBERTS

PHOTOGRAPHS BY PIERRE-GILLES VIDOLI

WILLIAM MORROW AND COMPANY, INC. • NEW YORK

Library of Congress Cataloging-in-Publication Data

Roberts, Michael, 1949–
    Parisian home cooking : conversations, recipes, and tips from the
cooks and food merchants of Paris / Michael Roberts.
        p.   cm.
    Includes index.
    ISBN 0-688-13868-3
    1. Cookery, French.   2. Cookery—France—Paris.   I. Title.
TX719.R588   1999   98–41750
641.5944—dc21   CIP

Printed in the United States of America

First Edition

1   2   3   4   5   6   7   8   9   10

BOOK DESIGN BY DEBORAH KERNER

www.williammorrow.com

In appreciation

of all

my Parisian friends

Acknowledgments

This book is the result of a few years' worth of shopping, cooking, dining, and discussing cooking and recipes with friends and acquaintances in Paris, among them Jean-Loup Champion, Pierre Piacentini, Giselle and Claude Rummel, Philippe Gautier, Hubert Legall, Jean-François Ferrandiz, Deborah Irmas, Jane Sigal, Corinne Megy, Charlotte Gardère, Babette Hullin, Odile Bernard-Schröder, Agnès and Hubert Matignon, Claude Deloffre, la famille Perrier, la famille Beltrans, Eric Busch, Suzy and Philippe Dubot, Sylvaine Lacoste, Jacques Bibonne, my cousins Huguette and Guido Prischi, Phielomena Nowlin, Peter Goss, Ron Stefano, Erna Jacquillat, and Mary and Philip Hyman. In the markets, I was fortunate enough to chat with many Parisian cooks, nearly all of whom remain anonymous, as well as merchants—Dominique Angelillo, Jean-Pierre Lesfolle, Michel Arras, Karin Lespoque, Monsieur Dambert, Monsieur Ducheval, Monsieur Zamba, Jean-Claude Desormeau, Michel Felten, Jean-Pierre Ducotte, Patrick Hayée, André Martin, the crew at Daguerre Mares and Didier Bertrand, as well as many others who remain anonymous to me. At l'École Supérieure de Cuisine Ferrandi, Gabriel Bousquet, Alain Paton; and my cooking professor Roger Lallemand. Infinite thanks to my dear friend Nicole Conte for being there, and to Martin Hyland; the recipe testers, all talented cooks, Nancy Jackson, Edward Cella, and Mark Haggard. Also in Los Angeles, Marysa Maslansky. Some of these recipes first appeared on the menu of Twin Palms Restaurant. Special thanks to the staff at William Morrow, Judith Sutton for copyediting, Deborah Kerner, who designed the book, Ann Cahn, Karen Lumley, Christy Stabin, and especially my editor, Justin Schwartz; my agents, Maureen and Eric Lasher; and Ann Bramson, who always believed in this project. Very special thanks to my friend Pierre-Gilles Vidoli, who photographed Paris with me and who shares a passion for things *culinaire;* and Daniel Adams for his loving support and hearty appetite.

Contents

Les Petits Plats — Les Soupes, les Oeufs, les Salades, les Petits Plats de Légumes, et les Gratins

Small Dishes—Soups, Egg Dishes, Salads, the Vegetable Course, and Gratins 26

And soon, mechanically, dispirited after a dreary day with the prospect of a depressing morrow, I raised to my lips a spoonful of the tea in which I had soaked a morsel of the cake. No sooner had the warm liquid mixed with the crumbs touched my palate than a shudder ran through me and I stopped, intent upon the extraordinary thing that was happening to me. An exquisite pleasure had invaded my senses, something isolated, detached, with no suggestion of its origin. And at once the vicissitudes of life had become indifferent to me, its disasters innocuous, its brevity illusory—this new sensation having had on me the effect which love has of filling me with a precious essence; or rather the essence was not in me it was me. I had ceased to feel mediocre, contingent, mortal. Whence could it have come to me, this all-powerful joy?

— MARCEL PROUST

Parisian

HOME COOKING

Paris Retrouvé

Bringing Paris Home

ooking at home? It's not the first thought that comes to mind when one thinks of Paris. It certainly was not what I was thinking about when I went to Paris to study cooking at Centre Jean-Ferrandi, the professional school for chefs. I was interested in the glories of French cuisine, which I believed existed only in the kitchens of two- and three-star restaurants. To me, Paris was one big restaurant, cooking an art, and dining its apogee. Lost as I was in some naïve illusion, completely oblivious to the way most Parisians lived, it never occurred to me to explore how Parisians cooked and ate at home, or even that they did. After all, people only ate at home because they couldn't get reservations, right? The city's shopping streets and open-air food markets were just part of the color, yet another of Paris's charms. I was a student. I had the arrogance of youth. I had listened to *La Bohème* too many times.

More recently, during a long visit after some years' absence, I discovered a Paris that had eluded me during my student days, and to which shopping, cooking, and dining at home are central. At dinner parties, in restaurants, whenever Parisians sit down to table, they talk about food, about a new shop they've discovered, the talent of the local cheeseman, where to find forest mushrooms, or how to prepare a perfect omelette. When they discuss the pending European Union, what worries them is the effect the new standards will have

Rustic country loaves in the window of Poilâne, rue du Cherche-Midi, 6th arrondissement

on farm production of cheese in France. They're less worried about American sitcoms polluting their airways than they are about the insidious effects that *les fasts* have on the sanctity of dinnertime. When they complain about the deterioration of culture, what's highest on their list is the way people don't cook as much or as well as in years past. Gossip? They exchange recipes like courtesans sharing confidences. Food is allegory for all that's good or bad. The realization that I had learned to cook but not to nourish, that I hadn't grasped the gastronomic world of the average Parisian, disheartened me. So, I returned several times for long stays, to live *à la parisienne,* to shop, to cook, to eat, to renew myself, to indulge my favorite pleasures among people who valued them more than I.

My old friends, who once had combed the flea markets at Porte de Vanves and Porte de Montreuil for the perfectly *immonde* clothing accessory that would, for twenty-five francs, turn them into fashion *provocateurs,* were now combing the neighborhood food markets for a freshly dug head of garlic, not yet dry, to prepare *poulet de Bresse à l'ail nouveau.* They traveled across Paris to buy a lemon tart at Christian Constant. They bought their veal on Saturday morning in the *marché biologique,* the organic market on the Boulevard Raspail. They had joined the legion of Parisians eating white asparagus nearly every day from mid-April to late June, when it disappears for another year. They were aware that French scallops, protected from harvesting during their reproductive months, are only available from October to May, and they prepare them with fall and winter accompaniments or the first vegetables of spring. The gray light and damp drizzle of winter are not so dreary, because they're the color of the oysters fished out of the sea in Brittany. New Year's Eve no longer meant dancing until dawn, but getting home by one A.M. for a bowl of steaming *soupe à l'oignon* and a *coupe de champagne,* the year's first meal. Tuna appears in the markets at the end of April, when the days start to become long again—large fierce-looking fish with tough, silvery skin and deep red meat the color of thick Roussillon wine. They prepare it *à la provençale,* and it reminds them that the summer holiday is not far off, that they might do well to begin searching for a house to rent by the sea.

*B*eyond the fact that the intervening years had brought careers and family to my formerly street-chic set of friends, it was as if a yet-to-be-discovered gene that causes "French" had activated. I had forgotten (or perhaps had failed to distinguish from other qualities that make my French friends French) that all life's occurrences, major or minor, happy or sad, somehow involve sitting down to a meal and some wine, that an appreciation of food is central to the French cultural identity. Charentes butter, Bresse chickens, Agen prunes, Normandy apples, Niçoise olives, Roquefort cheese—the list goes on—are all part of the French patrimony, like the Eiffel Tower or the

Arc de Triomphe or pasteurization or Johnnie Halliday. The art of cooking is a proud occupation, not only for the star chef in the place Vendôme, but for the young matron in Passy, the bachelor in Saint-Germain-des-Prés, and the concierge in Belleville.

*I*n the markets, I found superior ingredients, full of flavor. (And I remembered that our own great products go unappreciated by too many of us.) Vegetables, only a step away from the garden, picked at their peak of ripeness; whole fish brought to Paris straight from coastal ports; chickens that had been allowed to roam free and peck at the ground; meat from animals fed a diet of nutritious grains.

Two days a week I'd shop in the *marché volant,* one of the sixteen twice-weekly roving open-air markets around Paris. They operate from seven in the morning until two o'clock in the afternoon. Other days I'd shop on the *rue commerçante,* the shopping street in my neighborhood. The shops are open from eight in the morning until one o'clock, when they close for lunch; they reopen at four and close at seven-thirty. On Sundays, a favorite marketing day, everything closes at one in the afternoon, when people disappear for the family dinner and Paris becomes a still city. And everything except the *supermarché* and the local convenience store is closed all day Monday. Forget the schedule, and you don't eat very well.

Very quickly, I got to know the merchants, who taught me about their products, where they came from, how they arrived in the market, how to discern quality. I mingled with shoppers, talked about food and about cooking. We exchanged recipes. I got tips on how to make cooking less time-consuming. The sociability in the markets is infectious.

At home in my apartment, I'd empty my purchases from their little paper sacks and plan dinner, for I had gotten into the habit of inviting people around. It was the only feasible way to cook everything that I wanted to buy. And Parisians are excellent at reciprocating. Every invitation of mine was answered by another. So, not only did I end up in the market at least three days of the week, but as the weeks passed, I received more and more invitations to dine at the homes of other Parisians and saw how they cooked.

Invariably, dinner conversation would turn to shopping and cooking: You start with fine ingredients. You cook things in a way that coaxes out the flavors. No need to complicate a recipe with many ingredients, because they only end up fighting each other. The Parisian home cook and the Parisian star chef share the same principles of cooking, the same love of the table. Let the ingredients speak to you, tell you what to cook. Sit down with friends and family and savor the results of your efforts.

*P*arisians keep their everyday cooking simple and straightforward. They have to. Kitchens are small. They don't try to do too much, since few have the luxury of time. Parisian cooks, the women especially, cook in an offhanded manner, relying on intuition and experience, not worrying about a dish coming out perfectly. "Women attach less importance to appearance than to tradition, to long-simmering dishes like bouillabaisse," says Gisèle Berger, who has a restaurant in Clichy. "It's less method, more love." On the other hand, men approach cooking as if it were a problem to solve, an obstacle to overcome. They have the luxury of cooking on the weekend, and for them it's a hobby, not a

responsibility. Says Erna Jacquillat, a cooking teacher, "They follow recipes. Their cooking is methodical and their dishes are usually well presented and impressive. They have, after all, role models—the great French chefs, part of the national treasure of the country. I can look at a *mirepoix* [a finely chopped flavoring mixture of carrots, celery, and onions] and tell you the gender of the person who chopped it up."

I've learned as much about French food during the course of writing this book as I did as a cooking student. In the process, French food lost its mystique because it became an everyday way of cooking and eating for me. I understand haute cuisine better because I know where its roots are. Parisians appreciate the culinary inventions of their chefs because they are the mothers of invention. The charm of a French meal lies in their insistence on quality ingredients and balanced flavor, in respecting those ingredients by not overcomplicating the cooking, in the balance and variety of dishes that comprise the menu. The rules apply to all.

*T*ake a cue from Parisians and shop in different markets for different things. For household supplies and basic staples, take advantage of the supermarket. Stock your pantry and freezer with an emergency stash of family favorites. After all, no one, not even the most persnickety cook, not even the most careful eater, is perfectly organized. For people who work, convenience is a necessity, and for most of us, saving money a priority. So save time by shopping at the supermarket, and buy wisely, for quality can be found there. But take the time to spend your savings on really high-quality foods. Happily, for us Americans, there are ever more greenmarkets opening in cities around the country; there are organic growers and those who are rescuing heirloom varieties of tomatoes, potatoes, corn, and apples. While the variety doesn't rival that of the Parisian markets, we should support them. They'll only get better. Support cottage industries—the artisans who produce local handmade cheeses, the small family-owned dairies whose milk, cream, and butter have the flavor of the pasture, the growers who press their own olives, the fishmonger whose fish arrives fresh from the dock, the poultry rancher whose chickens roam at liberty, pecking at the ground, the ranchers of hormone-free veal and corn-fed cattle. Here in the States, the conduit between farm producers and market is not as developed as in France, but many of the artisans accept mail orders. Some cities, like Philadelphia and Seattle, have long had central markets, and there's a new breed of supermarket specializing in these products as well as in locally made pâtés, fruit preserves and jellies, honey, and condiments.

*M*ake marketing an adventure. After all, it's a wonderful kind of tourism. Shop the ethnic groceries and markets in your area. Chat with the shopkeepers. You'll discover a parallel universe of people and customs that you may not have realized existed. For instance, I buy fish and seafood in Japantown in my hometown of Los Angeles. The variety is always greater than at the supermarket or even my favorite seafood specialty shop. I find fresh eels for making a classic *matelote,* the red wine stew. There are periwinkles and other sea snails just like the *bigorneaux* and *bulots* I buy in Paris to put out with garlicky aïoli.

I buy fresh ducks, squab, quail, chicken, and capon in Chinatown. They're locally raised birds that have never seen the inside of a freezer. The skins have a matte finish, as if they've been slightly cured or dried. They become crisp, giving up their fat during cooking, which bastes the bird and protects the flesh, just like French birds.

In the neighborhood Italian grocery, I find olives, olive oil, anchovies, pasta, rice, and grating cheese. The Indian grocery is where I buy chickpea flour for making *socca,* a Niçoise crepe. It is also the source for the tiny lentils that I use for preparing

Madame Gautier's carrot and lentil terrine. In the Greek shops, I buy *tarama,* salted carp roe, for the whipped concoction that Parisians serve with the aperitif. Don't think that you need access to a French market or gourmet emporium to cook French food. What you need is access to fresh, high-quality ingredients. After all, they're the basis of all good meals, French or otherwise.

I worry that the joy of shopping for food is lost on most Americans, that it's a chore. People shop with lists and try to get it over with as quickly as possible. Why not browse the markets and buy what looks most appealing, most seasonally appropriate? Like Parisian cooks, go without a list, but with an idea for a kind of dish, and fill in the recipe ingredients with what looks brightest.

What's so impressive about Parisian home cooking is its naturalness. Mostly, Parisians rely on simple cooking techniques to prepare easy meals. They'll buy part of their dinner at the *traiteur,* or caterer/take-out shop—things like eggs in aspic, salmon mousse, a slice of pâté—that take too long to prepare. Then they'll prepare a quick-and-easy dish to serve. It's a shame to attempt a complicated recipe when you're rushed. But when you have the time, attempt something more challenging. Cooking should be a joy. Enjoy it as Parisians do. It's a worthwhile activity that enhances the day.

In the habits of the average Parisian—the daily routine of shopping for food, the careful way in which they vary menus, the time they take to share meals—the recipes and the dishes I've collected become something else; part of a rhythm, part of a synchronicity, part of the fabric that is Paris. If you think that good cooking takes time, that eating well is more difficult than simply eating, that sitting down to enjoy a meal has little value, I hope to change your mind.

When Marcel Proust dunked his madeleine into a cup of tea, unlocking the memory of his childhood, he experienced what most Parisians do nearly every time they sit down to table. For Parisians especially, a large part of the pleasures of the table lies in the nostalgia that it evokes and the tradition that it represents. For me, writing this book evoked the nostalgia of a couple of glorious youthful years spent in Paris. Now, having rediscovered Paris day to day, I've figured out how to bring Paris home.

L'Apéritif et
les Amuses-Gueules

Small Plates
to Whet the Appetite

*I*t's a little after seven o'clock and in the salon or *cuisine américaine* (open kitchen) of apartments all over the city, people are setting out platters of snacks—dried salami or a thick slice of pâté; a small jug of *rillettes,* pork or goose meat cooked in fat, then mashed to a spreadable delight; or *radis au beurre,* tiny, crunchy radishes served chilled and accompanied by soft butter and a little bowl of rock salt. Perhaps they've stopped at the *traiteur* for some bite-sized quiches, pizzas with tomatoes and anchovy, and an assortment of other little savories to warm in the oven.

For Americans, it's the six o'clock cocktail. In Paris, it's a glass of white or rosé wine, Champagne, or pastis at seven or eight o'clock in the evening along with small bites of food. This ritual, *l'heure d'apéritif,* whether with friends before going to a restaurant or with family, is a time to decompress from the day's travails. The food, usually salty and full-flavored, and the drink, normally slightly sweet or bitter, anticipate dinner, increasing rather than sating the appetite.

As one Parisian put it, *"L'apéritif, c'est ça.* Something to open the pores, the canals, the vessels of the body, letting down the defenses so that another mood seeps in."

Buying olives. Each bowl holds a different kind.

Acras | Senegalese Salt Cod Fritters

Every market in Paris has a stall or two selling prepared specialties from the former West African and Indochinese colonies. These Senegalese fritters—crispy curried nuggets of creamy salt cod—are sold in paper cones for munching while shopping, or to take home to serve with the aperitif. They're perfect to wash down with a kir royale, the lovely aperitif of Champagne sweetened with crème de cassis.

1/2 pound salt cod

2 tablespoons unsalted butter

2 tablespoons all-purpose flour

1/2 cup milk

1 teaspoon curry powder

1/8 teaspoon cayenne pepper

Pinch of freshly grated nutmeg

2 large egg yolks

Vegetable oil for deep-frying

1. Desalt the cod by soaking in a bowl of water for 36 to 48 hours, refrigerated, changing the water several times. Drain.

2. Place the cod in a pot of cold water, place over high heat, and bring to a boil. Reduce the heat and simmer for 5 minutes, or until the cod is falling apart. Drain the cod, place it in a mixing bowl, and mash well using two forks.

3. Melt the butter in a small saucepan over medium heat and whisk in the flour. Pour in the milk and cook, stirring with a wooden spoon, until the mixture thickens, about 1 minute. Remove from the heat and stir in the curry, cayenne, nutmeg, and yolks. Using a rubber spatula, transfer this mixture to the bowl of salt cod and mix together.

4. Heat a 2-inch depth of oil in a deep skillet over medium heat. When the oil is hot, drop tablespoon-sized balls of the cod mixture into the oil and fry until golden on all sides. Drain on paper towels. These can be kept warm in a 250°F oven until ready to serve (but no more than 45 minutes).

Acras

Gougères | Cheese Puffs

Gougères are traditional Burgundian snacks, but everyone in Paris, indeed all over France, makes them. They're simply choux paste nuggets flavored with cheese. These are best served hot from the oven, so divide the dough between two baking sheets. Bake and serve the first batch, then, about ten minutes later, put the second batch in to bake. Your *gougères* will be piping hot. They freeze well too.

1 cup milk

5 tablespoons (1 stick) unsalted butter

¼ teaspoon salt

Pinch of cayenne pepper

1 cup all-purpose flour

4 large eggs

¼ pound Gruyère cheese, grated

1 egg white, for brushing

1. Preheat the oven to 400°F.

2. Place the milk, butter, salt, and cayenne pepper in a deep saucepan and bring to a boil. Immediately remove from the heat. Pour in the flour and mix well with a wooden spoon. Return the saucepan to medium heat and cook, stirring, to dry the mixture, 2 to 3 minutes. The mixture is ready when it begins to form a ball and pulls away from the sides of the saucepan. Remove from the heat. Add the eggs one at a time and mix to incorporate; each one should be completely absorbed before the next one is added. This can be accomplished in a mixer. Mix in all but 2 tablespoons of the Gruyère.

3. Spoon or pipe tablespoon-sized mounds of batter onto ungreased cookie sheets, leaving about 2 inches between each one. Brush lightly with the beaten egg and dot the tops with the remaining cheese. Place in the oven, turn the oven down to 350°F, and bake until the *gougères* are puffed, crisp, and golden. Serve hot. *Gougères* can be reheated in a hot oven.

Tapenade | Black Olive Spread

Olives, anchovies, and capers—the main ingredients in tapenade—have their own characteristic flavors in addition to the sharp saltiness they share. Intense is the only way to describe this Provençal condiment, its black color warning that this is not a wallflower of a dip. I like it best spread on toasted bread and accompanied by crisp raw vegetables that cut the intensity—scallions, carrots, cauliflower, broccoli, and celery. It's also a favorite dip for chilled shrimp, crab, and lobster.

½ cup pitted black olives,
*   such as Kalamata*
2 cloves garlic
¼ cup drained capers

8 anchovy fillets
¼ cup fresh parsley leaves
3 tablespoons olive oil
2 tablespoons fresh lemon juice

Combine all the ingredients in a food processor or blender and process to a chunky paste. Transfer to a small serving bowl.

PARISIANS ALSO USE TAPENADE TO MAKE A SIMPLE PAN SAUCE FOR POULTRY OR FISH BY SWIRLING A SPOONFUL INTO THE PAN JUICES.

Cervelles d'Aubergine
Eggplant and Goat Cheese Caviar

MAKES 3 CUPS

Eggplant, the sponge of the vegetable kingdom, soaks up immense quantities of oil when you sauté slices of it. Roasting it whole in its skin changes its nature and the flesh makes a creamy, moist purée without the addition of oil. Mash it together with goat cheese, and you have something that resembles speckled white sea coral. Without the addition of goat cheese, these eggplant "brains" (or *cervelles*) are known as eggplant caviar. Whatever you call it, this is a divine spread to serve with little toasts.

1 large eggplant (about 1 1/4 pounds)
3 tablespoons olive oil
2 tablespoons minced shallots
1 tablespoon minced garlic

1 teaspoon fresh savory or thyme
1/4 cup goat cheese, softened
Salt and freshly ground black pepper

1. Preheat the oven to 400°F.
2. Poke a few holes in the eggplant with a fork or the tip of a knife and place it in a baking dish. Bake until the eggplant is completely shriveled and soft to the touch, about 50 minutes. Remove from the oven, slit one side of the eggplant lengthwise, and let stand for 5 minutes.
3. Cut the eggplant in half, scoop the seeds and flesh into a mixing bowl, and discard the skin. Mash the eggplant with a fork and set aside.
4. Heat the olive oil in a small saucepan over medium heat. Cook the shallots and garlic, without coloring, until soft, about 1 minute. Add to the eggplant. Add the savory or thyme and goat cheese and mix well to distribute the cheese evenly. Season with salt and pepper, cover, and refrigerate until well chilled, about 2 hours.

I'VE USED THIS DELICIOUS SPREAD TO FILL PASTA SHELLS, RAVIOLI, AND MANICOTTI. IT BAKES NICELY WHEN LAYERED WITH LASAGNA NOODLES. I'VE ALSO STUFFED TOMATOES WITH IT, BAKED THEM, AND SERVED THEM AS A FIRST COURSE, DRIZZLED WITH SOME VINAIGRETTE.

The cheese vendors buy
farm-made cheeses from
small producers.

Aïoli | Garlic Mayonnaise

Aïoli is both the heady garlic mayonnaise from Provence and the name of a main-course platter of boiled vegetables, served with salt cod, roast chicken, or boiled beef. In Paris, it's also an aperitif platter of carrot sticks, celery sticks, scallions trimmed of their green tops, tiny boiled new potatoes, and young, tender green beans. Here's how to make the famous mayonnaise into which everything is dipped.

6 cloves garlic, minced
1 large egg yolk
1 teaspoon salt

⅔ cup extra virgin olive oil
1 tablespoon fresh lemon juice

Mix the garlic, yolk, and salt together in a mixing bowl. Using a flexible wire whisk, whisk in the oil in a thin stream a little at a time, until it is completely absorbed and the aïoli has the consistency of a thick mayonnaise (which, of course, is what it is). Mix in the lemon juice. Let the aïoli sit, covered, for at least 15 minutes and up to 2 hours before serving to allow the garlic to "blossom." Don't refrigerate for more than 1 hour or the oil will congeal and break down the mayonnaise.

Taramasalata | Carp Roe Mousse

When you're invited for aperitifs in Paris, you can't avoid being served this purée of salted carp roe—it's as popular there as onion dip is in the States. All *traiteurs* prepare their own version, but everyone "doctors" the contents. Parisians feel it their obligation to add something of themselves to a store-bought preparation. These fish roes are intensely flavored—too fishy on their own for a tame, cultivated French palate—so slightly sour crème fraîche, chopped shallots, and a squeeze of lemon dilute the intensity of the roe and allow you to partake heartily of this intoxicating delicacy.

2 ounces tarama (salted carp roe)

1 tablespoon minced shallots

2 ounces cream cheese, at room temperature

2 tablespoons crème fraîche or sour cream, plus extra if needed

2 tablespoons extra virgin olive oil

2 tablespoons fresh lemon juice

Pinch of cayenne pepper

Crackers, toasts, or pita for serving

Combine all the ingredients in a food processor and purée until smooth and light in texture. If the purée seems too thick, add additional crème fraîche or sour cream by the tablespoon. Scrape the purée into a small serving bowl and accompany with crackers, toasts, or pita bread.

Rillettes de Porc | Potted Pork

This pork spread is the most popular "potted" meat in France. It's seasoned like a pâté with thyme, clove, and brandy, and then the meat cooks slowly until "fossilized" in its fat. Use a soft well-marbled cut from the shoulder or butt. It's best to prepare your *rillettes* a couple of days in advance and let the flavors develop in the refrigerator. Be sure to take the *rillettes* from the fridge two hours before serving to allow them to soften.

$1/2$ pound fatback, lard, or chicken fat

$1\,1/2$ pounds pork butt or shoulder

$1\,1/2$ teaspoons kosher salt

$3/4$ teaspoon dried thyme

$1/2$ teaspoon ground coriander

3 bay leaves

2 teaspoons freshly ground black pepper

$1/4$ teaspoon allspice

6 cloves garlic, crushed

$1/4$ cup brandy

$1/2$ cup water

Cornichon pickles and sliced baguette
   for serving

1. Cut the fatback, if using, and the pork butt into 1-inch cubes and place in dish with all the other ingredients except the water, the lard or chicken fat, and serving accompaniments. Cover and marinate overnight in the refrigerator.

2. The next day, preheat the oven to 300°F.

3. Transfer the contents of the dish to a Dutch oven. If you're using lard or chicken fat, add it to the marinated meat. Add the water, cover, and roast for 4 hours. Place the casserole over medium heat and boil off the liquid so that only the fat remains. Discard the bay leaves and garlic.

4. Transfer the meat to a mixer fitted with a paddle.

5. Running the mixer on low speed, break up the meat while slowly pouring in all but 3 tablespoons of the fat from the casserole. Pack the meat into a crock and press down to compact it. Pour the remaining fat over the surface and refrigerate overnight.

6. Remove the rillettes from the refrigerator and let sit at room temperature for 2 hours before serving. Accompany with cornichon pickles and rounds of fresh baguette.

Pork butchers, Marché Saxe-
Breteuil, 7th arrondissement

Escargots au Vin Rouge
Snails Braised in Red Wine

MAKES 6 TO 8 SERVINGS

The delightful thing about *escargots* is their ability to show off other flavors, although they actually do have a very subtle vegetal flavor of their own. If you like them broiled in garlic butter, you'll like this recipe with red wine sauce—all the favorite flavors are in here. Serve buttered bread with the snails and supply cocktail forks or picks for spearing them.

2 tablespoons minced shallots

2 tablespoons minced garlic

3 tablespoons unsalted butter

32 canned escargots, drained

1 tablespoon all-purpose flour

$^1\!/_4$ cup robust red wine, such as Merlot

1 teaspoon Pernod

$^1\!/_4$ teaspoon dried savory

1 teaspoon finely chopped fresh chervil

In a small skillet over medium heat, cook the shallots and garlic in 1 tablespoon of the butter until soft but not browned, about 1 minute. Add the *escargots,* sprinkle with the flour, and toss to mix the flour into the butter. Add the wine, Pernod, and savory, cover, and cook until the sauce thickens, about 2 minutes. Remove from the heat and whisk in the remaining 2 tablespoons butter. Pour into a small serving bowl, sprinkle with the chervil, and serve.

Rillettes de Saumon | Potted Salmon

The derivation of this relatively modern dish is not the country farm, where peasants developed *rillettes* as a way of preserving pork, duck, and goose through the long winter months. It's a Parisian restaurant variation on the theme, a marvelous spread, silky smooth and with great flavor. You can buy it at the *traiteur,* but many Parisians prepare it at home with leftover salmon. If you use cooked or drained canned salmon, omit the first step, but do bring the wine to a boil and simmer it to get rid of the alcohol, then proceed with the recipe.

½ pound skinless, boneless
  salmon fillets

3 tablespoons dry white wine, such as
  Sauvignon Blanc

½ pound smoked salmon, finely chopped

⅛ teaspoon freshly ground white pepper

Pinch of allspice

2 tablespoons unsalted butter

1 tablespoon olive oil

Croutons, toasts, or crackers for serving

1. In a small pot over medium heat, cook the salmon in the wine, covered, until cooked through, 7 to 10 minutes, depending on the thickness. Place the contents in a mixing bowl. Add the smoked salmon and the seasonings and mash together.

2. Melt the butter in a small saucepan and add the oil. Pour into the salmon mixture and mash with a fork to incorporate. Tightly pack the salmon mixture into a crock, cover, and chill for at least 4 hours before serving. Accompany with croutons, toasts, or crackers.

Salpicon de Crevettes | Potted Shrimp

MAKES 6 SERVINGS

Serve this chunky spread of minced shrimp on toast or in endive spears. Any left over can be tossed with pasta or rice, or melted and served as a sauce for poached fish.

2 tablespoons olive oil

12 jumbo shrimp, peeled and deveined

2 tablespoons minced shallots

1 teaspoon salt

1/4 teaspoon freshly ground black pepper

1/4 cup dry sherry

1/2 teaspoon dried thyme

6 tablespoons unsalted butter, at room temperature

1 tablespoon chopped fresh parsley

Toast points, crackers, or endive spears for serving

1. Heat the oil in a medium saucepan over medium heat. Add the shrimp, shallots, salt, and pepper and cook, tossing, for 1 minute. Add the sherry and thyme and cook for another 2 minutes. Remove the shrimp and set aside on a plate. Allow the liquid to boil down to a glaze, another 2 minutes or so, then scrape the glaze over the shrimp. Allow to cool to room temperature.

2. Transfer the shrimp to a food processor and add the butter and parsley. Pulse until the shrimp is chopped and incorporated into the butter. Scrape the contents of the processor into a serving bowl. Accompany with toast points, crackers, or endive spears.

Gâteau aux Foies de Volailles, Beurre Madère

Warm Chicken Liver Cake

MAKES 8 TO 10 SERVINGS AS AN APPETIZER

This liver "cake" is an astounding preparation, with the texture of a steamed bread pudding and a subtle liver flavor. Serve it warm to best appreciate the balance of thyme and Madeira with liver. It's perfect with both sweet and bitter aperitifs. Sliced leftovers can be gently sautéed in butter and served for lunch with salad.

1 tablespoon all-purpose flour

2 tablespoons fresh bread crumbs

3 large eggs

½ cup Madeira or dry sherry

¾ teaspoon salt, or more to taste

¼ teaspoon freshly ground black pepper, or more to taste

¼ teaspoon dried thyme

½ teaspoon baking powder

6 ounces chicken livers, trimmed

1 small onion, quartered

6 tablespoons milk

¼ cup heavy cream

4 tablespoons butter, cut up

1. Preheat the oven to 375°F. Grease a 3-cup small Bundt pan or round cake pan.

2. Place the flour and bread crumbs in a large mixing bowl and whisk in the eggs one at a time. Stir in ¼ cup of the Madeira, the salt, pepper, thyme, and baking powder.

3. Purée the livers and onion together in a food processor until smooth. Transfer to the mixing bowl and mix well. Stir in the milk and cream.

4. Pour the mixture into the prepared pan. Cover, place in a water bath with boiling water, and bake for 35 minutes, or until the center is firm to the touch. Remove the cake from the oven, remove from the water bath, and set aside for 5 minutes.

5. Meanwhile, bring the remaining ¼ cup Madeira to a boil in a small saucepan and boil for 1 minute. Remove the saucepan from the heat and whisk in the butter. Add salt and pepper as desired.

6. To serve, unmold the cake onto a serving platter and pour the sauce in over the center.

Les Petits Plats — Les Soupes, les Oeufs, les Salades, les Petits Plats de Légumes, et les Gratins

Small Dishes—Soups, Egg Dishes, Salads, the Vegetable Course, and Gratins

I eat everything, just not all the time. If I did, I'd be the size of the Arc de Triomphe." Like many Parisians, my old friend Philomena is a gourmand. "During the week I have a fairly large lunch, at about one or one-thirty. But our main meal of the day is dinner, which we sit down to at eight-thirty or nine o'clock, after our aperitifs. It's the main meal not because it's more serious dining, but because we (my husband and I) share it with each other and, when they were young, with the children. Often I serve small dishes. It may be some *mousse de foie,* followed by an omelette, then cheese and salad, and perhaps a *compote d'abricots.* It's a lighter meal than lunch, unless we're having people in for dinner or going out to a restaurant. Eating a variety of things satisfies the senses with lots of textures and tastes. You see how it is, Mick? When you eat many delicious things, you only want to eat a little of each one. Boring food, that's the culprit. You eat and eat and eat, hoping, waiting for the moment of satisfaction that never comes.

"We don't spend thirty minutes at the table, but, rather, more than an hour. We take our time, savor the pleasure. *Nous regalons de nos dîners* [we feast], even though dinner may be an omelette."

Small dishes are among the most traditional recipes in the Parisian cook's repertoire, the core of the everyday cuisine. I cannot tell you that the small dishes you'll find in this section are always eaten at lunch or at dinner, or even that they're either first or second courses. For a Parisian, they may be any of these.

Chanterelles come to the market in the fall.

Les Soupes
Soups

*P*arisians love soup for lunch or dinner, and I quickly got into the habit of making it. A day that I had planned to stay home to write or read was often a soup day. I'd go to the market early in the morning, come back to the apartment, and cook my soup in a heavy orange ceramic pot. I was reassured knowing that there was soup on the stove, that I could stop at any time and have a bowl. I'd think, "Soup is something you don't mind eating alone."

On Thursdays, when the Louvre stays open late, I'd prepare a soup in the afternoon before going with friends. "Come to my place for soup," and it would be waiting for us when we got back to the apartment. We'd begin with a plate of charcuterie, then have our soup, followed by a green salad and cheese.

Garbure
Cabbage, Bean, and Winter Vegetable Soup

MAKES 4 TO 5 SERVINGS

The ingredients for this soup are found year-round, but this is really a late autumn and winter main course, robust and heavy with vegetables. Most Parisians use *rillons,* a salted pork made from boneless rib ends, for flavor, and moisten the soup with water. To give the soup its traditional flavor in the States, a small ham hock will suffice. A pig's tail or calf's foot, if you have one, adds a gelatinous richness.

1 tablespoon unsalted butter

½ small onion, finely diced

½ small carrot, finely diced

½ medium turnip, finely diced

1 stalk celery, finely diced

5 cups water

½ cup dried white beans, soaked in water overnight and drained

1 small ham hock

4 bay leaves

2 teaspoons ground sage

1 teaspoon freshly ground black pepper

1 small new potato, peeled and thickly sliced

¼ head green cabbage, thinly sliced

¼ pound green beans, cut into ¼-inch rounds (½ cup)

Salt

4 to 5 slices French bread

1. Melt the butter in a soup pot over medium heat. Cook the onion, carrot, turnip, and celery, stirring occasionally, until softened, about 5 minutes. Add the water, beans, ham hock, bay leaves, sage, and pepper, cover the pot, and increase the heat to high. When the liquid comes to a boil, reduce the heat and let simmer gently for 45 minutes.

2. Add the potato and cabbage and continue to simmer for another 30 minutes. Add the green beans and cook for another 15 minutes. Add salt to taste.

3. To serve, remove the ham hock from the soup, remove the meat from the bone, chop it and replace in the soup. Discard the bone. Pour the soup into a tureen or individual bowls. Place the bread on top and bring to the table.

Potage à la Soissonnaise

White Bean Soup

MAKES 5 TO 6 SERVINGS

The white beans from the region of Soisson are famous for their small size and creamy texture. If you can find fresh navy or Great Northern beans in the market, by all means use them. If not, any dried white bean will give an excellent result. I like using cannellini beans because they fall to bits and give the porridgy texture for which this soup is known. Use water and wine for the broth, and, if you like, add a chicken bouillon cube for strength, as many Parisians do. The important ingredient is the bacon, added for its smoky flavor. Parisians rarely cook beans without it.

$1/4$ pound bacon, finely diced

2 tablespoons unsalted butter

1 medium onion, roughly chopped

2 medium carrots, peeled and
    roughly chopped

1 small turnip, peeled and
    roughly chopped

2 stalks celery, finely diced

2 cups dry white wine, such as
    Sauvignon Blanc

5 cups water

1 chicken bouillon cube, optional

$1/2$ cup dried cannellini beans,
    soaked for 2 hours

3 bay leaves

2 teaspoons fresh marjoram leaves
    or 1 teaspoon dried

1 teaspoon freshly ground white pepper

Salt

Crème fraîche or sour cream for serving

1. Combine the bacon and butter in a large pot, place over medium heat, and cook for 2 minutes, stirring. Add the onion, carrots, turnip, and celery and cook, stirring occasionally, until the vegetables are soft, about 5 minutes.

2. Pour in the white wine, increase the heat to high, and bring to a boil. Add the water, bouillon cube, beans, bay leaves, marjoram, and pepper. Cover the pot and bring the liquid back to a boil, then lower the heat and let the soup simmer for 1½ hours, or until the beans are falling apart. Taste for salt and add as desired.

3. Retrieve and discard the bay leaves, pour the soup into a tureen, and serve piping hot, accompanied by a bowl of crème fraîche or sour cream.

Dads shop, too.

Soupe Parisienne | Leek and Potato Soup

Leeks and potatoes are so often cooked together that, in my mind's palate, they've begun to taste similar, and whenever I taste a leek or potato alone, I sense the phantom taste of the missing ingredient. When you prepare this soup, you'll see what I mean: Leeks and potatoes were meant to be cooked together. Use a waxy new potato, such as red or White Rose, for this soup. Diced, as they must be for the soup, they don't fall apart.

1 large leek (about 3/4 pound)

2 bay leaves

1 teaspoon dried thyme

8 peppercorns

1 tablespoon unsalted butter

2 strips bacon, finely chopped

1 cup dry white wine, such as Sauvignon Blanc

4 cups water, Homemade Chicken Broth (page 237), or low-sodium chicken or vegetable broth

1 pound large new potatoes, peeled and cut into 1/8-inch dice

1/2 teaspoon salt, or to taste

1/2 cup crème fraîche or heavy cream

2 tablespoons chopped fresh chives

1. Trim off the green part of the leek and tie the greens, bay leaves, thyme, and peppercorns in a square of cheesecloth. Halve the white of the leek lengthwise, then cut into thin 1/4-inch half-moons. Wash well to rid the leek of sand.

2. Melt the butter in a soup pot over medium heat, add the leek and bacon, and cook for 5 minutes, stirring occasionally. Add the wine and simmer for 1 minute to burn off the alcohol. Add the water, potatoes, salt, and cheesecloth packet, cover, increase the heat to high, and bring to a boil. Reduce the heat and simmer for 20 minutes until the potatoes are tender. Remove from the heat and stir in the crème fraîche or cream.

3. To serve, pour the soup into a tureen or individual bowls and sprinkle with the chives.

What is he going to do with all those leeks?

Soupe aux Deux Choux
Sauerkraut and Brussels Sprout Soup

MAKES 4 TO 5 SERVINGS

You'll be surprised by how mellow the sauerkraut flavor is in this lovely soup. It's a fine winter meal whose origins are in Alsace, the region along the German border. The woman who shared this recipe adds quartered Brussels sprouts to a traditional sauerkraut soup, and then floats a few uncooked leaves as decoration. I've served this soup with a poached egg and a dollop of sour cream, making it a kind of French white borscht, and it gets raves. Accompanied by a bottle of Alsatian wine, it's like a re-creation of a memorable brasserie meal at home.

8 Brussels sprouts

1 tablespoon unsalted butter

4 slices bacon, chopped

1 medium onion, finely diced

1 cup drained sauerkraut,
   roughly chopped

1 cup dry white wine, such as
   Sauvignon Blanc

4 cups Homemade Chicken Broth
   (page 237), low-fat chicken or
   vegetable broth, or water

1 medium potato (about ½ pound),
   peeled and diced

2 bay leaves

2 teaspoons salt

Freshly ground black pepper

½ cup crème fraîche or sour cream

1. Remove and discard the 4 outermost leaves of each Brussels sprout and trim the bottoms. Carefully remove 3 more leaves from each sprout and reserve. Quarter the sprouts and set aside.

2. Melt the butter in a soup pot over medium heat, add the bacon and onion, and cook for 5 minutes, stirring occasionally. Add the sauerkraut and cook for another 5 minutes, stirring occasionally. Add the wine and let cook for 1 minute to burn off the alcohol. Add the broth, potato, bay leaves, and salt and pepper. Cover and bring to a boil, then reduce the heat and simmer for 20 minutes. Add the Brussels sprouts and simmer for 20 more minutes. (The soup can be made ahead to this point and reheated just before serving.)

3. Stir in the crème fraîche, if using. Or, if you're using sour cream, place it in a bowl, stir in 1 cup of the hot soup, and then stir this mixture into the soup. Do not reheat the soup at this point, or the sour cream will curdle. Pour the soup into a tureen or individual bowls, float the reserved Brussels sprouts leaves on top, and serve immediately.

Potage Germiny

Cream of Sorrel Soup

Sorrel, sometimes called sour grass (don't confuse it with lemongrass, a different thing entirely), is mostly used for flavoring fish sauces or making soup. The occasional bold cook will add some chopped leaves to the salad bowl. Its flavor is unique, in that it's very sour without being at all acidic. I was seduced by its flavor early in my childhood by my grandmother's Russian borscht called *schav*. But, be forewarned—sorrel is a powerful leaf. In this soup, the sour sorrel is softened by mixing it with spinach. The soup, which is a vibrant green color, is fresh tasting and has an exciting marriage of salty and sour sensations.

3 tablespoons unsalted butter

1 medium onion, minced

2 cloves garlic, minced

3 tablespoons all-purpose flour

6 cups Homemade Chicken Broth (page 237) or low-sodium chicken or vegetable broth

1 pound spinach, washed and stems removed, or ½ pound leaves, and leaves finely chopped

1½ pounds sorrel, center ribs removed and leaves finely chopped (¾ pound leaves)

¾ cup crème fraîche or heavy cream

1 teaspoon salt

Freshly ground black pepper

1. Melt the butter in a soup pot over medium heat. Cook the onion and garlic until soft, about 5 minutes. Add the flour, stirring to form a paste, and cook for another minute. Slowly add the broth, then cover and increase the heat to high. When the broth comes to a boil, reduce the heat, remove the cover, and simmer, skimming the surface occasionally, for 25 minutes, or until the soup is reduced to about 4 cups.

2. Add the spinach, sorrel, and crème fraîche and cook for another 5 minutes. Add the salt and pepper to taste. Serve immediately.

Soupe aux Fanes de Radis
Cream of Radish Leaf Soup

MAKES 4 TO 5 SERVINGS

As so often happens, while impatiently waiting to be served at a stand in the market, I learn something new. One Sunday morning after my weekly traipse through the flea market in the Porte de Vanves, I was nonplussed to hear a greengrocer suggest to the woman in front of me that she save the leaves from her radishes for soup. Well, when it was my turn, I pointed at the radishes and directed the grocer to choose bunches with the smallest, brightest-green leaves. "I'm going to make soup," I said. He did not find this unusual and I wondered why, if this is a typical thing to do, I had never heard about it. So, I went home and made some radish soup, and it was wonderful. The radishes lose their volatility when cooked and become nearly, but not quite, sweet; but the leaves maintain that favorite radish flavor.

2 bunches radishes

2 tablespoons unsalted butter

1 large leek, white part only, sliced
    and well washed

4 cups low-sodium vegetable broth
    or water

½ pound White Rose potatoes, peeled
    and roughly diced (about 1½ cups)

Salt and freshly ground white pepper

½ cup crème fraîche or sour cream
    (optional)

1. Remove the radish tops. Pick through the radish leaves and discard any yellow or otherwise discolored ones. Trim off and discard the stems. Slice the radishes.

2. Place the butter, radishes, and leek in a soup pot over medium heat and cook until the vegetables are soft but not browned, about 7 minutes. Add the broth, potatoes, and salt and pepper as desired, cover, increase the heat to high, and bring to a boil.

Reduce the heat to medium and simmer for 20 minutes. Add the radish leaves and continue simmering, uncovered, for another 5 minutes.

3. Purée the soup in a blender or food processor and replace it in the pot. Taste for salt and pepper and add if necessary. Heat the soup until piping hot, add the crème fraîche, and serve immediately.

Rue d'Aligre on market day, 12th arrondissement

Soupe Purée à l'Orge au Beurre Foie de Volailles

Purée of Barley Soup with Chicken Liver Butter

MAKES 4 TO 6 SERVINGS

On a drizzly Saturday afternoon in January, we gathered for a game of bridge at a friend's apartment. We played all afternoon, stopping around four o'clock for this barley soup and a platter of cheese. I could not at first determine what the soup was, so accustomed am I to seeing this favorite of mine with whole grains of barley. Melting the liver butter into the soup was a last-minute improvisation—there happened to be some in the fridge.

2 teaspoons cooking oil

1 small onion, diced

1 stalk celery, finely sliced

1 carrot, peeled and diced

2 cloves garlic, peeled

1/2 cup pearl barley

4 cups Homemade Chicken Broth
   (page 237), low-sodium chicken or
   vegetable broth, or water

1 cup white wine

1 1/2 teaspoons salt

1/2 teaspoon freshly ground pepper

1/2 teaspoon dried savory

2 ounces chicken livers

1/4 cup Madeira

3 tablespoons butter,
   at room temperature

1 cup milk

1 tablespoon finely chopped fresh parsley

1. Heat the oil in a 3-quart pot over medium heat. Add the onion, celery, carrot, and garlic and cook, stirring, until soft but not browned, about 10 minutes. Add the barley, broth, wine, salt, pepper, and savory. Cover, reduce the heat to medium-low, and simmer until the barley is completely tender, about 1 hour.

2. Meanwhile, combine the livers and Madeira in a small saucepan, and cook over medium heat, uncovered, until the liver is medium, about 3 minutes. Remove from the heat and let cool to room temperature.

3. Transfer the contents of the saucepan to the bowl of a food processor or blender, add the butter, and process until smooth. Scrape into a bowl and set aside.

4. Process the soup in a food processor or blender until smooth, then pour back into the pot. Add the milk, cover, and reheat the soup over medium heat, stirring to prevent it from sticking to the bottom of the pot. Taste for salt and pepper and add as desired. Pour the soup into bowls, sprinkle with the parsley, and place a spoonful of the liver butter mixture in the center of each. Serve immediately.

Soupe à l'Oignon | Onion Soup

Nicole Conte rang me one afternoon. "Come for dinner. It's cold. I want to make you my *gratinée à l'oignon*." I was so happy when dinner came to the table—a tureen of caramel-colored liquid garnished with only a film of melted cheese. The soup cooks slowly to develop its flavor and texture. Half the onions are boiled until they virtually melt into the liquid, the other half are caramelized on the stovetop with no liquid. Then the two batches are married. Parmesan cheese and crumbled stale bread thicken the soup, and a subtle sprinkling of grated Gruyère veils the surface.

2 pounds medium yellow onions,
  finely chopped (about 6 cups)

5 cups low-sodium beef broth

2 bay leaves

2 sprigs fresh thyme or 1 teaspoon dried

1/4 teaspoon freshly grated nutmeg

2 teaspoons salt

Freshly ground black pepper

3 tablespoons unsalted butter

1/2 cup medium-dry sherry (optional)

3 tablespoons bread crumbs

1/4 cup freshly grated Parmesan cheese

1/4 cup grated Gruyère cheese

1. Place 3 cups of the onions in a soup pot with the broth, bay leaves, thyme, nutmeg, salt, and pepper. Cover and bring to a boil over high heat. Lower the heat to medium and simmer for 2 hours, or until the onions have completely fallen apart.

2. Meanwhile, melt 1 tablespoon of the butter in a small heavy skillet over low heat. Add the remaining onions and the sherry, if using, and cook, stirring occasionally, until the onions turn a dark golden color, about 1 hour.

3. Scrape the onions in the skillet into the soup pot, add the bread crumbs, and simmer, uncovered, over medium heat for 30 minutes. Remove the bay leaves and thyme.

4. Preheat the oven to 300°F.

5. Add the Parmesan cheese to the soup and simmer for another 5 minutes. Place six ovenproof soup bowls on a baking sheet, pour the piping-hot soup into the bowls, sprinkle with the Gruyère cheese, and place on a rack in the oven. Leave in the oven for 5 minutes to melt the cheese before serving.

Potage Saint-Germain | Split Pea Soup

Of the many versions of this popular soup, this one, with its abundance of vegetables, is my favorite. Vegetables add such a nice sweetness that I've taken to adding chopped bits of spinach, chard, sorrel—whatever is calling out from the refrigerator to be cooked rather than thrown out. I include a nice chunk of bacon for each person and serve the soup and bacon separately, with some good mustard and crusty country bread.

2 tablespoons unsalted butter

1 medium onion, finely chopped

1 medium carrot, finely chopped

2 stalks celery, finely chopped

1 small turnip, peeled and
   finely chopped

1 teaspoon minced garlic

1 cup herbaceous dry white wine,
   such as Sancerre or Vouvray

5 cups water

1 cup split peas

2 bay leaves

1 teaspoon fresh or dried
   marjoram leaves

½ pound slab bacon, cut into 8 pieces

Salt and freshly ground black pepper

½ cup crème fraîche or heavy cream

1. Melt the butter in a soup pot over low heat. Add the onion, carrot, celery, turnip, and garlic and cook very gently until soft, about 15 minutes. Add the wine, water, split peas, bay leaves, marjoram, and bacon. Cover and bring to a boil, then reduce the heat to low and simmer for 50 to 60 minutes, until the peas are completely soft and falling apart.

2. Remove the bacon from the soup, cover, and keep warm. Retrieve and discard the bay leaves and add the crème fraîche to the soup. Taste the soup for salt and pepper and add as desired. Pour the soup into a tureen and serve the bacon separately.

Velouté de Champignons
Cream of Mushroom Soup

MAKES 4 TO 6 SERVINGS

My friend Jean Ferrandiz prepares this soup from his mother's recipe. What makes it unusual is that he adds puréed mushrooms to a rich chicken *velouté* and just heats it through enough to release the flavor of the mushrooms. It's a soup that retains a flavor freshness unlike any other mushroom soup that I've eaten.

3 tablespoons unsalted butter

3 tablespoons all-purpose flour

½ cup dry white wine, such as Chardonnay

3 cups Homemade Chicken Broth (page 237) or low-sodium chicken or vegetable broth

Salt and freshly ground white pepper

1 pound white mushrooms

½ medium onion

2 teaspoons fresh thyme leaves

½ cup crème fraîche or heavy cream

1. Melt the butter in a soup pot over low heat. Whisk in the flour and cook for 5 minutes. Stir in the wine, then add the broth. Increase the heat to medium, bring to a boil, reduce the heat, and simmer for 10 minutes. Add salt and pepper as desired.

2. Meanwhile, purée the mushrooms and onion together in a food processor.

3. Add the mushrooms and onion to the simmering broth. Add the thyme and cream, cover, and simmer for another 5 minutes. Serve hot.

Soupe Jardinière aux Fèves
Fava Bean Soup with Spring Vegetables

MAKES 4 TO 6 SERVINGS

Early spring is a wonderful time to shop for vegetables in Paris. The air is still crisp, but the days are beginning to get longer. Early crops of colorful vegetables, dug up while still young, begin replacing winter's staples. This soup, a confetti of vegetables cooked with the season's first creamy fava beans, is a favorite Lenten meal. When you go shopping, choose the youngest fava pods, those that are light green, springy to the touch, and supple, holding small, tender beans that don't require peeling. If small favas are not available, use the larger ones, but peel each bean.

2 tablespoons unsalted butter

1 small leek, white part only, thinly
   sliced and well washed

1 stalk celery, from the heart,
   thinly sliced

1 baby carrot, scrubbed and finely diced

3 cups water

1 teaspoon salt

Freshly ground black pepper

2 bay leaves, preferably fresh

1 teaspoon fresh thyme leaves

1 pound fava beans, shelled

2 small new potatoes, scrubbed and
   finely diced

12 haricots verts or very small green
   beans, sliced into thin rounds

1 tablespoon chopped fresh chervil

1 tablespoon chopped fresh parsley

Melt the butter in a pot over medium heat. Cook the leek, celery, and carrot until soft but not browned, about 5 minutes. Add the water, salt, pepper, bay leaves, and thyme, cover, and bring to a boil. Add the fava beans and potatoes, reduce the heat, and simmer for 15 to 20 minutes, until the favas are tender. Remove the cover, add the haricots verts, and cook for another 2 minutes. Remove from the heat, remove the bay leaves and thyme, add the chervil and parsley, and serve.

Soupe aux Caillettes, Façon Nicole Conte

Nicole Conte's Chicken Soup with Bread and Vegetable Dumplings

MAKES 6 TO 7 SERVINGS

"Everyone's asked me to prepare *caillettes* for supper tonight after the cinema. Michael, can you stay with me this afternoon? I don't feel like being *une prisonière* in the kitchen." I'd heard about Nic's *caillettes* from other friends, and whenever they were mentioned, Nicole's face became small, helpless as a suffering saint. I was intrigued to eavesdrop in the kitchen, for that's how I felt, while she prepared them. Although she sets about preparing this soup as if celebrating a secret rite, *caillettes* are not, I found, difficult to prepare. The trick is leaving the bread soaking in water to completely soften the stale crusts. When I got to Nic's, she was deep in so much stale bread that she had moved from the kitchen to the dining table. This dish becomes different meals over the course of a couple of days and in the Conte family when you make caillettes, you make a lot. However, here's a more manageable recipe.

6 ounces stale baguette, broken up

1/4 pound bacon, finely chopped, optional

1/2 small onion, peeled and finely
   chopped

1 teaspoon minced garlic

1/2 small leek, white part only, finely
   chopped and well washed

2 stalks celery, finely chopped

1/2 small head lettuce, chopped

3 teaspoons salt

1 teaspoon freshly ground black pepper

1/2 teaspoons fresh marjoram leaves

3 tablespoons flour

1 egg, lightly beaten

One 3-pound boiling hen

2 1/2 quarts water

1. Place the bread in a mixing bowl large enough to allow it to triple in volume. Add warm water to cover. Soak the bread for 30 minutes or until soft. As the bread absorbs the water, you may need to add more so that the water always covers the bread. Drain and wring out the water. Place the bread in a mixing bowl and tear up any large pieces.

2. Meanwhile, combine the bacon, onion, garlic, leek, and celery in a skillet or pot and cook, covered, stirring occasionally until soft but not brown, about 7 minutes. Add the lettuce, 1 teaspoon salt, $\frac{1}{4}$ teaspoon pepper, and the marjoram and cook until the lettuce is wilted, another minute or two. Remove from the heat, pour the contents of the skillet into the bread and sprinkle with the flour. Mix the contents of the bowl together. Add the egg and use your hands to mix, squeezing everything together. Cover and set aside for 15 minutes.

3. Rinse the chicken, place in a large soup pot, and cover with the water. Add the remaining salt and pepper, cover and bring to a boil over high heat. Reduce the heat to medium low and simmer, skimming the surface frequently, for 30 minutes or until the chicken is done.

4. Meanwhile, form the bread mixture into golf ball–sized dumplings. Carefully drop dumplings into the pot, cover, and simmer for 20 minutes.

5. Using a slotted spoon, transfer the dumplings to a large bowl or soup tureen. Remove the chicken, set aside to cool, cover, and place in the refrigerator for another meal. Pour the soup into the tureen and serve.

Velouté de Persil | Cream of Parsley Soup

Parsley root was one of my great market discoveries. There they were in the market one day, looking like very small parsnips, only about three inches long, with long-stemmed flat-leafed tops. "Ah, they're for soup," the vendor told me. "Or you can cook them in butter, like carrots." Unlike leaf parsley, whose flavor saddens when cooked, the root maintains its lovely essence.

6 parsley roots with tops

2 tablespoons unsalted butter

1 small onion, diced

1 tablespoon all-purpose flour

3 cups milk

1 teaspoon salt

$1/4$ teaspoon freshly ground white pepper

3 gratings whole nutmeg
    or a pinch of ground

1. Remove the parsley tops and reserve. Scrub the roots, grate them with a hand grater, and set aside. Remove the stems from the tops and tie them in a bundle. Finely chop the leaves and set aside.

2. Melt the butter in a soup pot over medium-low heat. Cook the onion and parsley root until soft, 3 to 5 minutes. Stir in the flour and cook for another minute.

3. Stir in the milk and season with the salt, pepper, and nutmeg. Cover and simmer for 10 minutes. Remove from the heat, discard the parsley stems, add the chopped parsley, and serve.

Les Oeufs
Egg Dishes

"Eggs for breakfast? Michel, do I look like an athlete in training?" Ghislaine feigned disbelief at the thought of an ordinary, healthy person eating eggs in the morning. French people in general have traditional ideas about which foods to eat when, with what, and in what order. Ghislaine's ideas are only slightly exaggerated from the norm.

"I serve eggs to the family for dinner. Sometimes I'll order an omelette for lunch, but only in very expensive restaurants where they know how to prepare them. There's nothing more horrifying than a poorly cooked egg, don't you agree? Maman had a whole mythology about eggs. She claimed that eggs should never be eaten before noontime. She would permit a rich egg dish midday—eggs baked with sauce in a ramekin, or an omelette, or even fried; but for the evening meal, they'd have to be lighter. She would have the cook make scrambled eggs for Papa if he had a particularly difficult day, because she claimed they had a soothing effect. I have no idea how she came up with her system, but she was a woman with a particular sensitivity to things, especially the effects certain foods caused on one's psychological well-being."

Astuce: Scrambled Eggs the French Way

When properly executed, *oeufs brouillés,* literally, "agitated eggs," bear slight resemblance to their American cousin, scrambled eggs. The scramble should result in small tender clumps of eggs suspended in an almost saucelike base. Most people prefer them creamy, with the consistency of oatmeal. Cooked until dry, they're more like small-curd cottage cheese but still springy and light. Use a small pot rather than a skillet for French-style scrambled eggs. It's pointless to cook less than 6 eggs; in fact, the larger the quantity, the better the scramble. For each egg, add 1 teaspoon of water, $\frac{1}{8}$ teaspoon salt, and $\frac{1}{2}$ teaspoon of butter to your bowl of eggs. Beat the mixture lightly, using a wooden spoon; use a whisk for scrambling. Scramble the eggs over low heat, whisking all the time. When the mixture begins to coagulate and form lumps, begin a little dance of removing your pot from the heat and replacing it, scraping the bottom and sides with the whisk to detach the particles that form there. If you loosely scramble 6 eggs in less than 9 minutes, you've not done it properly. For richer scrambled eggs, stir in 1 teaspoon each cream and butter per egg at the end of cooking.

Oeufs Brouillés à la Portuguaise
Scrambled Eggs with Tomatoes, Shallots, and Garlic

MAKES 4 SERVINGS

I'm always tickled when someone serves me these eggs, for this is one of the dishes I had to prepare for the practical exam part of my cooking diploma. Read the *astuce* about scrambled eggs and you'll understand the satisfaction that comes from preparing perfect eggs. Some people fancify the presentation of this dish by serving the eggs in puff pastry shells that they buy from the pastry shop. I like them better on buttered toast.

3 tablespoons olive oil

⅓ cup thinly sliced shallots

3 cloves garlic, thinly sliced

1¼ pounds Roma (plum) tomatoes,
    peeled, seeded, and chopped
    (see sidebar)

3 sprigs fresh thyme or
    ½ teaspoon dried

1½ teaspoons salt

Freshly ground black pepper

10 large eggs

3 tablespoons plus 1 teaspoon water

2 tablespoons unsalted butter,
    cut into bits

2 tablespoons chopped fresh parsley

1. Heat the oil in a medium skillet over medium heat. Cook the shallots and garlic, stirring, for 2 minutes. Add the tomatoes, thyme, 1 teaspoon of the salt, and pepper to taste and cook until the mixture is dry, about 10 minutes. Remove from the heat.

2. Break the eggs into a bowl. Add half the tomato mixture (keep the remaining tomatoes warm), the water, butter, and the remaining ½ teaspoon salt and beat with a wooden spoon. Pour the eggs into a saucepan, place over low heat, and whisk continuously until the eggs begin to thicken, about 6 minutes. Remove from the heat and continue whisking for 30 seconds, then replace over low heat and cook, always whisking, for 2 minutes. Remove again from the heat and continue whisking for 30 seconds, then replace over low heat and cook, always whisking, for 2 to 4 minutes more, to desired doneness.

3. Remove the eggs from the heat and mix in the parsley. Pour the eggs into a large serving bowl and mound the remaining tomato mixture in the center. Serve immediately.

Astuce : Peeling and Seeding Tomatoes

Peeling tomatoes is quite easy. Using a paring knife, cut out the cores, then make a small X in the bottom of each tomato. Drop the tomatoes into vigorously boiling water. When you see the skins beginning to crack, continue to boil the tomatoes for another 20 to 30 seconds, or until the peels begin to curl away from the crack. As each tomato is ready, immediately remove it and plunge into ice water. When the tomatoes are cool enough to handle, slip off the skins. Use a paring knife to remove any bits of skin that fight back. Halve the tomatoes crosswise and squeeze gently to remove the seeds and excess liquid. You now have tomato flesh that can be chopped or chunked according to the recipe instructions.

Oeufs Brouillés aux Cèpes
Scrambled Eggs with Porcini Mushrooms

MAKES 4 SERVINGS

One autumn weekend, my friends went foraging for mushrooms in the Fontainebleau Forest, about an hour's drive south of Paris. Dinner that evening promised to be built around the morning's gather. I arrived at Hubert's house near Neuilly, on the Seine side of the Bois de Boulogne, and unwrapped the cheese, my contribution to dinner. Over aperitifs in the kitchen, we set to brushing the large primeval-looking fungi with a special brush that he had for the job. You have to try Hubert's dish. The mushrooms are gently sautéed, yet when you bite into them, the stems are a bit chewy and the caps creamy. The eggs are cooked and served separately, almost like a sauce. Make sure you serve plenty of bread for wiping the plates clean.

10 large eggs

3 tablespoons plus 1 teaspoon water

2 teaspoons salt

1 pound porcini mushrooms

2 tablespoons olive oil

¼ cup thinly sliced shallots

2 cloves garlic, thinly sliced

1 teaspoon chopped fresh tarragon
  or ½ teaspoon dried

Freshly ground black pepper

2 tablespoons unsalted butter,
  cut into bits

2 tablespoons chopped fresh parsley

1. Break the eggs into a bowl. Beat in the water and 1 teaspoon of the salt and set aside. Separate the mushroom caps and stems. Trim and discard the sandy bottoms of the mushroom stems and wipe the caps and stems clean. Slice the stems into ⅛-inch-

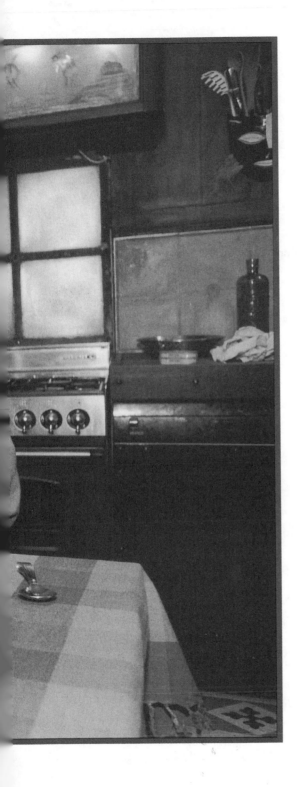

thick rounds. Cut the caps into ¼-inch-thick slivers.

2. Heat the oil in a skillet over medium heat. Cook the shallots and garlic for 1 minute, without browning. Add the mushrooms, tarragon, pepper to taste, and the remaining 1 teaspoon salt, cover, and cook until the mushrooms are soft, about 8 to 10 minutes. Arrange the mushrooms on four plates and keep warm.

3. Pour the eggs into a pot, place over low heat, and whisk continuously until the eggs have the consistency of very thick, lumpy gravy. Remove the eggs from the heat and mix in the butter and parsley. Pour the eggs into a large serving bowl and serve immediately with the mushrooms.

Hubert Legall's kitchen

Oeufs Pochés à la Crème d'Estragon
Eggs Poached in Tarragon Cream

MAKES 4 SERVINGS

We made this dish after a night of dancing at Queen, a club on the Champs-Elysées. Eggs have a quieting effect on our constitution, perfect for a four A.M. meal, but the tarragon cream really worked the taste buds, which needed rejuvenation after an evening in a crowded, smoke-filled place. The wine and vinegar spike the cream with an eye-opening edge.

8 slices brioche or white bread

¼ cup dry white wine,
   such as Chardonnay

¼ cup white wine vinegar

¼ cup minced shallots

¼ cup finely chopped carrot

¼ cup finely chopped celery

1 teaspoon salt

Freshly ground black pepper

2 teaspoons chopped fresh tarragon
   or 1 teaspoon dried

¾ cup heavy cream

8 large eggs

1. Preheat the oven to 200°F.

2. Using a round cookie cutter or an inverted cup, cut a 4- to 5-inch round from each slice of bread. Toast them, then place in wide-rimmed soup bowls and keep warm in the oven.

3. Combine the wine, vinegar, shallots, carrot, celery, salt, and pepper to taste in a saucepan just large enough to comfortably hold 8 eggs. If using dried tarragon, add it now. Bring to a boil over high heat, then lower the heat to medium, add the cream, and return to the boil. Add the eggs one at a time and poach for 3 minutes, or until the desired doneness. Using a slotted spoon, remove the eggs and arrange on the toasts in the bowls. Return the bowls to the oven.

4. Continue to boil poaching cream for 2 minutes, reducing it slightly. Remove the pan from the heat and add the fresh tarragon, if using it. Pour the cream over the eggs and serve immediately.

Astuce: Poached Eggs

The perfect poached egg requires a perfectly farm-fresh egg. A good poached egg requires a reasonably fresh egg, a supermarket egg. And you'll have greater success with a room-temperature egg than one that's just exited the refrigerator. You must use at least 6 cups of water to poach 4 to 6 eggs. Poach them in a 3-inch depth of water and do not crowd the pan. I use an 11-inch skillet to poach 4 to 6 eggs. Add $\frac{1}{4}$ teaspoon salt and $\frac{1}{2}$ teaspoon white vinegar for each cup of water used. The water should be at a nice simmer, not boiling. Break each egg into a ramekin, then, with the ramekin touching the surface of the water, slide in the egg. Try to agitate the water as little as possible while adding the eggs, then poach for another 2 to 4 minutes, or until the white is barely cooked. Carefully remove the eggs from the water as they are done. If not serving immediately, gently place them in a bowl of ice water. They can be reheated at the moment of serving by placing them in a skillet of gently boiling water for about 45 seconds.

Oeufs Meurette de Jacques

Soft-Cooked Eggs with Red Wine and Shallots

MAKES 4 SMALL SERVINGS

Visiting Paris from her place in Provence, Sylviane Lacoste introduced me to Jacques, a successful painter, who lived near the apartment I rented in Montmartre. He dropped by the evening of my arrival to cook this dish for us. He often treats his friends to this dish of soft-boiled eggs served out of their shells. The trick is peeling the soft-cooked eggs, and Jacques is more practiced at it than anyone who's not a professional chef. It takes a bit of practice, but once you've gotten the knack, you'll serve these eggs a lot. A few pointers: Bring the eggs to room temperature before cooking. Salt the water and keep it at a gentle boil. Cook large eggs for exactly six minutes, then drain and place the pot under cold running water. To peel, use the back of a spoon to crack the shells all around. Under cold running water, carefully remove the top of the shell from the pointed end. Insert a small spoon between the egg and the shell and scoop around the egg to release it from the shell. Then remove the shell.

4 tablespoons (½ stick) unsalted butter

1 tablespoon olive oil

4 slices country bread

½ cup minced shallots

2 teaspoons all-purpose flour

1½ cups red wine,
    such as Burgundy

1 sprig fresh thyme or ¼ teaspoon dried

½ teaspoon salt

Freshly ground black pepper

4 large eggs, at room temperature

1 tablespoon chopped fresh chervil

1. Melt 2 tablespoons of the butter with the olive oil in a large skillet over medium heat. Add the bread and cook until deep golden on the bottom. (If you have to cook the bread in batches, you'll need a bit more butter and oil to perform the task.) Remove and keep warm. Wipe out the skillet and return to medium heat.

2. Melt the remaining 1 tablespoon butter in the skillet, add the shallots, and cook until soft but not browned, about 5 minutes. Mix the flour into the shallots and add the wine, thyme, and salt. Give the mixture a grind of the peppermill and cook until it thickens and reduces by one third, 5 to 7 minutes. Remove from the heat, beat in the remaining 1 tablespoon butter, and set aside.

3. Bring a pot of salted water to a gentle boil and add the room temperature eggs. Cook for exactly 6 minutes. Remove the eggs and cool under cold running water. Set the pot aside. Carefully peel each egg (see headnote), then return them to the hot water for 2 minutes to warm them.

4. Arrange the slices of bread on plates, cooked side down. Place an egg on each slice and spoon over the sauce. Sprinkle with the chervil and serve immediately.

Oeufs en Cocotte au Madère
Coddled Eggs with Madeira

MAKES 4 SMALL SERVINGS

Baked eggs should have the texture of a delicate egg custard and should fall away from the spoon when you eat them. Cook them slowly in a water bath to avoid toughening the whites, and cook them only to the point that the whites are set. You'll need individual ramekins or soufflé molds to present this dish with the importance that it deserves, for, although easy to prepare, the eggs require a few minutes of the cook's vigilance. True elegance is never overcomplicated but lies in the graceful performance of a simple task, *n'est-ce pas?*

3 tablespoons unsalted butter

2 shallots, thinly sliced

1 tablespoon all-purpose flour

1/2 cup Madeira

1 teaspoon tomato paste

1 cup low-sodium beef broth

1/4 teaspoon salt

1/8 teaspoon freshly ground white pepper

1 bay leaf

4 large eggs

4 sprigs fresh thyme

1. Preheat the oven to 375°F.

2. Melt 1 tablespoon of the butter in a medium saucepan over medium heat. Add the shallots and cook for 1 minute, stirring. Stir in the flour and cook for another minute, stirring. Add the Madeira and tomato paste and cook for another 2 minutes, stirring to dissolve the paste. Add the broth, salt, pepper, and bay leaf and cook until the mixture thickens and is reduced by one third, about 5 minutes. Remove from the heat.

3. While the sauce is cooking, bring a quart of water to the boil. Remove from the heat and set aside. Melt the remaining 2 tablespoons butter and set aside.

4. Divide the sauce among four 4-inch ramekins. Break an egg into a small bowl, then carefully slide it into a ramekin. Spoon a little melted butter over each egg. Repeat with the remaining eggs, then place the ramekins in a shallow 2-quart baking dish. Carefully fill the baking dish with enough of the hot water to come halfway up the sides of the ramekins. Bake for 12 to 15 minutes, or until the whites are just set.

5. Remove the ramekins from the baking dish and place on servers or small plates. Place a sprig of thyme on each egg and serve immediately.

Une rue commerçante

Oeufs en Cocotte Brunoise

Coddled Eggs with Vegetables

MAKES 4 SERVINGS

This perfect dish was served at a literary lunch for one of the authors of Jean-Loup Champion, the Gallimard editor. The eggs put everyone at ease, as they made the somewhat formal repast seem more intimate, almost familial. The caterer followed with sautéed Dover sole accompanied by parsleyed boiled potatoes. I've served these eggs as a dinner opener and found it has a similar effect on my guests. Americans are unaccustomed to being served eggs at a dinner party, which makes them all the more special.

3 tablespoons unsalted butter

½ medium carrot, finely diced

½ small onion, finely diced

½ stalk celery, finely diced

¼ teaspoon salt

2 cups Homemade Chicken Broth
  (page 237) or low-sodium chicken
  or vegetable broth

4 large eggs

1 tablespoon chopped fresh parsley

Freshly ground black pepper

1. Preheat the oven to 375°F.

2. Melt 2 tablespoons of the butter in a small saucepan over medium heat. Add the carrot, onion, celery, and salt and cook, covered, until the vegetables are softened, about 5 minutes.

3. Meanwhile, place the broth in another small saucepan, place over medium heat, and cook until reduced to about ½ cup. As the liquid begins to reduce, reduce the heat to low. When the liquid is syrupy, remove from the heat and keep warm.

4. Use the remaining 1 tablespoon butter to butter four ramekins. Bring a quart of water to the boil.

5. When the vegetables are cooked, spoon them into the four 4-inch ramekins. Break an egg into a small bowl, then carefully slide it into a ramekin. Repeat with the remaining eggs, then place the ramekins in a shallow 2-quart baking dish. Carefully fill the baking dish with enough of the boiling water to come halfway up the sides of the ramekins. Bake for 12 to 15 minutes, or until the whites are just set.

6. Remove the ramekins from the baking dish and place on servers or small plates. Add the parsley to the reduced broth and spoon the mixture over the eggs. Give a turn of the peppermill over each ramekin and serve immediately.

Omelette Plate aux Poireaux et aux Fines Herbes
Flat Omelette with Herbs

MAKES 4 SERVINGS

Although French omelettes are renowned for their creaminess and lightness, it's rare that people prepare them at home, for they have to be prepared individually and must be eaten immediately. For a family dinner or lunch, most people make large flat omelettes, enough to serve three people or more. Begin them as scrambled eggs, then, as the eggs begin to set, cover the skillet and place it in the oven. The omelette should not brown; it should be rather wet in the center and fluffy. Comparing a flat omelette to scrambled eggs with a skin is the best way to describe what they're like. You'll have the most success if you use a Teflon or well-seasoned nonstick skillet. A nine- to eleven-inch skillet is best; you want a nice mass of eggs to cook slowly. An omelette meal may begin with some charcuterie or a soup and always includes salad and cheese.

½ cup dry white wine, such as
    Sauvignon Blanc

1 tablespoon tomato paste

1½ teaspoons salt

½ cup heavy cream

2 tablespoons unsalted butter

1 large leek, white and light green
    parts only, quartered lengthwise, cut
    crosswise into ¼-inch pieces, well
    washed, and dried

8 large eggs

3 tablespoons water

1 teaspoon chopped fresh tarragon

1 tablespoon chopped fresh parsley

1 teaspoon chopped fresh chervil

1 tablespoon chopped fresh chives

¼ teaspoon freshly ground black pepper

1. Preheat the oven to 325°F.

2. Combine the wine, tomato paste, and 1 teaspoon of the salt in a small saucepan, place over high heat, and boil for 2 minutes. Add the cream and cook until the mixture reduces to a saucelike consistency, about 3 minutes. Remove from the heat and keep warm.

3. Melt the butter in a 10-inch nonstick ovenproof skillet over medium heat. Add the leek and cook, stirring occasionally, until soft, about 5 minutes.

4. Meanwhile, break the eggs into a mixing bowl, add the water, tarragon, parsley, chervil, chives, the remaining ½ teaspoon salt, and the pepper, and beat together.

5. Pour the egg mixture into the skillet and cook, stirring vigorously with a wooden spoon, for 2 minutes. Once the eggs begin to set, shake the pan in a circular motion for 1 minute. Cover the pan, transfer it to the oven, and bake until the center of the omelette is barely set, about 8 to 10 minutes.

6. Remove the skillet from the oven and invert a large plate over it. Grab the skillet handle with the inside of your wrist facing up, place your other hand on the plate, and quickly turn upside down to remove the omelette from the skillet. Drizzle the tomato cream over the omelette and serve immediately.

Les Salades Simples
Green Salads

*E*ric answered the door, his usual natty self, and took our scarves. (When there's a chill in the autumn evening air but it's not yet cold enough for coats, out come the cashmere scarves that people wrap around their necks, men tucking the ends between the lapels of their jackets, women contriving to form shawls.) We joined the others in the salon. Dinner talk at Sandra and Eric's apartment always begins with the subject of fashion and eventually turns to food, but not usually over the aperitifs.

"The perfect green salad is like the perfect black dress or blue suit," expounded Sandra, "always presentable, never out of place, perhaps not exciting, but one of the marks of a well-served meal." Sandra is a stylist, *très comme il faut,* one of the very fashionable people.

"I keep it simple. In spring and summer, there are tender salad greens with good flavor, such as *laitue,* equivalent to butter lettuce, watercress, and small young heads of romaine. I dress them with some old red wine vinegar and good extra virgin olive. During the winter, there are crisp salads and bitter ones too. As for the chicories—frisée, or curly endive and escarole—these I usually dress with a simple mustard vinaigrette, flavored with minced garlic. Belgian endive gets either my mustard vinaigrette or a delicate douse of lemon juice and walnut oil. I usually dress larger, mature heads of romaine, not a tasty lettuce, with a cream vinaigrette. Then there are the field salads, the mixture of young leaves called mesclun. I like these with mustard vinaigrette.

"There are other salads that we make, too, but they're not standard, not the perfect black dress or blue suit of the salad repertoire. Sometimes I make an arugula salad, spicy and strong. Eric is fond of the peppery flavor of watercress. I make a shallot vinaigrette or a vinaigrette with lemon juice for these spicy lettuces. And I have to mention bitter dandelion, which was a childhood horror for me, but which I have since developed a fondness for. I make a cream vinaigrette for it.

"Preparing the salad is the last thing I do before serving the first course. When I prepare my mustard or cream vinaigrette, I make it directly in the salad bowl and pile the lettuce on top. I keep it covered, in the refrigerator, so the leaves don't discolor, and I toss the dressing with the salad when I bring it to the table. Warm vinaigrettes and a simple oil and vinegar dressing must be tossed at the last moment, though."

Sandra stopped, but I could tell she wasn't finished. Turning to me, the only American, she made her last pronouncement on the subject of salad and dressing. "I think it makes no sense starting a meal with salad, Michel; the vinegar taints the palate and can even upset the stomach. And don't forget that wine and vinegar don't mix. Starting a meal with salad, you would not be able to serve wine. Salad is taken after the main course. It cleanses and prepares the palate for cheese, which, of course, is the reason for having it. We never serve it on its own." Sandra's life, it would seem, is a fashion statement.

Salade Verte, Vinaigrette Simple
Green Salad Dressed with Oil and Vinegar

MAKES 4 TO 5 SERVINGS

I am always amazed at the oohs and ahs a great green salad elicits. Use Bibb, Boston, or butter lettuce for this, the most simple, the ideal green salad. These varieties of spring and summer lettuces are characterized by light green, tender leaves. Parisians don't dress their salads with much vinaigrette, but what there is must be in perfect balance—tangy, with just enough oil to make the leaves shine and to mitigate the vinegar. A touch of chervil or tarragon combined with flat-leaf parsley gives the lettuce a clean, faintly licorice flavor. Flake or coarse salt and freshly ground pepper are indispensable. Toss the salad at the table, not a minute before.

2 heads Boston, Bibb, or butter lettuce

1 clove garlic, minced

1 shallot, minced

3 tablespoons canola, peanut, grapeseed, or extra virgin olive oil

2 tablespoons red wine vinegar

1/2 teaspoon flake or coarse sea salt

1 1/2 teaspoons fresh chervil or tarragon leaves, finely chopped

1 1/2 teaspoons fresh flat-leaf parsley leaves, finely chopped

Freshly ground black pepper

1. Remove and discard the outer layer of leaves from the lettuce. Separate the tender leaves, tearing the larger ones into 2-inch pieces. Wash the lettuce and dry completely. Place in a salad bowl, cover, and place in the refrigerator.

2. Place the garlic and shallot in a small bowl, add the oil, and let infuse for at least 15 minutes and up to 45 minutes.

3. When it's time to serve the salad, vigorously beat the vinegar into the oil. Remove the salad from the refrigerator, pour over the vinaigrette, and sprinkle with the salt, chervil, and parsley. Give a few grinds of the peppermill over the salad. Toss well and serve immediately.

Vinaigrette Moutardée
The Perfect Mustard Vinaigrette

MAKES 1 CUP, OR 6 TO 8 SERVINGS

Cooks gain their reputations from the way they prepare the simplest of things—scrambled eggs and mustard vinaigrette being two of the tests.

A proper vinaigrette is light and doesn't wilt the salad. Use either the lightest flavorless salad oil—first-pressed canola, peanut, or grapeseed—or an extra virgin French olive oil, or a combination. The quality of the vinegar is of the utmost importance. If you buy a French vinegar, the best ones come from Orléans. Vinegars marked only *à l'ancienne* are not aged. The ones marked *vieux* have been aged in wood casks and are less acidic. Crushed shallots and garlic are a must for most people, and everyone has their own dose. Some use only shallots, some only garlic. Care should be taken with the salt. I find that a vinaigrette containing mustard is usually salty enough and so I add salt and pepper to the lettuce itself. *Fleur de sel*, literally the upper crust of a flake sea salt from Brittany, is the preferred choice, with its iodine tang. The pepper must be freshly ground. Chopped chervil and tarragon are optional, but they contribute a fine fresh flavor that I really like.

1 clove garlic, minced

1 shallot, minced

1 tablespoon Dijon mustard

3 tablespoons aged red wine vinegar

5 tablespoons canola, peanut, grapeseed, or extra virgin olive oil

1/2 teaspoon salt

1 1/2 teaspoon finely chopped fresh chervil leaves, optional

1 1/2 teaspoons finely chopped fresh tarragon leaves, optional

Freshly ground black pepper

In a small bowl, whisk together the garlic, shallot, mustard, and vinegar. Gradually beat in the oil until it is incorporated, then mix in the salt, chervil, and tarragon. Give a grind or two of the peppermill, as desired.

Salade de Scarole, Vinaigrette à la Moutarde

Escarole Salad with Mustard Vinaigrette

MAKES 4 TO 5 SERVINGS

This is a great winter green salad, with leaves that are crisp and chewy. The mustard vinaigrette should be of a heavy enough consistency that it will coat the leaves. This vinaigrette is heady with garlic.

2 small heads escarole

2 cloves garlic, minced

2 teaspoons Dijon mustard

2 tablespoons red wine vinegar

3 tablespoons vegetable oil, preferably canola, or extra virgin olive oil

¼ teaspoon salt

Freshly ground black pepper

1. Remove and discard the outer lettuce leaves and trim any dark green tops. Using a small knife, cut out the core and discard. Separate the remaining leaves, tearing the larger leaves into manageable pieces. Wash the lettuce and dry completely.

2. Combine the garlic and mustard in the salad bowl. Stir in the vinegar, then slowly beat in the oil. Place the lettuce on top of the vinaigrette, cover, and place in the refrigerator until serving time.

3. To serve, bring the salad to the table, sprinkle with the salt, give a few grinds of the peppermill, and toss.

Coeurs de Romaine, Vinaigrette Crème à la Ciboulette
Hearts of Romaine with Creamy Chive Vinaigrette

MAKES 4 TO 5 SERVINGS

In springtime, romaine is at its best, small young heads of firm lettuce that are moderately crisp. If you don't succeed in finding small heads of romaine, simply peel off the outer leaves until you're left with only the light green heart. The creamy vinaigrette that dresses this salad is familiar in Normandy, the dairy-producing region of France. I like to add a squeeze of anchovy paste to the dressing instead of salt, a variation that is definitely not Normande. American sour cream is thicker than crème fraîche, and if you're using it, you may need to add a tablespoon or two of milk to thin the dressing.

2 small or 1 large head romaine
   (about 1 pound)
2 tablespoons crème fraîche
   or sour cream
1 tablespoon grainy mustard
2 tablespoons fresh lemon juice

1 teaspoon anchovy paste
1/4 cup minced fresh chives
2 tablespoons peanut, canola,
   or grapeseed oil
Freshly ground black pepper
1 teaspoon salt, or to taste

1. Trim off and discard the outer leaves of the romaine until the light green centers are exposed. Halve small heads or quarter large ones, depending on their size, and cut out the core. Wash the romaine, dry thoroughly with kitchen towels, and place in the refrigerator.

2. In a small bowl, combine the crème fraîche, mustard, lemon juice, anchovy paste, and chives and mix well. Beat in the oil and give a few grinds of the peppermill, as desired. Taste for salt and add as desired.

3. To serve, arrange the romaine on plates and spoon over the dressing.

Salade de Roquette aux Croûtons, Vinaigrette Tiède aux Echalotes

Arugula Salad with Warm Shallot Vinaigrette and Garlic Croutons

MAKES 4 SERVINGS

Following a spate of Provençal restaurants opening in the capital, spicy arugula has become a popular salad choice. Parisians use it alone or mix it with mild-flavored, tender summer lettuces. Some people simply dress the arugula with lemon juice, extra virgin olive oil, and a sprinkling of salt, because lemon doesn't interfere with the strong arugula flavor. I like this version, which uses a shallot-and-vinegar reduction to similar effect. Heating vinegar softens it, so it's not imperative to use the finest aged vinegar for the dressing. This tasty salad should follow a simply cooked main course, one without a rich sauce. Buy young arugula with small leaves and trim the stems well.

4 bunches arugula (about ¾ pound)

6 tablespoons olive oil

2 cloves garlic, minced

8 thin slices French bread

3 shallots, minced

6 tablespoons red wine vinegar

½ teaspoon sea salt (flake or coarse)

1. Trim off and discard any large arugula stems. Wash the arugula and dry well. Place in a salad bowl and place in the refrigerator.

2. Heat ¼ cup of the olive oil in a large skillet over medium heat. Add the garlic, then add the bread in one layer. Cook the bread for about 1 minute on each side, or until lightly golden on both sides. Remove the bread and drain on paper towels. Retrieve the garlic and scatter it over the bread.

3. When you're ready to serve the salad, remove the arugula from the refrigerator. Combine the shallots and vinegar in a small saucepan, place over high heat, and boil for 2 minutes. Remove from the heat and add the remaining 2 tablespoons oil. Pour the dressing over the arugula, sprinkle with the salt, and toss well. Arrange the croutons on the salad and serve immediately.

Neighbors visiting in the market, rue Monge, 5th arrondissement

Salade de Chicorée à l'Huile de Noix

Belgian Endive and Walnut Salad

MAKES 4 SERVINGS

This is a classic combination, bitter Belgian endive with a smoky walnut oil. Lemon juice balances the flavors. Choose compact heads of Belgian endive. The heads should not have any green edges that are beginning to curl, but a bit of brown discoloration, which you should trim off, is common.

¼ cup walnut pieces	4 teaspoons dark walnut oil
3 medium heads Belgian endive	½ teaspoon sea salt (flake or coarse)
2 tablespoons fresh lemon juice	Freshly ground black pepper

1. Preheat the oven to 350°F.

2. Spread the walnuts on a cookie sheet, place in the oven, and toast until lightly colored and fragrant, about 10 minutes. Remove from the oven and let cool.

3. Remove and discard any discolored outer endive leaves. Halve the endive lengthwise and cut out the bottom core. Lay the endive cut side down on a work surface and cut crosswise into ½-inch pieces. Place the cut endive in a salad bowl, toss with the lemon juice, cover, and place in the refrigerator until ready to serve.

4. To serve, add the oil to the salad, sprinkle with the salt, give a few grinds of the peppermill, and toss.

$\mathscr{S}$OME PEOPLE DRESS THIS SALAD WITH A MUSTARD VINAIGRETTE. USE A TEASPOON MORE MUSTARD THAN YOU WOULD NORMALLY AND OMIT THE TRADITIONAL GARLIC — THE RAW GARLIC AND BITTER ENDIVE FLAVORS FIGHT.

$\mathscr{A}stuce:$ Instead of Vinegar

Substitute verjus, juice from unripened white wine grapes, for the vinegar for a delicate salad dressing to avoid the tainting character that vinegar can have on the palate. For those of you who make vinegar at home, use some that's only started to turn. It's mildly acidic and very pleasing for its fruitiness. Or try adding one part wine to four parts vinegar for a softer vinegar.

Salade de Tomates | Tomato Salad

It may seem silly to give a recipe for tomato salad, but there are little tricks I picked up from Parisian cooks that make this simple plate tastier. Most important is never refrigerate a tomato and always serve tomatoes at room temperature to maximize flavor. Slice tomatoes from tip to stem rather than across—the ratio of pulp to seed is more agreeable. Lightly season the sliced tomatoes with salt fifteen minutes before serving them, then drain off the excess juice on the plate. When you season the tomatoes for serving, use sea salt in flakes rather than ordinary table salt. Finally, when you make the vinaigrette, use a tarragon-flavored vinegar and an herb-infused oil. These little pointers may seem bordering on obsession, but they are the key to a perfect plate of tomatoes.

6 vine-ripened tomatoes

½ teaspoon salt

Freshly ground black pepper

Flake sea salt

1 teaspoon Dijon mustard

1 clove garlic, minced

1 tablespoon tarragon or white
   wine vinegar

1 tablespoon fresh lemon juice

¼ cup herb-infused olive oil

3 tablespoons finely chopped
   fresh chives

1. Core the tomatoes and slice them from tip to stem into ½-inch slices. Lay the slices on a large plate, sprinkle with the ½ teaspoon salt, and let sit for 15 minutes.

2. Drain any juice that has accumulated on the plate and arrange the slices on serving plates. Give a few turns of the pepper grinder over the tomatoes and sprinkle with sea salt.

3. Combine the mustard and garlic in a small bowl and stir in the vinegar and lemon juice. Slowly beat in the oil. Spoon the vinaigrette over the tomatoes and sprinkle them with chives.

Les Salades Composées
Composed Salads

o, I take it your meeting was a mess," I ventured.

Marianne dropped herself down on the little café chair and ordered a glass of rosé. She had just come from the monthly co-op meeting of apartment owners in the building where she lives, in the Marais.

"Mais, quelle salade! A confusion of people that I would never have believed had I not witnessed it myself."

The French approach composed salads, those with more than just lettuce greens, with trepidation, for they signify the possibility of confusion, irregularity, and oddness. And to say that someone would sell you salad, in familiar talk, means that they're indiscriminate and would sell you anything.

At home in Paris, composed salads are rarely the kind of jumble that is popular in the States. They're mostly simple, to be served as light dinner or lunch, the menu rounded out with a plate of cold cuts or a soup, or perhaps an omelette.

Salade de Mâche, Endive, et Betteraves
Mâche, Belgian Endive, and Beet Salad

MAKES 4 SERVINGS

Cultivated mâche, also known as corn salad or lamb's tongue, is in the Paris markets around the year in little plastic containers, cleaned and ready to serve. From early Fall through the winter, it grows wild in the fields. It's a relatively delicate salad green and is used as a contrast to crisper lettuces. Here in the States, it's a bit more difficult to find and, even when available, rather expensive. However, it's simple to grow in pots and well worth the effort.

1 medium beet

½ pound mâche (lamb's tongue)

2 heads Belgian endive

1 tablespoon Dijon mustard

2 tablespoons red wine vinegar

¼ cup extra virgin olive oil

½ teaspoon flake sea salt

Freshly ground black pepper

1. Trim and discard the beet top. Place the beet in a pot of salted water, cover, bring to a boil, and cook until tender, about 40 minutes. Drain.

2. When the beet is cool enough to handle, place under cold running water and rub off the skin. Cut the beet into ½-inch cubes and place in a salad bowl in the refrigerator to chill.

3. Twist off and discard the bottoms of the bunches of mâche. Wash the leaves, dry them well, and add to the beets. Trim and discard any discolored outer endive leaves. Halve the endive lengthwise, cut out the root core, and cut each half crosswise into ½-inch pieces. Add the endive to the salad bowl.

4. In a small mixing bowl, combine the mustard and vinegar, then beat in the oil. Set aside.

5. When it's time to serve the salad, remove it from the refrigerator and pour over the vinaigrette, sprinkle with the salt, and give a few turns of the pepper grinder. Toss well and serve.

Salade de Fenouil, Artichaut, et Petits Pois

Fennel, Artichoke, and Pea Salad

MAKES 4 SERVINGS

It's funny how blind one can be to something, then once it's been discovered, it seems to pop up everywhere. I was introduced to small Provençal artichokes at a luncheon at the weekend house of Madame Champion, mother of my friend Jean-Loup. We had gone touring the châteaux of the Loire Valley and were staying the weekend. I was amazed, first, that it was possible to eat raw artichokes and, second, that their taste was so unlike that of cooked. We pulled off the individual leaves, spread them with butter, and sprinkled them with sea salt. When I arrived at the naked bottom, there was no choke, just the reward of a delicious pure artichoke heart nugget.

Here in the States, you should be able to find these little thistles in the market from early spring through late fall, but they begin to turn bitter as the weather gets colder. Both the artichokes and fennel must be sliced paper-thin; a Japanese mandoline makes the job easier. The fennel shouldn't pose a problem, but you might find that the artichoke bites back, so eat a slice before tossing the ingredients together. If you find the texture too chewy, blanch the slivers in salted boiling water for one minute, drain, and run under cold water.

1 lemon, halved
6 baby artichokes
2 medium fennel bulbs
½ cup fresh or frozen peas
¼ cup minced fresh chives

2 teaspoons grainy mustard
1 tablespoon red wine vinegar
2 tablespoons virgin olive oil
½ teaspoon salt
Freshly ground black pepper

continued

1. Squeeze the juice of the lemon into a bowl. Trim and discard the outer layers of green leaves from the artichokes and snip off about ½ inch from the top of each. Trim and discard the stems. Halve each artichoke from tip to stem, lay the halves cut side down on a work surface, and slice as thin as possible. As each half is sliced, add to the lemon juice and toss well.

2. Trim and discard the fennel stalks and remove and discard the tough outer layer. Halve the fennel bulbs from tip to stem and cut out and discard the solid cores. Lay the fennel cut side down on a work surface and slice into paper-thin slivers. Add the fennel to the artichokes and place in the refrigerator.

3. Bring a pot of salted water to the boil and add the peas. Cook frozen peas for 1 minute, fresh ones for 3 minutes. Drain and run under cold water until cool, then drain well and add the peas to the bowl with the artichokes and fennel.

4. Add the chives. Stir in the mustard, then the vinegar, oil, and salt. Give a few turns of the peppermill, as desired. Toss and serve.

A former ballerina, now a greengrocer, in the Marché Jeanne d'Arc, 13th arrondissement

Salade Frisée aux Lardons
Chicory and Poached Egg Salad, with Bacon Vinaigrette

MAKES 4 SERVINGS

In France *frisée* is the very curly, flat-stemmed chicory similar to curly endive. It's harvested young in France and is a favorite because of its slight bitter tang and chewy texture. I was chatting with a young man in the market who was looking over some *frisée*. He was telling me that his mother always trimmed off the greenish top of the *frisée* and only used the very whitest center, barely 50 percent of the head. This discards went into soup or were sautéed in butter and served as a vegetable. This warm bacon vinaigrette "fatigues" the salad, as they say in Paris, wilting it slightly. Serve this salad as a luncheon main course or a dinner first course followed by soup or charcuterie. It's a favorite staple of Parisians at the café and at home.

2 small heads frisée lettuce or
   1 ½ pounds curly endive
4 large eggs, poached (see page 57)
¾ pound bacon, cut into ½-inch pieces
1 tablespoon grapeseed, canola, or extra
   virgin olive oil

3 shallots, minced
5 tablespoons red wine vinegar
¼ teaspoon salt
Freshly ground black pepper

1. Trim off all the green tops from the lettuce and reserve for another use. Cut out the center cores, separate the leaves, and cut the longer ones into 3-inch-long pieces. Wash the lettuce, dry it well, and divide among four soup or pasta bowls. Place a poached egg on each salad.

2. Place the bacon and oil in a large skillet and cook over medium-high heat. Cook, stirring occasionally, until the bacon is crisp, about 5 minutes. Add the shallots to the skillet. Cook, stirring, for another 30 seconds, then add the vinegar and salt and cook for another minute.

3. Using a slotted spoon, remove the bacon from the skillet and divide equally among the four salads. Spoon the vinaigrette over the salads, give a few turns of the pepper grinder, and serve immediately.

The Sunday market at Bastille, 11th arrondissement, one of the best and largest

Salade aux Délices de Volailles
Bibb Lettuce with Chicken Livers and Gizzards

MAKES 4 SERVINGS

Jane Sigal, the food writer and journalist, took me to a neighborhood bistro and wine bar near the market in the rue Daguerre, where I encountered this salad. The *propriétaire* of this five-table place is a redoubtable presence, a temperamental chef who's forever getting into arguments with customers when they try to order something other than the two or three dishes that he prepares daily. He's fond of using the kind of ingredients that have long passed from fashion, which he cooks unabashedly and with wild abandon. This salad is actually a combination of two dishes that his mother used to prepare at home. I think it represents a brilliant kind of cooking that one seldom sees nowadays. Plan ahead, for the livers and gizzards need to marinate for at least twelve hours before you prepare the confit.

³/₄ pound chicken gizzards

2 tablespoons kosher salt

¹/₄ cup brandy

¹/₂ pound chicken livers

2 teaspoons fresh thyme leaves or dried

12 peppercorns

3 bay leaves

3 cloves

1 medium onion, peeled

About ¹/₂ cup olive oil

16 cloves garlic, peeled

2 teaspoons Dijon mustard

2 tablespoons aged red wine vinegar

1 tablespoon chopped fresh tarragon
   (do not use dried)

2 heads Bibb lettuce, washed, dried,
   and leaves torn

1. One day in advance, rinse the gizzards. Lay them flat on a work surface, silverskin down. Beginning in the center, remove as much silverskin as you can easily, cutting each gizzard in half. Place the gizzards in a small bowl, mix with half the salt and half the brandy, and place in the refrigerator for 12 to 18 hours. Rinse the livers and trim them of any green or discolored bits. Place in another bowl with the remaining salt and brandy and place in the refrigerator for 12 to 18 hours.

2. The next day, tie up the thyme, peppercorns, bay leaves, and cloves in a square of cheesecloth and place in a heavy 1-quart casserole. Halve the onion from tip to stem, lay it flat, and slice it lengthwise. Add the onion to the casserole. Drain and rinse the gizzards; discard the marinade. Add the gizzards to the casserole, add enough oil to cover, and place the casserole, covered, in the oven. Turn the oven on to 325°F and cook for 1½ hours.

3. Drain and rinse the livers; discard the marinade. Add the livers and garlic to the casserole and cook for an additional 30 minutes.

4. Strain out the gizzards, livers, onion, and garlic and allow the cooking fat to drip off; discard the herb packet. Reserve the cooking fat. Allow everything to cool to room temperature.

5. Stir the mustard, vinegar, and tarragon together in a salad bowl. Whisk in about 3 tablespoons of the reserved fat. Place the lettuce in the bowl and add the gizzard and liver mixture. Toss the salad at the table.

Pissenlit au Jambon de Pays
Dandelion Greens with Prosciutto

MAKES 4 SERVINGS

Home-style cooking is one of the hallmarks of Paris bistros. There, we find many specialties that are part of most Parisians' cooking repertoire, such as this salad. And, as with any folk dish, there are endless variations. My favorite version of this salad uses the fat covering of a cured ham, such as jambon de Bayonne or prosciutto, for the vinaigrette. Have the deli man slice the ham thicker than usual, into eighth-inch-thick slices. The clove flavors and the delicate fat make this salad a *merveille* (marvel). Try to find young, tender dandelion greens, or use the white part of curly endive, another nice bitter green.

$1/2$ pound prosciutto, cut into
  $1/8$-inch slices

$2^1/2$ cups loosely packed chopped
  dandelion greens

1 teaspoon coarse sea salt

2 tablespoons olive oil

$1/4$ cup thinly sliced shallots

2 cloves garlic, thinly sliced

$1/4$ cup red wine vinegar

Freshly ground black pepper

1. Trim the outer fat from the prosciutto and finely dice it. Trim and discard the interior fat and dice the meat. Toss the prosciutto meat, dandelion greens, and salt together in a large salad bowl.

2. Place the diced prosciutto fat and the oil in a nonreactive skillet over medium heat and cook for 1 minute, stirring. Add the shallots and garlic and cook for another couple of minutes to render some of the fat. Do not allow the shallots or garlic to brown. Pour in the vinegar, swirl everything together, and pour over the salad. Give a few turns of the peppermill and serve immediately.

Les Petits Plats de Légumes
The Vegetable Course

*I*f there's one thing that perturbs a Frenchman, it's being presented with a crowded plate of food. As if good sense and reason (not to mention the cook) have flown out the window, one is left to create a menu out of the food on the plate. This defies convention. It's fair neither to the food, which fights for an organizing menu, nor to the guest, who is forced to suspend good manners. Much better to eat one's meal in separate courses, to take the time to enjoy, for order and balanced variety are as important to a French meal as ingredients are to a recipe. So in France, one rarely finds vegetables served with the main course except when the vegetable is part of the dish, as in *poulet chasseur,* chicken with mushrooms, or *tournedos de veau Clamart,* veal medallions with artichokes and peas. Otherwise, vegetables, which demand a cook's special attention, are accorded a place of privilege and are served on their own.

Gâteau de Tomates d'Été

Upside-down Tomato Tart

MAKES 4 SERVINGS

This upside-down tomato tart reminds me of a weathered, bougainvillea-covered barn, not in Paris, of course, but in the South. The pastry bubbles and browns to crispness, as if it were the sun that parched it, not your oven, and the tomatoes dry out and caramelize to their essential sunny flavor. Don't refrigerate this tart.

¼ cup packed dark brown sugar

¼ cup red wine vinegar

12 ripe but firm Roma (plum) tomatoes (about 3 pounds)

2 teaspoons salt

½ teaspoon freshly ground black pepper

3 sprigs fresh oregano, leaves only

2 tablespoons extra virgin olive oil

½ recipe Savory Tart Crust (recipe follows)

Fresh basil sprigs for garnish

1. Combine the sugar and vinegar in a saucepan, place over medium-high heat, and boil the mixture until it turns dark and syrupy, about 3 minutes. Set aside.

2. Cut out the tomato cores, quarter the tomatoes from tip to stem, and gently squeeze out the seeds (see page 52). Place the tomato quarters in a bowl, add the vinegar syrup, salt, pepper, oregano, and olive oil, and toss well.

3. Arrange the tomatoes in a tight rose-petal pattern in a 7-inch-round, 2-inch-deep nonstick baking dish and pour over any syrup remaining in the bowl. Place in a cold oven, turn the oven to 375°F, and bake for 1 hour.

4. Roll out the pastry into a 7-inch circle. Cover the tomatoes with the pastry, replace in the oven, and bake for another 30 to 35 minutes, or until the pastry is golden.

5. Let the tart cool for 20 minutes, then invert it onto a plate. Decorate with fresh basil and serve at room temperature.

Pâte Brisée | Savory Tart Crust

MAKES ONE 9-INCH TART SHELL

1½ cups pastry flour

¼ teaspoon salt

¼ teaspoon sugar

3 tablespoons unsalted butter,
chilled and cut into 9 slices

1 large egg yolk

1 to 2 tablespoons ice water,
if needed

Combine the flour, salt, and sugar in the bowl of a food processor or mixer. Add the butter and yolk. Pulse the food processor or run the mixer until the mixture just begins to hold together; it should resemble coarse meal. If the mixture seems too crumbly and won't hold together, add a tablespoon or 2 of water. Do not overwork the dough. Transfer the dough to a work surface and press it into a ball. Wrap in plastic wrap and refrigerate for 1 hour before using. (It may be frozen for up to one month.)

Tomates au Four | Roasted Tomatoes

In all French cooking other than the cooking of the Midi, tomatoes are used for adding color and sweet acidity to stocks, sauces, and vegetable concoctions—more condiment than vegetable. I did find some recipes for tomato side dishes and first courses, though. This one, from a produce vendor in the Marché Saint-Quentin, is a favorite I've adapted for the average American tomato, firmer than the tomatoes in Parisian markets and requiring longer, slower cooking. Roasting tomatoes gives them a concentrated, jammy flavor and texture. Serve these tomatoes with fish or poultry in sauce, or use olive oil rather than butter and serve the tomatoes at room temperature with vinaigrette. Either way, you'll appreciate this marvelously simple dish.

8 ripe but firm Roma (plum) tomatoes
½ teaspoon fine sea salt
Freshly ground black pepper
1 teaspoon dried thyme

2 cloves garlic, finely slivered
2 tablespoons unsalted butter
or olive oil

1. Cut out the tomato cores, cut a deep X in the tip of each and gently squeeze out the seeds. Sprinkle the incisions with the salt, pepper to taste, and the thyme and insert the slivered garlic. Place the tomatoes in a shallow baking dish, stem side down, place in the oven, and turn the oven to 300°F. Bake the tomatoes for 1½ to 2 hours, or until shriveled but not dried out. Remove from the oven and set aside.

2. When you're ready to serve the tomatoes, preheat the broiler. Place a nut of butter (or a drizzle of oil) in the incision of each tomato and place the baking dish under the broiler until the butter (or oil) is bubbling. Serve immediately.

Fenouil et Oignons Rôtis au Vermouth

Fennel and Onions Baked with Vermouth

MAKES 4 SERVINGS

Fennel, a celerylike vegetable with a licorice flavor, can be tough and stringy when cooked. I learned from one of the greengrocers in the market that cooking it in liquid before roasting breaks down some of the fiber and tenderizes the stalks so it can absorb the vermouth and butter as it bakes.

4 small fennel bulbs (about 1 pound)

1 large yellow onion, quartered

1 cup dry vermouth

⅛ teaspoon allspice

1 teaspoon salt

2 tablespoons unsalted butter

Freshly ground black pepper

1. Preheat the oven to 375°F.

2. Trim and discard the fennel stalks. Remove the core and discard the tough outer layer. Quarter the bulbs from tip to stem.

3. Bring a pot of salted water to a boil. Add the onion and fennel, cook for 5 minutes, and drain.

4. Place the onion and fennel in a baking dish just large enough to hold them. Add the vermouth and allspice, sprinkle with the salt, dot with the butter, and give a few turns of the peppermill. Cover tightly and place in the oven for 45 minutes.

5. Remove the baking dish from the oven and preheat the broiler. Place the dish under the broiler for about 10 minutes, or until the vegetables take on a golden color. Transfer to a serving dish and serve.

Choufleur Rôti à la Vinaigrette
Whole Roasted Cauliflower with Vinaigrette

MAKES 4 TO 6 SERVINGS

The French call cauliflower "cabbage flower," because it reminds them of cabbage, especially when boiled. Shopping at the greengrocer one afternoon, I noticed some beautiful cauliflower, tinged with purple and only slightly larger than a baseball. The buds were symmetrically formed into little triangular ridges, more like pavé-set diamonds than the common convolution of free-form bud masses.

Wanting me to take advantage of the visual impact we both knew this ordinary vegetable could make, the grocer urged me to roast the whole cauliflower. I was happily rewarded with a cauliflower that tasted more like hazelnuts than the cabbagy boiled cauliflower that one often masks with cheese sauce. I've never boiled cauliflower since, and this has become one of my most popular standards. Here at home, you can occasionally find the pretty cauliflower that I saw in Paris. Otherwise, look for the smallest heads of white cauliflower at the local greenmarket. Don't despair if you can only get a larger head; simply parcook it in a microwave or steam it to soften (but only slightly) before roasting.

2 small or medium cauliflower
   (about 1 pound)
2 tablespoons extra virgin olive oil
3 tablespoons unsalted butter
2 tablespoons fresh lemon juice

1 teaspoon salt
½ teaspoon freshly ground black pepper
Pinch of freshly grated nutmeg
The Perfect Mustard Vinaigrette
   (page 69)

1. If using one large cauliflower, place it in a steamer over boiling water, cover, and steam for 20 minutes.
2. Preheat the oven to 375°F.
3. Combine the oil, butter, lemon juice, salt, pepper, and nutmeg in a small saucepan and heat over low heat until the butter is melted. Set aside.
4. Place the cauliflower in a small roasting pan, baste with the butter mixture, cover, place in the oven, and roast for 30 minutes, basting several times. Remove the cover and continue to cook for another 10 to 25 minutes, depending on the size of the head. The cauliflower is cooked when a knife can easily be inserted into the core. Serve hot or at room temperature, with the vinaigrette.

Broccoli à l'Étuvée

Casserole-Roasted Broccoli

MAKES 4 SERVINGS

Parisians, who peel most vegetables, esteem broccoli as much for its stem as for the florets. Peel off the tough, woody outside and you'll discover another vegetable lurking inside. You'll adore its tender texture, slight hazelnut flavor, and pale cucumber color. Shopping for broccoli now, I look not only for heads of compact florets, but for those with a thick base that I can peel with little problem.

2 pounds broccoli (about 2 bunches)

1 medium onion

2 ounces prosciutto, ham, or bacon,
  finely chopped

7 cloves garlic, thinly sliced

½ teaspoon salt

Freshly ground black pepper

1 teaspoon dried thyme

1 teaspoon dried summer savory

2 tablespoons unsalted butter, melted

1. Preheat the oven to 350°F.

2. Trim and discard the bottom ½ inch from the broccoli stalks. Cut off the tops, separating them into large florets. Trim off the leaves and set aside. Peel and discard the outer dark green skin from the long stems and cut the stems lengthwise (as best you can) into ½-inch-thick sticks. Halve the onion from tip to stem and cut out the core. Lay each half cut side down on a work surface and sliver from tip to stem.

3. In a baking dish just large enough to hold all the ingredients, place the prosciutto, onion, and broccoli stems in one layer, followed by a layer of the leaves, then the florets, and finally the garlic. Season with the salt, pepper, thyme, and savory and drizzle with the butter. Cover tightly and place in the oven for 45 minutes, or until the florets are tender.

4. Transfer the contents of the baking dish, including any cooking juices, to a serving bowl and serve.

Garlic

Choux de Bruxelles aux Échalotes
Glazed Brussels Sprouts and Shallots

MAKES 4 SERVINGS

Madame Demoquet never boils Brussels sprouts, and when you prepare this recipe, you'll understand why. Her sprouts are tender but not at all soggy, and they lose any noxious aroma of boiled cabbage. The trick is to cook them in a saucepan or skillet that's just large enough to hold them and the shallots in one layer. As the cooking liquid reduces, it becomes concentrated with flavor. When the liquid is completely evaporated, continue cooking. The sprouts will continue to lose moisture from inside. After a minute or so, the sprouts and shallots become glazed. Keep cooking them until they turn dark golden. When the kitchen fills with an aroma reminiscent of chestnuts roasting, they're done.

1 pound Brussels sprouts
1/2 pound shallots
1 tablespoon unsalted butter

1/2 teaspoon salt
1 teaspoon sugar
Freshly ground black pepper

1. Trim the outer leaves from the Brussels sprouts and cut an X in the root end of each one. Peel the shallots, without cutting into the root end, separate the cloves, and cut an X in the root end of each.

2. Place the Brussels sprouts, butter, salt, sugar, and pepper to taste in a skillet. Add enough water to cover the sprouts by three quarters, place over high heat, and boil for 5 minutes. Add the shallots and continue to boil until all the liquid has evaporated, another 7 to 10 minutes. Reduce the heat to medium and continue cooking, shaking the pan occasionally, until the sprouts and shallots turn a dark golden color. Transfer to a serving dish and serve.

Oignons Nouveaux aux Lardons
Glazed Spring Onions with Bacon Vinaigrette

MAKES 4 SERVINGS

The new onions that come to Parisian markets in April are like large scallions with round or teardrop bulbs that haven't yet formed a dry skin. People take advantage of their season to prepare them as a vegetable. Heat destroys the volatile oils and leaves them sweet. Cook them slowly, without browning, with bacon. A little vinegar balances the salt in the bacon and makes the onions taste sweeter. In the States, I sometimes find these lovely onions in the supermarket, and they're always at the greenmarket in early spring. If need be, you can approximate the dish by using the largest scallions you can find. Serve these to accompany simply prepared lamb chops, fish, or chicken.

12 spring onions or 36 large scallions

6 slices bacon, cut into $\frac{1}{2}$-inch strips

3 tablespoons red wine vinegar

1 tablespoon unsalted butter

$\frac{1}{4}$ teaspoon salt

Freshly ground black pepper

1 tablespoon fresh chervil leaves

1. Trim the spring onions or the scallions, leaving about $1\frac{1}{2}$ inches of the green tops. Trim the root tips, being careful not to cut into the bulb, and cut a small X in the bulb tip of each spring onion.

2. Place the bacon in a skillet over medium heat and cook, stirring, until crisp, 5 to 6 minutes. Add the onions and cook for about 5 minutes, turning once. The exact cooking time depends on the size of your onions or scallions. When the X that you've cut into the tip of the bulb opens up and the onion is soft to the touch, it's ready. If the onions begin to brown or the bacon becomes too dark before the onions are done, cover the skillet and reduce heat to low. Remove the onions and bacon bits to a platter and keep warm.

3. Add the vinegar and butter to the skillet and cook, stirring constantly, until the butter is melted. Remove from the heat and pour over the onions and bacon. Add the salt, give a few turns of the peppermill over the platter, and sprinkle with the chervil leaves. Serve immediately.

Brioche aux Asperges
Asparagus on Toasted Brioche

MAKES 4 SERVINGS

In France, certain vegetables are so special that people attribute qualities to them usually reserved for pets or small animals such as lambs and goats. Asparagus is one of these vegetables. People choose the spears individually in the market, and they describe them with adjectives such as *bien gros,* meaning stout, or *de jolie tête,* with a pretty face (to describe a nicely formed top). So, it's no wonder that asparagus is too important to be a side dish. If you've been steaming asparagus your entire life, you'll love this way of cooking it in its own juices. Choose really fat asparagus. (Length is not as important as thickness.) Peel them about three quarters of the way up, but don't bother trimming the ends—Parisians pick up asparagus with their fingers and eat the stalks down to the woody end. When the asparagus is cooked, most of the cooking liquid will have evaporated. If the water in the saucepan evaporates too rapidly, add a bit more.

1¾ pounds thick asparagus,
stalks peeled
Salt and freshly ground black pepper

3 tablespoons unsalted butter
Four ¾-inch-thick slices brioche,
challah, or egg bread

1. Place the asparagus in a single layer in one or two large saucepans and add enough water to come three quarters of the way up the asparagus. Season with salt and pepper and add the butter. Place the skillet(s) over high heat, bring to a boil, and boil until the asparagus is tender and the liquid becomes buttery, about 8 minutes.

2. Meanwhile, preheat the broiler. Toast the brioche on one side only and keep warm.

3. To serve, place the brioche toasted side down on plates, arrange the asparagus spears on top, and spoon over the juices.

Talking about bread with the artisan baker
in the Saxe-Breteuil market; 7th arrondissement

Sauté de Petits Artichauts
Panfry of Baby Artichokes

MAKES 4 SERVINGS

Sautéing these small thistles produces a nutty flavor. Don't be afraid of cooking them too long—they caramelize, crisp, and turn a nice dark golden color. Undercook them, and you risk toughness. Make certain to trim the artichokes well of all dark green leaves, and serve them while still hot and crispy, with aïoli or tapenade. These artichokes can be served in place of fried potatoes. They are also good served as a hot hors d'oeuvre with aperitifs.

16 baby artichokes	1/2 teaspoon fine sea salt
3 tablespoons olive oil	Freshly ground black pepper
2 tablespoons unsalted butter	4 lemon wedges

1. Trim and discard the outer layers of leaves from each artichoke until the light green leaves are exposed. Trim and discard any dark bits from the base. Halve the artichokes tip to base and trim and discard the top 1/4 inch.

2. Heat the oil and butter in a skillet over medium heat. Add the artichokes and cook, uncovered, for 15 minutes, shaking the pan, or turning the artichokes, so that both surfaces become a dark golden color. Remove from the heat, sprinkle with the salt, and give a few turns of the peppermill. Arrange on plates and accompany with the lemon wedges.

Petits Artichauts à la Moëlle
Baby Artichokes Sautéed with Beef Marrow

For this incredible dish, you'll have to ask your butcher to order some marrow bones sawed into two-inch rounds. The jiggly marrow has only a faint flavor, but it has great "mouth feel" that complements the chewy artichokes perfectly. This dish is herby and tart, and the marrow drippings make a wonderful sauce for the artichokes.

³⁄₄ pound beef marrow bones
16 baby artichokes
2 tablespoons unsalted butter
2 tablespoons minced shallots
¹⁄₄ cup dry white wine,
  such as Chardonnay

1 teaspoon salt
Freshly ground black pepper
1 tablespoon chopped fresh parsley
1 tablespoon chopped fresh chervil

1. Place the marrow bones in ice water and place in the refrigerator for 20 minutes. When the bones are well chilled, pop the marrow centers out of the bones. (Save the bones for making stock or for adding to stews.) Slice the marrow into ¹⁄₂-inch rounds and set aside in the refrigerator.

2. Trim and discard the outer layers of leaves from each artichoke until the light green leaves are exposed. Trim and discard any dark bits from the base. Halve the artichokes tip to base and trim and discard the top ¹⁄₄ inch.

3. Melt the butter in a skillet over medium heat. Add the shallots and artichokes, cover, and cook for 5 minutes. Add the wine, salt, and pepper to taste and continue to cook, uncovered, for another 5 to 7 minutes, until the wine reduces and the artichokes are tender. Add the marrow and cook, stirring, another 1 minute, or until the marrow turns translucent. Remove the skillet from the heat and add the parsley and chervil. Transfer the contents of the skillet to a serving dish and serve immediately.

Artichauts Braisés
au Jambon de Pays

Braised Artichokes
with Prosciutto

MAKES 4 SERVINGS

I was at Jacques Bibonne's atelier for lunch. Spring was in the air, but it was still chilly. He served me these braised artichokes, and then he prepared his *Oeufs Meurette* (page 58). What a perfect meal it was. And, you know, his kitchen is the size of a bread box, but it didn't matter. When you try his recipe, you'll see that the prosciutto adds its wonderful clove flavor to the astringent artichokes. Be sure to serve plenty of bread to soak up the buttery sauce.

4 purple or green globe artichokes

White vinegar

4 cloves garlic, minced

2 tablespoons minced shallots

3 cups Homemade Chicken Broth
   (page 237), or low-sodium chicken
   broth

1 lemon, halved

$\frac{1}{2}$ teaspoon dried savory

$\frac{1}{2}$ teaspoon salt

$\frac{1}{2}$ teaspoon freshly ground black pepper

2 ounces prosciutto, finely chopped

3 tablespoons unsalted butter

2 tablespoons finely chopped fresh
   flat-leaf parsley

1. Pull off the outer two layers of leaves from each artichoke. Trim an inch off the top of each artichoke and snip off the prickly tips of the remaining leaves. Halve the artichokes from tip to stem and, using a paring knife, cut out the chokes. To avoid darkening, keep the trimmed artichokes in cold water to which you've added some white vinegar, until ready to cook them; drain well when ready to cook.

2. Place the artichokes in a nonreactive skillet large enough to hold them in a single layer (or use two skillets) and add the garlic, shallots, broth, lemon, savory, salt, and pepper. Cover, bring to a boil over high heat, reduce the heat to medium-low, and simmer, turning once, until the artichokes are tender in the center, 25 to 30 minutes. Transfer the artichokes to a warm serving platter.

3. If you've used two skillets, combine the cooking liquids in one. Remove and discard the lemon. Add the prosciutto and cook for a minute to warm through. Beat in the butter, add the parsley, and remove from the heat.

4. To serve, arrange the artichokes on plates. Serve the sauce in ramekins or small cups for dipping the leaves.

Place d'Aligre, 12th arrondissement

Petits Artichauts Citronnés
Slivered Artichokes in Lemon Butter

The secret to this dish is in the cutting, for the artichokes must be slivered paper-thin. I use a little Japanese mandoline for this job, though most Parisians cut them by hand. You'll also have good luck using a thin-bladed flexible stainless-steel knife designed for filleting fish. Be sure to trim all the green outer leaves, to avoid any toughness. Top the artichokes with poached eggs for a lovely luncheon course. Or, use as a bed for chicken or turkey breasts, grilled or broiled salmon, or veal or pork cutlets. If you substitute extra virgin olive oil for the butter, you'll be able to serve the artichokes at room temperature or chilled.

4 teaspoons fresh lemon juice
12 baby artichokes
2 tablespoons unsalted butter
*   or extra virgin olive oil*

1 shallot, finely chopped
2 tablespoons dry white wine
Salt and freshly ground black pepper

1. Place 2 teaspoons of the lemon juice in a mixing bowl. Trim and discard the outer layers of leaves from each artichoke until the light green leaves are exposed. Trim and discard any dark bits from the base. Trim and discard the top ¼ inch. Halve each artichoke from top to stem, lay each half flat on a cutting board, and cut into the thinnest slivers possible. Toss the slivers in the lemon juice as you work.

2. Melt the butter in a nonreactive skillet over medium heat. Add the shallot and cook, stirring, to soften, about 2 minutes. Add the wine, artichokes, and the remaining lemon juice. Cook, tossing, for about 3 minutes, or until the artichokes are just wilted. Remove from the heat, season with salt and pepper, scrape into a serving dish, and serve.

Pain Tiède de Champignons, Sauce à l'Estragon

Warm Mushroom Loaf with Tarragon Sauce

MAKES 8 SERVINGS

The mushroom vendor in the Marché Passy, near the Bois de Boulogne, prepares this loaf when wild mushrooms are available. For the mushroom "bread," she uses ordinary cultivated mushrooms. She sautés a mixture of chanterelles, morels, and pleurottes to garnish the loaf and may serve it as a main course at lunch. The texture of this warm "bread" is like that of Boston brown bread straight from the steamer.

3 pounds white mushrooms

3 medium onions, minced

¾ cup dry sherry

¾ teaspoon dried thyme

2 teaspoons salt

1 teaspoon freshly ground black pepper

1 cup fresh bread crumbs

½ cup all-purpose flour

1 teaspoon baking powder

4 large eggs

½ cup heavy cream

6 tablespoons unsalted butter

2 pounds assorted mushrooms, such as
   oyster, shiitake, chanterelle, morel,
   portobello, and/or porcini

½ to ¾ cup dry white wine

1 tablespoon chopped fresh tarragon
   or 1 teaspoon dried

1. Purée the white mushrooms and onions together in a food processor. Place in a large skillet, add the sherry, thyme, 1½ teaspoons salt, and ¾ teaspoon pepper, and place over medium heat. Cook, stirring occasionally, for about 45 minutes, or until the mixture is dry.

2. Preheat the oven to 375°F. Grease a 9- by 5-inch loaf pan or a Bundt pan.

3. Transfer the contents of the skillet to a mixing bowl and stir in the bread crumbs, flour, and baking powder. Add the eggs one at a time, mixing well. Stir in the cream. Pour the mixture into the prepared pan. Cover, place in a water bath with boiling water, and bake for 2 hours, or until a toothpick inserted into the center comes out clean. Remove the loaf from the oven, remove from the water bath, and set aside. (It should cool for 10 minutes before being unmolded.)

4. Meanwhile, melt 1 tablespoon of the butter in a large skillet. Add the assorted mushrooms and cook, stirring occasionally, for 5 minutes. Add the wine and season with the remaining salt and pepper. If using dried tarragon, add it now. Continue cooking until the liquid is reduced by half. If using fresh tarragon, add it now. Remove from the heat and whisk in the remaining 5 tablespoons butter. Set aside and keep warm.

5. Unmold the mushroom loaf and slice into 1½-inch slices. Arrange the slices on plates, spoon over the sautéed mushrooms, and serve.

*I*N OLDER FRENCH COOKBOOKS, MUSHROOMS ARE LISTED UNDER CONDIMENTS, LIKE MUSTARD OR HORSERADISH, INGREDIENTS THAT ENLIVEN THE FLAVORS OF A DISH, LENDING A MYSTERIOUS, EARTHY FLAVOR TO STEWS AND SAUCES.

Cèpes à la Bordelaise
Porcini Mushrooms in Red Wine with Marrow

MAKES 4 SERVINGS

Porcini, or cèpes, are the most prized of all mushrooms. They can be enormous, and, until you get to know them, they don't seem very attractive, with their squat meaty stems and mottled caps. Everyone says they cook up like a steak. But they remind me more of lobster, with their greenish undersides that become creamy like tomalley. At any rate, this recipe uses them in a classic steak dish, instead of filet mignon. They're pan-grilled, then sauced with a red wine sauce and garnished with beef marrow. (Ask your butcher to order you some marrow bones, sawed into 2-inch rounds.) Follow this rich and delicious starter with a seafood main course.

1 $\frac{1}{2}$ pounds beef marrow bones	2 tablespoons minced shallots
1 pound fresh porcini	$\frac{1}{2}$ cup dry red wine
2 tablespoons unsalted butter	$\frac{1}{2}$ teaspoon fresh thyme leaves or dried
2 tablespoons olive oil	1 tablespoon chopped fresh chervil
$\frac{1}{2}$ teaspoon salt	Freshly ground black pepper

1. Place the marrow bones in ice water and place in the refrigerator for 20 minutes to chill. When the bones are chilled, use your thumb to pop the marrow centers out of the bones. Save the bones for making stock or for adding to stews. Cut the marrow into $\frac{1}{4}$-inch rounds and replace in the refrigerator until needed.

2. Trim and discard the sandy bottoms of the mushroom stems. Wipe the caps and stems clean, then slice into $\frac{3}{8}$-inch cross sections. Remove and discard any spongy bits from the slices.

3. Heat 1 tablespoon of the butter and the oil in a large skillet over medium heat. Cook the mushrooms for 3 minutes, turning once. Remove from the skillet, sprinkle with $\frac{1}{4}$ teaspoon of the salt, and keep warm on a plate.

4. Add the shallots, wine, thyme, and the remaining ¼ teaspoon salt to the skillet, increase the heat to high, and cook until the liquid is reduced by half, about 2 minutes. Add the marrow to the sauce and cook for another minute or until the marrow becomes translucent. Swirl in the remaining 1 tablespoon butter and add the chervil.

5. Arrange the mushrooms on plates and spoon over the sauce and marrow. Give a turn of the peppermill over each plate and serve immediately.

Inspecting cèpes in the Bastille market, 11th arrondissement

Sauté de Morilles et de Haricots Verts

Green Beans and Morels

MAKES 4 SERVINGS

"The morels, when they are first in season, are such a treat," said Giselle. "Conversation stops when I bring this dish to the table. We savor the peaty taste and thick texture of these mushrooms and marvel at their strange appearance. When Eve was little, she marveled at their honeycomb shape and asked if we were eating a bee's house. I always think of that now when I make morels." The secret to this dish is to cook the mushrooms without losing the juices that bleed into the skillet. Cook them slowly, so that they make their own little sauce.

½ pound fresh morel mushrooms or 3 ounces dried

½ pound haricots verts or small green beans

2 tablespoons unsalted butter

1 tablespoon minced shallots

1 teaspoon salt

½ teaspoon freshly ground black pepper

3 tablespoons sherry

1. If using fresh morels, rub with a damp kitchen towel to remove any dirt particles. Or reconstitute dry morels by soaking in warm water for 2 hours; then remove them and squeeze them to get rid of excess water. Reserve a few tablespoons of the liquid for the sauce.

2. Bring a pot of salted water to a boil and add the beans. Cook haricots verts for 3 minutes, green beans for 5 minutes. Drain and run under cold water until cool. Place on kitchen towels to dry.

3. Melt the butter in a skillet over medium heat. Add the shallots, morels, salt, and pepper. If using dried morels, add 2 tablespoons of the water in which the mushrooms were reconstituted. Cover and cook for 5 minutes. Add the sherry, replace the cover, and cook for another minute. Remove the cover, add the beans, and cook, stirring a couple of times, until heated through, 1 to 2 minutes.

4. Mound the morels and beans on plates, spoon over the liquid that remains in the skillet, and serve immediately.

Shopping with Papa, Marché Père Lachaise, 11th arrondissement

Toasts de Champignons Sauvages
Forest Mushrooms on Toast

During the spring and fall, depending on the rains, mushrooms of all sorts come and go in the markets—honeycombed morels, dense orange chanterelles, and tiny *mousserons* and *philiots* are snatched up by Parisians, who take them home and cook them the simplest way possible. It gives city dwellers the illusion of having spent a Sunday foraging in a forest, when in reality they were strolling the Luxembourg Gardens.

Some people buy little puff pastry shells at the bakery and fill them with this mixture, but most people cut slabs from a dense country-style loaf of bread and cook them in butter to serve as a presentation "raft." Some people cook a couple of cloves of thinly slivered garlic with the mushrooms. One merchant suggested adding a point of sherry. Both are good ideas, but I prefer the unadorned flavor of the mushrooms, slightly enhanced by the sweetness of shallots and the acid piquancy of white wine.

4 ounces fresh morel mushrooms	2 shallots, minced
4 ounces fresh chanterelle mushrooms	1 bay leaf
4 ounces fresh shiitake mushrooms	2 sprigs fresh thyme
4 ounces fresh oyster mushrooms	1/2 teaspoon salt
4 tablespoons (1/2 stick) unsalted butter	Freshly ground black pepper
2 teaspoons vegetable oil, preferably canola	3/4 cup whole milk
4 slices rustic white bread	1 tablespoon unsalted butter

1. Rub, don't wash, the morels and chanterelles and halve or quarter the larger ones. Trim the stems off the shiitake and oyster mushrooms and reserve for another use.

2. Preheat the oven to 200°F.

3. Melt 1 tablespoon of the butter with 1 teaspoon of the oil in a large skillet over medium-low heat. Add the bread and cook until lightly golden around the edges, about 4 minutes. Add 1 more tablespoon butter and the remaining 1 teaspoon oil, turn the bread, and cook briefly on the other side, about 2 minutes. Remove the bread and keep warm in the oven.

4. Add the remaining 2 tablespoons butter to the skillet and increase the heat to medium. Add the shallots and cook, stirring, until they begin to soften, about 1 minute. Add the mushrooms, bay leaf, thyme, salt, and pepper to taste, cover, and cook, stirring once or twice, for about 2 minutes. Remove the cover, add the milk, increase the heat to high, and continue to cook for another 6 minutes. Remove the skillet from the heat and stir in the butter. Remove the thyme and the bay leaf.

5. Place the toasts on plates and spoon on the mushrooms and sauce. Serve immediately.

Terrine de Lentilles, Sauce Vinaigrette

Lentil Aspic with Vinaigrette

MAKES 8 TO 12 SERVINGS

"This is an old-fashioned dish, a recipe that most of the young don't prepare," said the woman who gave me this recipe. "Perhaps it's too plain for today's tastes." Traditionally, lentils and carrots simmer with *rillons,* a kind of ham hock, that gives a smoky flavor. A pig's tail is added for the gelatin that holds the terrine together. I think the pork flavor is too strong for most North American palates, so I re-created the terrine using finely chopped bacon and unflavored gelatin. People who say they never cook lentils have marveled at this simple dish. Here's a tip: When the lentils have finished cooking, the liquid in the pot should cover the lentils by about one inch. If necessary, add some broth or water to make up the difference.

2 tablespoons vegetable oil,
preferably canola

2 medium onions, finely chopped

2 medium carrots, finely chopped

3 stalks celery, finely chopped

¼ pound bacon, finely chopped

1¼ cups small French (du Puy) lentils

4 to 4½ cups Homemade Chicken Broth
(page 237) or low-sodium broth

½ teaspoon ground sage

2 bay leaves

2½ packets unflavored gelatin

¼ cup chopped fresh parsley

4 sprigs fresh thyme for garnish,
optional

The Perfect Mustard Vinaigrette
(page 69)

1. Heat the oil in a small pot over medium heat. Cook the onions, carrots, and celery until soft, about 12 minutes. Add the lentils, broth, sage, bay leaves, and bacon, cover, and cook for 1 hour, or until the lentils are tender and beginning to fall to pieces.
2. Meanwhile, soften the gelatin in ¼ cup of water. Add it to the pot about 5 minutes before the lentils are done.
3. When the lentils are cooked, if the broth does not cover the lentils by 1 inch in the pot, add more. Pour the contents of the pot into a large bowl and remove the bay leaves. Mix in the chopped parsley. Pour the mixture into a 1-quart loaf pan, cover, and refrigerate overnight.
4. To serve, unmold the terrine onto a work counter and cut into 1-inch slices. Arrange the slices on a platter or individual plates, spoon some mustard vinaigrette around the slices, and garnish with sprigs of thyme.

Blanquette de Légumes "Marysa"
Marysa's Creamed Vegetable Ragout in Puff Pastry

MAKES 4 SERVINGS

Vegetables in Parisian markets are often so small and tender that they require no pre-cooking. Even so, for this dish each vegetable is cooked on its own, then combined with the others to simmer in the sauce for a few minutes. This is a dish best prepared with vegetables from your garden or the local growers' market, but the blanquette is still delicious with less carefully grown candidates. To soften the cellulose and make a potentially tough vegetable tender, add one to four tablespoonfuls of water to the skillet with each one and cook until evaporated; the older and larger the vegetables, the more water you'll need.

12 scallions

3 leaves green Swiss chard

4 Brussels sprouts

3 tablespoons unsalted butter

3 stalks celery, cut into ½-inch slices

Salt

1 carrot, sliced into ¼-inch rounds

12 small radishes, tops removed
    and discarded

½ pound large asparagus, bottoms
    trimmed, stalks peeled, and
    cut into 1-inch pieces

½ cup dry white wine,
    such as Sauvignon Blanc

½ pound medium white mushrooms,
    rinsed and patted dry

1 tablespoon all-purpose flour

½ cup whole milk

¼ teaspoon freshly ground white pepper

¼ lemon

½ cup fresh or frozen peas

1 teaspoon chopped fresh savory
    or ½ teaspoon dried

3 tablespoons chopped fresh chervil
    or parsley

Four 6-inch puff pastry shells,
    prebaked

1. Trim and remove the green tops of the scallions, slice into rounds, and reserve. Trim and discard the roots and cut a small X in the base of each scallion. Remove the ribs from the chard leaves and slice into ¼-inch pieces. Roughly chop the chard leaves. Remove and discard the outer leaves from the Brussels sprouts and cut an X in the base of each one.

2. Over medium heat, melt 2 teaspoons of the butter in a lidded skillet large enough to comfortably hold each vegetable. Add the celery, season with a pinch of salt, cover, and cook until barely tender, about 1 minute. Using tongs or a slotted spoon, transfer the celery to a large flameproof casserole. Melt another teaspoon of butter in the skillet and add the carrot and 1 tablespoon water. Cover and cook until barely tender, about 2 minutes. Using the tongs, transfer the carrot to the casserole. Melt another teaspoon of butter in the skillet and add the Brussels sprouts and 2 tablespoons water. Cover and cook until barely tender, about 5 minutes. Using the tongs, transfer the sprouts to the casserole. Add the radishes to the skillet and cook, covered, until they lose their bright color and begin to soften. Using the tongs, transfer the radishes to the casserole. Melt another teaspoon of butter in the skillet and add the chard ribs. Season with a pinch of salt and cook for 2 minutes. Using the tongs, transfer the chard ribs to the casserole. Melt another teaspoon of butter in the skillet and add the asparagus and 2 tablespoons water. Season with a pinch of salt and cook, uncovered, until the asparagus turns bright green, about 2 minutes. Using the tongs, transfer the asparagus to the casserole.

3. Add the wine to the skillet, bring to a boil, and add the mushrooms. Season with salt, increase the heat to high, and cook for 3 minutes. Using the tongs, transfer the mushrooms to the casserole. Boil the liquid in the skillet until reduced to a few tablespoons and add to the casserole.

4. Melt the remaining 1 tablespoon butter in the skillet over medium heat. Sprinkle with the flour and cook, stirring, for 1 minute. Slowly stir in the milk. Season with the pepper and a pinch of salt, cover, and simmer until thick, about 3 minutes. Add the lemon and chard leaves and cook for a minute, or until wilted. Pour the contents of the skillet into the casserole, add the peas and savory, and mix gently.

5. Cover the casserole and cook over low heat for 10 minutes. Remove from the heat and retrieve and discard the lemon. Stir in the chervil. Arrange the pastry shells on plates, fill with the vegetables and sauce, and serve immediately.

Tarte de Légumes aux Fèves, Façon Erna

Erna's Vegetable and Fava Bean Tart

MAKES 4 SERVINGS

Erna, a cooking teacher, teaches this dish because cooking the vegetables requires a careful eye. The zucchini, onions, and tomatoes must cook slowly until they melt together into a chunky purée consistency, like unsweetened preserves. The secret is to cook the vegetables for a long time. At first, the vegetables lose their water. Pour off the first liquid that accumulates in the pan, reserving it to sauce the tart. Eventually the remaining liquid evaporates and the flavors of the vegetables combine.

3 vine-ripened tomatoes

½ cup shelled fava beans

*4 medium zucchini, peeled, quartered
   lengthwise, and cut crosswise into
   ½-inch slices*

1 medium onion, roughly chopped

2 tablespoons olive oil

¼ cup dry vermouth or dry white wine

2 bay leaves

1 teaspoon ground sage

1 teaspoon salt

Freshly ground black pepper

2 tablespoons unsalted butter

*One 9-inch tart shell (page 89),
   prebaked*

1. Bring a pot of water to the boil, drop in the tomatoes, and leave for 1½ to 2 minutes, or until the skins begin to crack. Immediately remove the tomatoes from the water and peel them. Cut out the cores and cut the tomatoes into eighths. Drop the fava beans into the boiling water and cook for 1 minute. Drain and remove the skins.

2. Combine all the ingredients except the butter and tart shell in a lidded heavy skillet or saucepan, cover, and place over medium heat. After about 20 minutes, drain the vegetables and set the liquid aside. Return the vegetables to the skillet and continue to cook for 40 minutes, stirring occasionally. Remove the cover, stir the vegetables, and cook for another 10 to 15 minutes, stirring occasionally, until all the liquid has evaporated and the vegetables have the consistency of preserves.

3. Meanwhile, place the reserved liquid in a saucepan over medium heat and cook a few minutes to reduce and concentrate. Remove from the heat, swirl in the butter, and pour into a sauceboat.

4. Transfer the contents of the skillet to the tart shell and serve with the sauce.

A greengrocer in the place d'Aligre market, 12th arrondissement

Les Gratins
Gratinéed Vegetables, Fish, and Poultry

"Your Jerry Lewis, we French appreciate him more than you Americans. He is so *gratiné*, so extraordinary, so outrageously ridiculous."

Gratins, served bubbling hot from the oven, rate among the favorite traditional dishes for lunch and dinner, as either a first or second course. They are deceptively easy to prepare, the challenge lying in having only enough sauce and topping to bathe the main ingredients and give them a bit of crust.

Gratin de Courge

Gratinéed Winter Squash

Banana squash, celebrated in the Provençal *soupe à la potiron,* is the most widely cooked of the hard squashes. I asked greengrocers how else to prepare it and most of them suggested this gratin, a dish that goes well on a menu with game, lamb, and poultry. Because of the subtly flavored squash, this gratin benefits from aromatic herbs. Fresh bay leaves, as easy to find in Paris as dried, impart a flavor that I can only describe as eucalyptus. My favorite recipe uses fresh leaves of lemon verbena. Since it's most likely that you'll be using dried bay leaves, and may have to omit the verbena, I suggest adding ground cardamom and coriander for the missing flavor. Butternut squash and other hard squashes also cook up nicely in this recipe.

1 pound banana squash

1 medium onion, finely chopped

2 cloves garlic, minced

1/2 cup heavy cream

3 bay leaves

1/8 teaspoon freshly grated nutmeg

1/4 teaspoon ground cardamom

1/4 teaspoon ground coriander

1 teaspoon salt

1/2 teaspoon freshly ground white pepper

1/2 cup grated Gruyère cheese

1. Preheat the oven to 375°F.

2. Peel the banana squash. (If using a whole squash or butternut squash, peel, halve, and remove the seeds.) Slice the squash into strips about 1/4 inch thick.

3. Mix together all the ingredients except the cheese. Place in a baking dish, cover tightly, and place in the oven for 35 minutes, or until the squash is tender.

4. Preheat the broiler. Uncover the baking dish and retrieve and discard the bay leaves. Sprinkle with the cheese and place under the broiler until the surface bubbles and turns golden. Serve immediately.

Gratin d'Aubergine

Eggplant and Onion Gratin

MAKES 4 SERVINGS

Serve this great vegetable dish as a separate course or as an accompaniment. If habit won't permit you to accept the idea of preparing eggplant in a casserole without tomatoes, halve four or five drained canned tomatoes and arrange them in the baking dish with the eggplant.

1½ *pounds large eggplant*	1 *cup milk*
Kosher salt	⅛ *teaspoon freshly grated nutmeg*
3 *tablespoons olive oil*	½ *teaspoon dried thyme*
2 *tablespoons unsalted butter*	½ *teaspoon freshly ground black pepper*
1 *onion, finely chopped*	1 *cup grated Gruyère cheese*
1 *tablespoon all-purpose flour*	

1. Peel the eggplant and slice it into ½-inch rounds. Layer the slices in a colander, sprinkling each layer with a little kosher salt. Set the colander in the sink or over a plate and leave for 1 hour. Press down occasionally to help rid the eggplant of its liquid.

2. Preheat the oven to 375°F.

3. Firmly press each slice of eggplant between kitchen towels to get rid of the salt. Brush the eggplant slices on both sides with the oil and arrange in a single layer on baking sheets. Place in the oven for 25 minutes, turning once. Remove from the oven and set aside. (Leave the oven on.)

4. Meanwhile, prepare the béchamel: Melt the butter in a saucepan over medium heat. Add the onion and cook, stirring, for 5 minutes, or until softened. Mix in the flour and cook for another minute. Add the milk, nutmeg, thyme, and pepper. Simmer, stirring, until thick, about 5 minutes.

5. Lightly oil a 6- by 8-inch baking dish. Arrange a layer of eggplant in the bottom of the baking dish and spread with a little of the béchamel. Sprinkle with some grated cheese. Repeat until all the eggplant is layered, using about half the cheese and ending with a layer of béchamel. Sprinkle the surface of the gratin with the remaining cheese. Place the baking dish in the oven for 40 minutes, or until bubbling. Remove from the oven and serve immediately.

Gratin de Sole aux Asperges
Gratin of Sole and White Asparagus

MAKES 4 SERVINGS

Potluck is not a very Parisian custom, but Gabriel Bousquet, who teaches cooking at Centre Ferrandi, the École Supérieure de Cuisine (my alma mater), insisted on bringing this simple dish to a little reunion at my apartment. He prepared it at home and we just slipped it into the hot oven to finish it.

$1^3/_4$ pounds skinless lemon sole
   or flounder fillets

$^1/_2$ teaspoon salt

$^1/_4$ teaspoon freshly ground white pepper

2 tablespoons chopped fresh parsley

1 medium onion, finely chopped

$^1/_4$ cup dry vermouth or dry white wine

$^3/_4$ pound white asparagus, bottoms
   trimmed, stalks peeled, and cut
   into $^1/_4$-inch rounds
   (substitute green if necessary)

$^1/_2$ cup heavy cream

3 large egg yolks

$^1/_4$ cup freshly grated Parmesan cheese

1. Preheat the oven to 375°F.

2. Halve each fillet lengthwise. Lay them skinned side up and sprinkle lightly with the salt and pepper, then with the parsley. Roll them up and arrange standing on end in a baking dish; they should fit snugly in the dish. Cover, place in the oven, and cook for 7 minutes. Remove from the oven and pour the liquid that has accumulated in the baking dish into a saucepan. Set the baking dish aside.

3. Add the onion and vermouth to the saucepan, place over medium heat, and cook for 3 minutes. Add the asparagus and cream and cook, uncovered, for another 3 minutes. Using a slotted spoon, retrieve the asparagus and arrange over the fish fillets. Continue cooking the liquid until reduced to a saucelike consistency, about another 5 minutes. Pour the liquid into a bowl, whisk in the yolks, and set aside.

4. Preheat the broiler. Spoon the sauce over the fish and asparagus, sprinkle with the cheese, and place under the broiler to brown the surface, about 3 minutes. Serve immediately.

White asparagus is in season
from April to June.

Gratin de Morue aux Pommes de Terre
Salt Cod and Potato Gratin

MAKES 4 SERVINGS

I'll go anywhere for salt cod. Even out to Saint-Denis, a working-class suburb just north of Paris. We profited from Madame Quetsch's dinner invitation to visit the Basilica there, the burial site of the kings of France. We had simple aperitifs—kirs—accompanied by radishes with butter. This delicious gratin was the main event, followed by a green salad and a copious platter of cheese. Choux puffs filled with praline buttercream were served for dessert.

1 $\frac{1}{2}$ pounds salt cod

1 medium onion, finely diced

3 cloves garlic, thinly sliced

2 tablespoons unsalted butter

2 tablespoons all-purpose flour

1 cup dry white wine

1 cup milk

$\frac{1}{2}$ pound russet potatoes, peeled and sliced into thin rounds

3 bay leaves

1 teaspoon fresh thyme leaves or
  $\frac{1}{2}$ teaspoon dried

$\frac{1}{2}$ teaspoon freshly ground black pepper

$\frac{1}{2}$ cup heavy cream

3 large egg yolks

$\frac{1}{4}$ cup fresh bread crumbs

1. Soak the cod for 36 to 48 hours in cold water, changing the water several times. Drain.
2. Place the cod in a pot with fresh cold water, place over high heat, bring to a boil, and cook for 1 minute. Drain, flake the meat, and set aside.
3. In a large skillet, cook the onion and garlic in the butter over medium heat until soft, but not brown, about 5 minutes. Stir in the flour, then add the wine and cook for 1 minute. Add the milk, potatoes, bay leaves, thyme, and pepper. Cover and cook until the potatoes are tender, about 10 minutes. Remove the lid, mix in the salt cod, and continue to cook for another minute. Remove from the heat. Remove and discard the bay leaves.
4. Preheat the broiler. Transfer the contents of the skillet to a broiler-proof dish. Beat the cream and yolks together and spoon over the top of the casserole, then sprinkle with the bread crumbs. Place the dish under the broiler until the top browns, about 2 to 3 minutes. Serve immediately.

On a *rue commerçante* in
Edith Piaf's neighborhood
in Gambetta

Gratin de Broccoli Rave

Broccoli Rabe Gratin

Broccoli rabe, also called rapini or broccoli radish, is a relative of broccoli with rather small individual bud clusters on thin, leafy stems. With its vaguely spicy bitterness and lingering hints of licorice and allspice, it bears little resemblance to the tame broccoli that we are more familiar with in the States. The stalks are a deep green color and always a little wilted in appearance. I like adding them, blanched, to salads, but Parisians prefer them steamed and served hot or cold with vinaigrette and especially in this creamy, cheesy gratin.

$1\frac{1}{2}$ pounds broccoli rabe

3 tablespoons unsalted butter

1 medium onion, finely diced

2 tablespoons all-purpose flour

$1\frac{1}{2}$ cups milk

1 teaspoon salt

Freshly ground black pepper

$\frac{1}{8}$ teaspoon freshly grated nutmeg

$\frac{1}{2}$ cup grated Gruyère cheese

1. Preheat the oven to 375°F.

2. Trim the bottom $1\frac{1}{2}$ inches of the broccoli rabe stems and discard. Bring a large pot of salted water to the boil, add the broccoli rabe, and cook for 4 minutes. Drain well.

3. To prepare the béchamel sauce, melt the butter in a saucepan over medium heat. Add the onion and cook, stirring, for 5 minutes, or until softened. Mix in the flour and cook, stirring, for 2 minutes. Slowly stir in the milk. Add the salt, pepper, and nutmeg and cook, stirring, until the mixture thickens, about 5 minutes.

4. Arrange the broccoli in a baking dish and pour over the béchamel. Cover and place in the oven for 15 minutes until bubbling in the center.

5. Preheat the broiler. Uncover the baking dish, sprinkle the surface with the cheese, and place under the broiler to brown, about 3 minutes. Serve immediately.

Gratin de Dinde aux Blettes
Chard and Turkey Gratin

MAKES 4 SERVINGS

Turkey is popular but not traditional in France. It's associated with no holidays, and one rarely finds the whole bird for sale. But Parisians, in their search for quick midweek meals, cook turkey *paillards,* or cutlets. Here's a nice recipe for serving them gratiné.

1 bunch green Swiss chard	½ cup heavy cream
2 tablespoons unsalted butter	4 thick-cut or 8 thin-cut turkey cutlets
1 teaspoon minced garlic	(1½ to 1¾ pounds)
1 tablespoon minced shallots	Freshly ground black pepper
1 teaspoon salt	½ cup grated Gruyère cheese

1. Wash the chard and pat dry. Remove the center ribs from the chard leaves and set aside. Roughly chop the leaves into two or three pieces each and set aside. Trim and discard the bottom of each rib as well as the narrow top. Slice the ribs crosswise into ¼-inch strips and set aside.

2. Preheat the oven to 375°F.

3. Melt 1 tablespoon of the butter in a large skillet over medium heat. Cook the chard ribs, covered, until soft, about 5 minutes. Remove and set aside. Melt the remaining 1 tablespoon butter, add the garlic and shallots, and cook for 1 minute, stirring. Add the chard leaves and ½ teaspoon of the salt and cook until the leaves are wilted, about 2 minutes. Add the cream and cook until the cream boils down and thickens, another 3 to 5 minutes. Remove from the heat and set aside.

4. If using thick-cut cutlets, halve each horizontally to make two flat pieces. Lay the cutlets on a work surface and season lightly with the remaining ½ teaspoon salt and pepper. Place a dollop of creamed chard in the center of each cutlet and roll up. Arrange the turkey cutlets, standing on end, in a broiler-proof baking dish. Sprinkle with the cheese and place in the oven for 20 to 25 minutes.

5. Preheat the broiler. Place the gratin under the broiler until golden, about 2 minutes. Serve immediately.

Buying lettuce, Marché Brune, 14th arrondissement

Gratin d'Endives au Jambon
Endive and Ham Gratin

Braised Belgian endive is arguably the most popular cooked lettuce in Paris. Here, the endive is cooked as for braised endive—blanched in water and then browned in butter. Next it's combined in a casserole with béchamel and ham, topped with bread crumbs, and baked until crisp on top. You'll appreciate how the bitterness of the endive cuts the saltiness of the ham and cheese.

2 tablespoons salt

6 medium heads Belgian endive

2 tablespoons unsalted butter

1 tablespoon vegetable oil,
   preferably canola

¾ cup heavy cream

2 bay leaves

2 sprigs fresh thyme or 1 teaspoon dried

Pinch of freshly grated nutmeg

2 tablespoons fresh bread crumbs

3 tablespoons freshly grated
   Parmesan cheese

6 slices ham, halved into
   12 small slices

Freshly ground black pepper

1. Add the salt to a pot of water and bring to a boil. Add the endive, cover, and cook for 5 minutes, then drain. Halve the endive lengthwise and press out the water using a kitchen towel.

2. Heat the butter and oil in a large skillet over medium heat. Add the endive, cut side up, in a single layer. Cook, turning once, until golden on both sides, about 10 minutes. Remove from the pan and set aside.

3. Meanwhile, combine the cream, bay leaves, thyme, and nutmeg in a small saucepan and place over medium heat. Bring to a boil and cook until reduced by a third, about 10 minutes. Remove the bay leaves and thyme sprigs, if using, and set the cream aside. In a small bowl, combine the bread crumbs and cheese; set aside.

4. Preheat the oven to 375°F.

5. Roll a slice of ham around each endive and arrange seam side down in a baking dish just large enough to hold the endive in one tightly packed layer. Sprinkle with a few turns of the peppermill. Spoon the cream over the endive. Sprinkle the bread crumb mixture over the top and place in the oven until the mixture bubbles and the top browns, about 20 to 25 minutes. Serve immediately.

The *traiteur* prepares complicated take-away food that people don't have time to make at home.

Hachis Parmentier | Shepherd's Pie

For a simple dish of mashed potatoes and leftover meat, this recipe borders on the baroque with its liberal use of wine, butter, and cream. If you're used to a shepherd's pie made with ground beef, you'll be happy that you made this *hachis parmentier*, for it's truly sumptuous. Using raclette cheese is a variation that I love, because, when melted, the cheese intoxicates with its overpowering aroma. Aged imported Gruyère or Emmenthaler will work fine, though. The dish is ready when the potatoes puff and the golden, bubbly surface cracks.

2½ pounds large new potatoes

6 tablespoons unsalted butter,
   cut into pieces

½ cup heavy cream

A few tablespoons milk as needed

Pinch of freshly grated nutmeg

Salt and freshly ground black pepper

1 onion, finely diced

1 carrot, finely diced

2 stalks celery, finely chopped

1 tablespoon all-purpose flour

1¼ cups dry robust red wine,
   such as Merlot

3 cups finely chopped cooked, beef, lamb,
   or pork (about 1¾ pounds)

½ teaspoon dried thyme

1 cup grated raclette, Gruyère,
   or Emmenthaler cheese

1. Preheat the oven to 375°F.

2. Boil the potatoes in their jackets until tender, 15 to 25 minutes. Drain, peel, and mash them. Mix in 4 tablespoons of the butter and stir in the cream. If the potatoes seem dry, add a little milk. Add the nutmeg and salt and pepper to taste. Cover and set aside.

3. Meanwhile, cook the onion, carrot, and celery in the remaining 2 tablespoons butter in a covered large skillet over medium-low heat until soft, 5 to 7 minutes. Stir in the flour and slowly add the wine. Cook until the mixture thickens, about 2 minutes. Add the beef, thyme, and salt and pepper to taste. Cover and cook for 2 minutes.

4. Transfer the contents of the skillet to a 2-quart baking dish. Spread the mashed potatoes on top and sprinkle with the cheese. Place the dish in the oven and bake until golden and bubbling, 30 to 40 minutes. Serve immediately.

Les Plats Principaux—
Les Poissons et les Crustacés,
les Volailles, et les Viandes

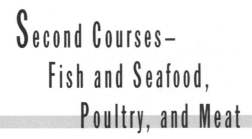

Second Courses–
Fish and Seafood,
Poultry, and Meat

ourquoi en faire un plat? "(Why make a big to-do?)," I said to a very put-out Corinne, who was seated at the wrong end of the table.

To appreciate French cuisine, you have to understand French habits. Often, when I'd be invited for dinner, my host or hostess would tempt me with, say, a poached turbotin, a Bresse hen, or a lamb roast—the *plat.* "Come for dinner. I'm preparing a family recipe." For an American unfamiliar with French meals, it's puzzling, because the Bresse hen, or whatever, is neither larger nor more weighty than the other courses served; but, coming after aperitif and entrée and before salad, cheese, and dessert, *le plat* is the apex of a meal, the *pièce de résistance,* a larger course only in concept and because it anchors the rest of a meal.

Any meal may lack a *plat principal,* be a sequence of *petits plats* instead, but when someone makes a big deal over something, plans their menu around a certain dish, you know to expect something special, usually something in sauce—for after all, what is French cooking if there's no sauce?

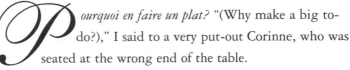

"Parisians are mad for fish."
—Alain Paton

Les Poissons et les Crustacés
Fish and Seafood

French people give meaning and significance to food beyond its life-sustaining value. I was having a conversation with Alain Paton, who teaches the fish specialty at Centre Ferrandi, the government cooking school, discussing the fact that Parisians seem to be buying more fish than ever before. Suddenly, he said, "Parisians are mad for fish simply because it's so perishable. Better to dine on fish while it's fresh, for life is fleeting. You could be crushed under the wheels of a speeding métro train, or hit by a taxi, or assassinated in the street. Ah, *oui,* monsieur, life in Paris can be like that. *Voilà. C'est tout.*" And he threw up his arms in a shrug.

Sardines Marinés au Muscadet
Marinated Sardines with New Potatoes

When cooked, sardines and their cousins mackerel and herring can be too strong for my palate, but when marinated, as they are for this dish, you avoid the heavy fish flavor that cooking the volatile fish oils gives to these fish. Pouring a hot marinade over these sardines barely cooks them and the acid in the marinade completes the process. Serve this dish well chilled in the summer or reheat and serve it hot during the cold months of the year.

1/4 cup kosher salt

1 1/2 pounds skinless sardine, herring, or small Spanish mackerel fillets

1/2 cup Muscadet or other herbaceous dry white wine

1/4 cup white wine vinegar

3 tablespoons extra virgin olive oil

1/2 small onion, finely minced

1 stalk celery, minced

2 bay leaves

1 teaspoon coarsely ground or crushed white pepper

16 coriander seeds or 1 teaspoon ground coriander

1 clove

2 sprigs fresh thyme

2 sprigs fresh tarragon

12 to 16 tiny new potatoes, boiled in their jackets and chilled

1 lemon, halved

1 tablespoon sea salt

2 tablespoons chopped fresh parsley

1. Using half the kosher salt, make a bed in a shallow nonreactive dish. Arrange the fish in a single layer on top and salt the surface with the remaining salt. Cover and place in the fridge for 1 hour, then rinse the fish, pat dry, and place the fish in a clean baking dish.

continued

2. Combine all the other ingredients except the potatoes, lemon, sea salt, and parsley in a small saucepan, cover, and bring to a boil over medium heat. Pour the contents of the pan over the fish and let cool to room temperature. Cover and place in the refrigerator for 2 hours before serving, turning the fillets once if necessary so they marinate evenly.

3. To serve, arrange the fish on a platter with the chilled boiled potatoes, spoon over the marinade, squeeze the lemon juice over the fish, and sprinkle with the salt and parsley.

Boiled crabs at the Raspail market, 6th arrondissement

Pain de Poisson, Beurre Fondu
Seafood Loaf with Butter Sauce

MAKES 4 TO 6 SERVINGS

This is inspired by the fishmonger's recipe, using ends of various fish left from filleting and portioning the daily arrival. It's unlikely that you will be able to buy fish scraps, except, perhaps, if you have a reputable fish supplier who cuts his own fish, so I adapted the recipe using a combination of salmon and cod. Not only is this a wonderful dinner starter or main course, but it's wonderful the next day, chilled and served with some horseradish mayonnaise.

1 pound skinless salmon fillets

2 pounds skinless cod fillets

3 medium onions, minced
  (about 2¼ cups)

½ cup fresh bread crumbs

½ cup all-purpose flour

1 teaspoon baking powder

¼ cup dry sherry

4 large eggs, lightly beaten

½ cup heavy cream

½ cup milk

¾ teaspoon dried thyme

2 teaspoons salt

¾ teaspoon freshly ground black pepper

¾ cup dry white wine

1 tablespoon chopped fresh tarragon
  or 1 teaspoon dried

6 tablespoons unsalted butter

1. Preheat the oven to 375°F. Grease a 9- by 5-inch loaf pan or 9-inch Bundt pan.

2. Finely chop the fish by hand and combine with the onions in a mixing bowl. Add the bread crumbs, flour, baking powder, sherry, eggs, cream, milk, thyme, salt, and pepper and mix well.

continued

3. Pour the mixture into the prepared pan. Cover, place in a larger pan of boiling water to create a water bath (the water should come three quarters of the way up the sides), and place in the oven for 1½ hours, or until the center is springy to the touch. Remove the loaf from the oven, remove from the water bath, and set aside.

4. Meanwhile, place the wine in a saucepan. If using dried tarragon, add it now. Place over medium heat and cook until the wine is reduced by half. If using fresh tarragon, add it now. Remove from the heat, whisk in the butter, and set aside. Keep warm.

5. Unmold the loaf and slice into 1½-inch slices. Arrange the slices on plates, spoon some tarragon sauce over the corner of each slice, and serve.

Moules à la Marinière
Mussels Steamed in White Wine

MAKES 4 SERVINGS

Parisians use medium-to-large mussels for this, the most common mussel dish. The tiny ones that you sometimes find in the market don't have enough natural juices to make a good broth. A nice nut of butter and a spoonful of crème fraîche keep the mussel meats shiny and moist. The trick is to start the mussels with no liquid and to add the wine just after the first mussels open. If the wine and cream cook together too long, you risk curdling the broth. This dish must be devoured immediately.

3 shallots, thinly sliced

2 cloves garlic, thinly sliced

2 tablespoons unsalted butter

3 pounds medium-to-large black
   mussels, scrubbed and debearded

2 bay leaves

2 sprigs fresh thyme

1/2 cup herbaceous dry white wine,
   such as Muscadet or Vouvray

2 tablespoons heavy cream
   or crème fraîche

Freshly ground black pepper

Salt

2 tablespoons chopped fresh parsley

1. Place the shallots, garlic, and butter in a large pot, place over medium heat, and cook, covered, for 1 minute. Add the mussels, bay leaves, and thyme, replace the cover, and cook until the mussels begin to open, about 1 minute. Add the wine and cream and give a few turns of the peppermill. Cover and cook for another minute. Remove from the heat and taste the liquid. Add salt as necessary.

2. To serve, divide the mussels among four soup bowls, discarding any that have not opened. Add the parsley to the cooking juices and pour over the mussels.

An Old-fashioned Way to Eat Mussels

Eating steamed mussels doesn't require tableware. Choose a large mussel from your bowl and, using your fingers, remove the meat from the shell. Then hold the empty shell as if it were a set of castanets and use it to pinch the mussels out of the other shells. When you've finished your bowl of mussels, separate the two halves of the shell and use one half as a spoon to sip the broth.

A dog with its owner in a Sunday market

Moules au Beurre d'Escargots
Mussels with Garlic Butter

"I can't stand snails of any kind, not land snails, not sea snails. But I'm crazy for the butter that accompanies them." Thus pronounced a shopper who was buying a large sack of shiny black mussels at Marée Daguerre, the fish stand in the shopping street in the rue Daguerre. This recipe is for mussels broiled in the butter that usually accompanies snails. You can cook the mussels in the oven, covered, or under the broiler. Under the broiler, the mussels open quicker and the butter sizzles faster, cooking the garlic. Baked, covered, in the oven, though, they keep more of the mussel liquor. Either way, it's a divine way to prepare mussels.

16 cloves garlic, peeled
½ bunch fresh parsley leaves
6 tablespoons unsalted butter
2 tablespoons extra virgin olive oil
¼ cup Pernod

1 teaspoon salt
1 teaspoon freshly ground black pepper
3 pounds black mussels, scrubbed
   and debearded

1. Preheat the broiler or preheat the oven to 475°F.

2. Place the garlic and parsley in a food processor and process until finely chopped. Add the butter, olive oil, Pernod, salt, and pepper and pulse until smooth. Scrape the mixture into a bowl.

3. Place the mussels in a large roasting pan and distribute dollops of the butter around the pan. Cover tightly and place in the oven for 10 minutes, or until the mussels have opened.

4. Divide the contents of the roasting pan among four soup or pasta bowls, discarding any mussels that have not opened. Serve immediately.

La Mouclade Antillaise
Steamed Mussels West Indian Style

MAKES 4 SERVINGS

The first time I was served this dish, it was prepared by a friend who had grown up in Martinique. Her version was spicy with cayenne and had a nice background of curry flavors. Sometime later, I saw it on a restaurant menu, ordered it, and was disappointed to find that it was more or less a dish of mussels steamed in white wine and cream. Delicious, but not what I expected. Whatever the authentic *mouclade* may be (and I have a feeling it's closer to the restaurant version), I infinitely prefer the spicy tomato-based version that I was first served. I think you will too.

3 tablespoons unsalted butter

¼ cup finely chopped shallots

12 Roma (plum) tomatoes, peeled
   (see page 52), seeded, and chopped,
   or 4 cups canned chopped
   tomatoes, drained

¼ teaspoon ground coriander

1 teaspoon curry powder

½ teaspoon red pepper flakes

¼ cup herbaceous dry white wine,
   such as Muscadet or Vouvray

¼ cup heavy cream

3 pounds black mussels, scrubbed
   and debearded

Salt

2 tablespoons minced fresh parsley

1. Melt the butter in a nonreactive casserole over medium heat. Cook the shallots until soft but not browned, about 2 minutes. Add the tomatoes, coriander, curry, and pepper flakes and cook until the tomatoes are soft, about 10 minutes. Add the wine, cream, and mussels, cover, and cook for about 3 minutes, then remove the cover and continue to cook, removing the mussels to a large serving bowl as they open.

2. When all the mussels have opened (discard any that do not open), taste the cooking liquid for salt and add as needed. Ladle the cooking liquid over the mussels, sprinkle with the parsley, and serve immediately.

Pilaf de Praires au Curry
Curried Clams with Rice Pilaf

Praires are the size of cockles, Manila clams, or the smallest cherrystone clams that I remember from growing up in New York. Pilaf refers to a way of cooking rice in which the rice is lightly sautéed, almost toasted in oil, then simmered in stock until tender. Sautéing the rice intensifies its flavor and gives it a nutty edge. The almost unanimously preferred method for achieving this is cooking the rice in the oven, rather than boiling it on the stove.

¾ cup fish broth, Homemade Chicken
  Broth (page 237), or water
4 tablespoons olive oil
1 small onion, minced
2 teaspoons curry powder
½ cup long-grain rice
4 pounds cockles or Manila or small
  littleneck clams, scrubbed

½ cup fruity white wine,
  such as a dry Riesling
½ teaspoon freshly ground white pepper
2 tablespoons butter, in pieces
1 tablespoon chopped fresh parsley

1. Preheat the oven to 350°F.
2. Place the broth in a small pot, cover, and bring to a boil.
3. Meanwhile, heat the oil in a small ovenproof pot over medium heat. Add the onion and curry powder and cook until the onion is soft, about 2 minutes. Add the rice and cook, stirring, another 2 minutes, until the rice becomes aromatic. Add the boiling broth and stir once. Cover, transfer the pot to the oven, and cook for 12 minutes.

continued

4. Ten minutes after placing the rice in the oven, place the cockles or clams, wine, and pepper in a pot, cover, and cook over high heat until the clams have opened, about 6 minutes or so. Remove from the heat and set aside. Discard any that haven't opened.

5. Remove the rice from the oven and divide it among four ramekins or coffee cups, pressing the rice down gently. Invert the ramekins onto plates, tap gently in the center, and lift off the ramekins. Arrange the clams around the rice and place the plates in the turned-off oven to keep warm.

6. Return the pot with the clam cooking liquid to the stove, bring to a boil over high heat, and add the butter. Boil until the butter melts, whisking all the time. Remove from the heat and stir in the parsley. Spoon the sauce over the clams and serve immediately.

Cassolette de Coquilles St-Jacques à l'Estragon

Small Casserole of Scallops with Tarragon

MAKES 4 SERVINGS

I was not prepared for the way this dish felt in my mouth. "It's all in the temperature and the timing," said Odile, who served these for lunch one freezing Sunday in early March. She was careful to cook them in a tightly sealed casserole at a high temperature. When you make the sauce, it will be rather thick, in order that the *jus* released from the scallops will bring it to the proper consistency. These scallops are so creamy that the sauce seems to be an extension of their essence. Serve them with rice pilaf.

4 shallots, thinly sliced

2 tablespoons unsalted butter

1 tablespoon plus 1 teaspoon
   all-purpose flour

1 cup dry vermouth or herbaceous
   dry white wine, such as Muscadet
   or Vouvray

1 teaspoon Dijon mustard

½ cup heavy cream

1 teaspoon salt

¼ teaspoon freshly ground black pepper

2 teaspoons fresh tarragon leaves,
   chopped, or 1 teaspoon dried

1½ pounds large sea scallops

⅓ cup chopped fresh chives

1. Preheat the oven to 500°F.

2. In a small saucepan, cook the shallots in the butter over medium heat until soft, about 2 minutes. Stir in the flour. Add the vermouth and mustard and cook, stirring, until the liquid thickens, about 8 minutes. Add the cream, salt, and pepper. If using dried tarragon, add it now. Cook until the mixture thickens again, then remove from the heat.

3. Place the scallops in a small Dutch oven, sprinkle with the fresh tarragon, if using, and pour the sauce over the scallops. Cover and place in the oven for 10 minutes.

4. Remove from the oven, stir in the chives, and serve immediately.

Scallops

Scallops, *coquilles St-Jacques* in French, are named for Saint James, whose shrine in Compostela, Spain, was a major site of pilgrimage during the Middle Ages. Pilgrims to the shrine carried few belongings and the round deep shell of the scallop served as a kind of mess kit—to sip water from and to place food on. Owning a scallop shell was a sign that one had made the pilgrimage and it gave one a certain status.

Odile Bernard-Schröder in her kitchen

Coquilles St-Jacques Bonne Femme

Scallops and Mushrooms

MAKES 4 SERVINGS

I cooked this dish in school, a restaurant version of what a traditional *bonne femme,* or housewife, would prepare at home. The recipe is deceptively simple, and easy for entertaining. The trick is to be patient, allowing each liquid to reduce after you add it. The sauce is rich and concentrated. Scallops and sauce are easily prepared up to an hour in advance and can be finished under the broiler at the last minute.

1 cup dry white wine, such as Sauvignon Blanc

2 shallots, minced

½ teaspoon dried thyme

½ teaspoon salt, or more to taste

Freshly ground black pepper

1 ¼ pounds large sea scallops (about 16 scallops)

¾ pound mushrooms, thinly sliced

½ cup fish or vegetable broth or Homemade Chicken Broth (page 237)

½ cup heavy cream

2 tablespoons unsalted butter

1. Combine the wine, shallots, thyme, salt, and pepper to taste in a nonreactive skillet and bring to a boil over high heat. Add the scallops and cook, covered, for 1 minute. Immediately remove the scallops and set aside on a plate. They should be rare.

2. Add the mushrooms and broth and cook until the liquid is reduced by half, about 10 minutes. Add the cream and any juices that have collected around the scallops. Reduce the heat to medium and cook until the liquid thickens and becomes sauce-like, another 5 minutes or so. Remove the skillet from the heat and swirl in the butter. Check the seasonings and add salt as desired.

3. Preheat the broiler. Arrange the scallops in a large gratin dish or in four scallop shells and spoon over the sauce. Place the dish under the broiler until the top begins to show small areas of golden color, 2 to 3 minutes. Serve immediately.

Coquilles St-Jacques aux Nouilles et au Basilic
Scallops with Noodles and Basil

MAKES 4 SERVINGS

This is a lovely luncheon or dinner dish of lightly sautéed scallops served over buttered vegetables and noodles. Use egg noodles, not pasta, for this dish. Semolina makes pasta too chewy a partner for the scallops. Tear the large basil leaves by hand, so as not to bruise them, and leave small leaves whole.

¼ pound dry egg noodles

2 tablespoons olive oil

1¼ pounds large sea scallops
    (about 16 scallops)

Salt

All-purpose flour for dusting

4 tablespoons (½ stick) unsalted butter

1 medium zucchini, finely diced

1 medium carrot, finely diced

2 medium onions, finely diced

3 shallots, finely diced

½ cup dry white wine, such as
    Sauvignon Blanc

2 tablespoons Pernod or aquavit

1 bunch fresh basil, leaves only
    (about ½ cup), large leaves
    torn by hand

Freshly ground black pepper

2 tablespoons crème fraîche
    or sour cream

1. Bring a pot of salted water to a boil and cook the noodles according to the package directions. Drain the noodles well and toss with a little olive oil to prevent them from sticking together. Cover and set aside.

2. Meanwhile, halve the scallops crosswise, sprinkle with salt, and dust with flour, shaking off the excess. Heat the remaining oil and 2 tablespoons of the butter in a large

skillet over medium-high heat. Add the scallops, without crowding the pan, and cook for 1 minute on each side. Remove the scallops and keep warm.

3. Add the vegetables, wine, and Pernod to the skillet, bring the liquid to a boil, and cook until reduced by half, about 3 minutes. Add the noodles, along with the basil, pepper to taste, crème fraîche, and the remaining 2 tablespoons butter and toss well.

4. To serve, mound the pasta and vegetables on plates and place the scallops on top.

Salt Cod

La morue, or salt cod, is one of the staple foods of France, so common that to call a woman a *morue* is worse than calling her a tramp. It connotes an image of dried-up infertility, and it implies that the poor dear in question is the most common of the common, that she is, in fact, completely dispensable.

Fresh cod is not a terribly tasty fish, and it has always been considered unworthy by chefs and gourmands alike. But salted and dried, it becomes a truly remarkable product, one that's stewed, fried, mashed, roasted, or served in salads by cooks all over France. In Paris, it's been given a *coup d'élégance* and become the reverse-chic fish of choice of restaurant chefs. The fishmongers in Paris sell both dried and desalted fish. It's a typical dinner for Friday, still the traditional fish day in Catholic countries. And it's the dish of choice for *Vendredi Saint,* or Good Friday, as ubiquitous as America's Thanksgiving turkey.

Morue "Ile-de-France"
Sautéed Salt Cod with White Wine

MAKES 4 SERVINGS

This is probably the most satisfying salt cod I've ever eaten. The cod first poaches in wine and vinegar, absorbing their flavors. Then it's cooked *à l'anglaise,* after a dusting of flour and a dip in some beaten eggs.

1¼ pounds salt cod fillets,
    cut into 12 pieces

½ cup dry white wine, such as
    Sauvignon Blanc

½ cup white wine vinegar

1 medium onion, finely chopped

1 clove garlic, minced

1 bay leaf

½ teaspoon dried thyme

½ teaspoon dried rosemary

3 tablespoons unsalted butter

Vegetable oil, preferably canola,
    for panfrying

All-purpose flour for dusting

3 large eggs, lightly beaten

1 tablespoon finely chopped
    fresh parsley

1. Soak the cod in cold water for 36 to 48 hours, changing the water several times, then drain.

2. Place the salt cod in a pot and add the wine, vinegar, onion, garlic, bay leaf, thyme, and rosemary. Cover, place over medium heat, and simmer—do not boil—for 15 minutes. Remove the pot from the heat and transfer the salt cod to a plate.

3. Replace the pot over medium-high heat and cook until the liquid reduces by two thirds. Drain any liquid that has collected around the cod into the cooking juices. Whisk in the butter, remove the pot from the stovetop, and keep the sauce warm.

4. Heat a 1-inch depth of oil in a large heavy skillet. Pat the cod dry, then dust it in the flour and dip in the eggs, letting the excess drip off. When the oil is hot, fry the cod until golden on both sides, about 2 minutes per side. Remove the cod fillets from the skillet as they are done, and place on absorbent towels.

5. Add the parsley to the sauce, pour onto a platter, and serve the cod on top.

Brandade de Morue
Salt Cod and Potato Mousse

MAKES 4 SERVINGS

Sylviane Lacoste prepared her *brandade* for me during a visit to Paris. I've always pre-pared it with mashed potatoes, but Sylviane insists her deconstructed version is the real one. I say deconstructed because she serves potatoes with her *brandade,* not as part of it. The liaison of salt cod and olive oil makes this *"véritable" brandade* moist and fluffy. It should reek of olive oil and garlic. Present it surrounded by the smallest waxy new potatoes you can find as well as some small green Picholines, the olives of Provence.

³/₄ pound salt cod

1 small onion, quartered

1 small carrot, cut into medium chunks

1 stalk celery, cut into pieces

4 bay leaves

1¹/₂ pounds fingerling or new potatoes

6 tablespoons extra virgin olive oil

¹/₄ cup heavy cream

6 cloves garlic, minced

¹/₄ to ¹/₂ cup milk

Freshly ground white pepper

¹/₂ cup Picholine olives or Spanish green olives

2 tablespoons chopped fresh parsley

1. Soak the cod in cold water for 36 to 48 hours, changing the water several times, then drain.

2. Fill a large pot with fresh water, add the onion, carrot, celery, and bay leaves, cover, and bring to a boil over high heat. Reduce the heat to low and simmer for 10 min-utes. Add the cod and, if necessary, more water to cover it. Simmer, covered, for 20 minutes. Remove from the heat, drain the cod, and place it in a mixing bowl. Dis-card the cooking liquid and vegetables.

3. Meanwhile, place the potatoes in a pot, cover with salted water, place over medium heat, and boil until tender. Remove from the heat and set aside.

4. Heat the oil and cream in a small saucepan over medium heat and cook the garlic for 1 minute. Remove from the heat. Heat the milk.

5. Using a wooden mallet or a potato masher, mash the salt cod. Slowly add the oil and cream mixture, mashing vigorously until incorporated. Add pepper as desired. Beat in the hot milk until the mixture smooths but is still stiff enough to hold a shape. Mound the *brandade* on a platter and use a fork to shape the mound without compacting it. Drain the potatoes and arrange them around the *brandade.* Arrange the olives among the potatoes, sprinkle with the parsley, and serve.

A more common Brandade

Boil ¹/₂ pound potatoes in their jackets. Remove and discard the jackets and rice or mash the potatoes. Combine the potatoes with the mashed, cooked salt cod before beating in the oil/cream mixture.

The café in the Rue de Seine market, 6th arrondissement

Pot-au-Feu de Morue à l'Aïoli

Cod, Shrimp, and Scallops Simmered in Broth with Aïoli

MAKES 4 SERVINGS

Pot-au-feu is a French boiled dinner. This seafood version is traditional, but I've changed the procedure slightly to ensure that the baby vegetables that are the nicest for this soup meal are cooked in a modern American style—well done, but not mushy. If baby vegetables are not available, cut large vegetables into two-inch pieces.

1 pound salt cod

2 large egg yolks

6 cloves garlic, minced

1/2 cup extra virgin olive oil

1 tablespoon fresh lemon juice

Salt and freshly ground black pepper

2 quarts low-sodium vegetable or
   fish broth, or Homemade Chicken
   Broth (page 237)

8 small waxy new potatoes, peeled

4 baby carrots, scrubbed

4 baby turnips, peeled

8 pearl onions, peeled

1 celery heart, quartered lengthwise

4 baby zucchini

1/4 pound sugar snap peas,
   strings removed

2 tablespoons white wine vinegar

1 teaspoon dried marjoram

2 bay leaves

8 large sea scallops (about 1/2 pound)

12 medium shrimp, peeled and deveined

4 teaspoons chopped fresh chervil
   or parsley

1. Soak the salt cod in cold water, for 36 to 48 hours, changing the water several times. Drain.

2. Place the salt cod in a pot, cover with fresh water, bring to a gentle boil over medium heat, and cook for 10 minutes, or until tender. Drain. Cut the cod into 8 chunks and set aside.

3. Meanwhile, place the yolks and garlic in a mixing bowl and, using a flexible wire whisk, beat in the olive oil in a thin stream, a little at a time, until it is completely incorporated and the mixture has a mayonnaise consistency. Stir in the lemon juice and season with salt and pepper. Transfer the aïoli to a small serving bowl and set aside.

4. In a large pot, combine the broth and 2 teaspoons salt and bring to a boil. Add the potatoes, cover, and cook for 5 minutes. Add the carrots, turnips, onions, and celery and continue cooking, covered, another 5 minutes. Add the zucchini and sugar snap peas and cook for 4 minutes more, or until all the vegetables are tender. Using a slotted spoon, remove the vegetables, set aside, and keep warm.

5. Add the vinegar, marjoram, and bay leaves to the broth. Give a few turns of the peppermill as desired. Add the scallops and shrimp and cook for 2 minutes; do not overcook. Remove the scallops and shrimp and set aside. Remove and discard the bay leaves.

6. To serve, divide the vegetables, cod, scallops, and shrimp among four wide-rimmed soup bowls. Ladle the boiling broth into the bowls and sprinkle with the chopped chervil. Serve immediately and offer the aïoli separately.

Bar Rôti en Cocotte aux Poireaux
Casserole-Roasted Sea Bass and Leeks

MAKES 4 SERVINGS

This is a marvelous way to cook thick fillets of firm-fleshed fish, which can sometimes be tough and sinewy. Just enough natural moisture is trapped in the Dutch oven to keep the fish juicy while it cooks.

¼ pound bacon, finely chopped

3 tablespoons unsalted butter

3 large leeks, white part only, sliced into thin rounds and well washed

¼ cup herbaceous dry white wine, such as Sancerre or Vouvray

1 tablespoon Dijon mustard

Four 7-ounce sea bass fillets

½ teaspoon salt

Freshly ground black pepper

1 tablespoon chopped fresh chives

1. In a heavy-bottomed skillet, cook the bacon in 1 tablespoon of the butter over medium heat, stirring occasionally, for 3 minutes. Add the leeks, cover, and cook, stirring occasionally, until barely tender, about 5 minutes. Add the wine and stir in the mustard.

2. Season the bass with the salt and pepper and arrange on top of the leeks. Cook, covered, until the fish is cooked to the desired doneness, 8 to 10 minutes, depending on the thickness of the fillets. Transfer the fish to a plate. Reduce the heat under the skillet to low and stir in the remaining 2 tablespoons butter.

3. To serve, mound the leeks on a platter and arrange the fish on top. Sprinkle with the chives and serve.

The Fishmonger

Parisians have never contented themselves with the local trout, shad, and pike from the Seine, Marne, Eure, and Oise rivers. In Roman times, the elite of Lutétia dined on oysters and turbot from the Atlantic. During the Middle Ages, Charlemagne built artificial lakes at the outskirts of Paris for raising eels and carp. Peruse the fishmongers' stands in the Paris markets today, and you would believe yourself in a coastal port city, the variety is so great.

The *poissonier* has by far the most colorful stall in the market. Fish are arranged logically, by family, on mounded beds of crushed ice and laboriously decorated with various seaweeds, parsley, and lemon. There are flatfish—the sole, flounder, turbot, *carrelet, limande,* and *cardine;* red fishes—snapper, mullet, *rascasse, rouget, grondin;* the cods—*lieu noir, cabillaud, églefin, merlan, lingue;* and skate wings, which he'll tell you should "rest" a day in the refrigerator before cooking (skate is probably the only denizen of the sea that gets better with a little age).

She also sells cooked langoustines, shrimp, lobsters, and crabs, ready to take home and eat, and cooked *bulots* and *bigorneaux,* types of sea snails that you dip in a garlicky aïoli mayonnaise. When I told the fishmonger in the rue de Bretagne that I loved *brandade,* she offered to soak a nice piece of salt cod for me to cook two days hence.

Most neighborhood fishmongers provision their shops through suppliers at Rungis, the huge wholesale food market on the outskirts of Paris, but many have direct connections as well to small aquaculturists who raise oysters, scallops, lobsters, trout, and salmon. Craftsmen-fishers, *les pêches artisanales,* are independent owners who fish from lines on boats that stay out at sea for only two or three days at a time. They also supply much of the sought-after Dover sole; *lieu noir,* a kind of scrod; and *bar,* a striped bass caught at night under a new moon, when the fish come nearer to the surface to feed.

At the fish stand, marketers choose their whole fish from among the many strange and familiar specimens. Lickety-split, off come the scales, out come the entrails. The fishmonger tries to convince nearly everyone to cook the fish whole. "*Mais*, madame, you know it's so easy to lift off the fillets after you've cooked the fish. And it cooks so much tastier." But, no, most want filleted fish. The *poissonier* grudgingly obliges. It's not that he is annoyed by the extra work (after all, it only takes him seconds to lift off the fillets), but he's concerned about how your dinner is going to turn out. Parisians do insist, however, that he include the bones and head for making their *fumet,* a quick fish stock used as a sauce base.

The variety of fish you find in the markets is more abundant from September to April, making the fishmonger's job more difficult. All that ice is nice in the heat of summer, but to stand in the damp cold air of Paris—well, you forgive them their vulgarities.

Astuce: Perfectly Poached Fish Fillets

Place your fillet of fish in a boiling court bouillon, cover the pan, and remove from the heat. Leave the fish in the court bouillon for about 6 minutes for each $\frac{1}{2}$ inch of thickness.

Court Bouillon

3 cups cold water

1 cup dry white wine

1 small onion, peeled and sliced

1 small carrot, peeled and sliced

1 celery stalk, sliced

2 bay leaves

1 teaspoon salt

12 black peppercorns

Combine water, wine, onion, carrot, celery, bay leaves, salt, and peppercorns in a large saucepan, cover, place over high heat, bring to a boil, and cook 5 minutes. Strain the liquid.

Turbotin à l'Oseille

Turbot with Sorrel

MAKES 4 SERVINGS

Béatrice and Monique occupy neighboring stalls in the Port-Royale market, selling cheese and fish, respectively. Béatrice admits that she couldn't permit herself the luxury of poaching a *turbotin,* one of the most highly prized and expensive fish, if she actually had to buy it. But the neighbors exchange fish and cheese, a mutually beneficial arrangement. Here's Monique's traditional recipe for turbot. As it's rare to find true turbot in the States, especially the whole fish, I substitute halibut when it's in season, or other flatfish, such as flounder or lemon sole. A five-pound fish will net about two and a quarter pounds of fillets. If you're lucky enough to find one, poach the whole fish. The gelatin in the bones permeates the flesh and the skin protects the delicate flesh, sealing in flavor.

*2 cups dry white wine, such as
    Sauvignon Blanc*

1 carrot, roughly chopped

1 onion, roughly chopped

2 stalks celery, roughly chopped

12 peppercorns

½ teaspoon salt

2 bay leaves

1 sprig fresh thyme

*4½ to 5 pounds whole turbot,
    or 2 to 2¼ pounds fillet*

½ cup heavy cream

*12 sorrel leaves, center ribs removed and
    leaves finely chopped (about ½ cup)*

1 tablespoon fresh lemon juice

2 tablespoons unsalted butter

*Lemon slices and parsley sprigs
    for garnish*

1. Place the wine, carrot, onion, celery, peppercorns, salt, bay leaves, and thyme in a fish poacher or roasting pan just large enough to hold the turbot. Cover, place over high heat, and cook for 5 minutes. Lower the heat to medium and add the turbot, white skin down, then add enough cold water so that the turbot is half submerged in liquid. Cover and simmer until the turbot is tender to the touch, 8 to 10 minutes. Remove the pan from the heat and carefully transfer the turbot to a platter. Using a soupspoon, gently remove the dark skin. Cover with a damp cloth and keep warm in a 200°F oven while you finish the sauce.

2. Strain the poaching liquid, discarding the vegetables and seasonings. Pour the poaching liquid into a saucepan, place over high heat, and cook until the liquid is reduced to 1 cup, about 15 minutes. Add the cream, reduce the heat to medium, and simmer until the liquid thickens to a saucelike consistency, about 7 minutes. Remove from the heat, stir in the sorrel and lemon juice, and whisk in the butter. Uncover the turbot and pour any liquid that has collected around the fish into the sauce.

3. Decorate the platter with lemon and parsley and serve the sauce separately.

Loup de Mer Poché, Sauce Verte
Poached Striped Bass with Green Sauce

MAKES 4 SERVINGS

Philippe Lapeyre teaches special education to disabled children. Since he's home by four o'clock every day, he is the cook in his family. His method for cooking fillets of fish is to place them in simmering liquid, turn off the heat, and let the fish cook by themselves in the hot liquid until done. Since the temperature of the water is never more than about 200°F, the flesh maintains a creamy texture. I have tried this method with John Dory, sole, flounder, cod, and even frozen fish, and they all come out more succulent. Philippe's method also allows him to serve a first course without having to constantly monitor the fish cooking on the stove. Since he cooks fish about four times a week, Philippe likes to save the poaching liquid the first time around and reuse it two or three more times by adding some water to it as necessary.

3 cups cold water

1 cup dry white wine, such as
    Sauvignon Blanc

1 small onion, sliced

1 small carrot, sliced

1 stalk celery, sliced

2 bay leaves

1 teaspoon salt

12 black peppercorns

1 1/2 pounds striped bass fillets

1 bunch watercress, leaves only

1/2 bunch sorrel, stems and center
    ribs removed

2 tablespoons fresh lemon juice

2 shallots, minced

2 tablespoons unsalted butter

1/2 bunch fresh chives, minced

1. Make a court bouillon by combining the water, wine, onion, carrot, celery, bay leaves, salt, and peppercorns in a large saucepan, cover, bring to a boil over high heat, and cook for 5 minutes. Reduce the heat to low and add the fillets. If there's not enough liquid to cover the fillets, add hot water to cover. Replace the cover and cook for 1 minute. Remove from the heat and let the fillets sit in the hot liquid, covered, for 10 to 15 minutes, depending on their thickness (allow about 6 minutes per $\frac{1}{2}$ inch).

2. Meanwhile, place the watercress and sorrel leaves in a food processor and process until finely chopped. Transfer the chopped leaves to a saucepan and add the lemon juice, shallots, butter, and $\frac{1}{3}$ cup of the fish poaching liquid. Place over medium heat, bring to a boil, and cook for 3 minutes.

3. Pour the sauce onto a serving platter and sprinkle with the chives. Remove the fish from the poaching liquid, arrange on the sauce, and serve.

Jurer Comme un Poissonier

In English we swear like sailors, but in French you swear like a fishmonger. Just question the quality of his fish, and see what happens. First, he insults you personally. Then, he proceeds to insult the good name of your mother and your wife, who must be questionable themselves to be associated with one so stupid as yourself, who is incapable of recognizing the freshness of his fish.

Saumon à la Gasconne
Salmon with Leeks, Potatoes, and Bacon

MAKES 4 SERVINGS

Salmon is a fish whose flavor pairs extremely well with bacon, as you'll see when you prepare this dish. In this recipe, the starch in the potatoes thickens the cooking broth and, when reduced on the stovetop, makes a kind of simple sauce.

2 large leeks, white part only, sliced
　　into ¼-inch rounds and well washed
¼ pound bacon, finely diced
1 pound waxy potatoes, peeled and
　　sliced into ¼-inch rounds
1 teaspoon dried thyme
2 bay leaves

2 cups fish broth or Homemade Chicken
　　Broth (page 237)
¼ cup white wine vinegar
1 teaspoon salt
Freshly ground black pepper
Four 7-ounce salmon steaks or fillets

1. Preheat the oven to 375°F.

2. Combine the leeks and bacon in a 3-inch-deep nonreactive ovenproof skillet and cook over medium heat, stirring, until the bacon begins to render its fat, about 3 minutes. Add the potatoes, thyme, and bay leaves and pour in the broth and vinegar. Season with the salt and give a few grinds of the peppermill. Cover and place in the oven for 20 minutes.

3. Lay the salmon on the potato/onion mixture, re-cover, and return to the oven for another 8 to 10 minutes, or until the salmon is cooked to the desired doneness.

4. Transfer the salmon to a plate. Remove the bay leaves from the potato mixture and pour the contents of the skillet onto the center of a platter. Place the salmon on top and serve immediately.

***Fraternité*, Daguerre Marée,
14th arrondissement**

Saumon Farci, Crème à la Ciboulette

Stuffed Salmon Steaks with Chive Cream

MAKES 4 SERVINGS

Bread crumbs and milk cooked together make what's called a panada, or *panade*, a sticky mass used as a thickener in the kind of nineteen-century classic cooking that has fallen out of favor. However, it's still used by French home cooks, who, buying bread on a daily basis, always have some left over. I became particularly fond of *panade* because it reminded me of holiday turkey dressing.

½ cup fresh bread crumbs

¾ cup milk

2 large eggs, lightly beaten

2 tablespoons chopped fresh parsley

1 tablespoon chopped fresh tarragon
  or 1 teaspoon dried

Salt and freshly ground black pepper

Four 7-ounce salmon steaks (see note)

3 tablespoons fresh lemon juice

3 tablespoons dry vermouth or
  herbaceous dry white wine,
  such as Sancerre or Vouvray

½ cup heavy cream

2 tablespoons unsalted butter

1 small bunch fresh chives, minced
  (about ¼ cup)

1. Place the bread crumbs and milk in a small saucepan. Cook over medium heat for about 4 minutes, stirring, until the mixture thickens and gets sticky, then scrape the mixture into a small mixing bowl. When cool, mix in the eggs, parsley, tarragon, ½ teaspoon salt, and ¼ teaspoon pepper.

2. Using a paring knife, remove and discard the center bones and any long bones from the belly flaps of the salmon steaks. Enclose the bread mixture in the two belly flaps, to form a round-to-oval medallion. Place the salmon steaks in a nonreactive saucepan or skillet just large enough to hold them. Pour in the lemon juice and wine and sprinkle with salt and pepper. Cover tightly, place over medium heat, and cook for about 15 minutes, or until the stuffing is firm to the touch.

3. Using a slotted spatula or spoon, remove the salmon, to a plate. Cover and keep warm. Add the cream and butter to the juices in the saucepan and cook over medium heat until the liquid boils down to a saucelike consistency. Taste for salt and pepper and add as desired. Mix in the chives and pour in any juices that have collected around the salmon. Arrange the salmon on a platter, spoon over the sauce, and serve immediately.

NOTE: At the market, choose center-cut salmon steaks, the ones with prominent belly flaps. You'll be able to remove the bones, place a handsome dollop of stuffing in the cavity of each, and then envelop it in the flaps.

La Portuguaise de Cabillaud
Portuguese-Style Cod

MAKES 4 SERVINGS

Although this is a classic French garniture, I was given this recipe by my housekeeper, whose family is Portuguese. All the ingredients for the *Portuguaise*—onion, garlic, peppers, and tomato—melt together into a nice compote, but what makes this preparation unique are the accents of orange peel and saffron. You can use other white-fleshed fish for this dish, such as halibut, monkfish, John Dory, red snapper, bass, or turbot. If you want to use delicate flatfish such as flounder or lemon sole, roll up the fillets and secure them with toothpicks so they don't fall apart.

1 onion, finely chopped

1 clove garlic, finely sliced

*1 green bell pepper, cored, seeded,
    and finely chopped*

*4 tomatoes, peeled (see page 52), seeded,
    and chopped*

1 teaspoon grated orange zest

½ teaspoon dried thyme

Pinch of thread saffron

*½ cup dry white wine, such as
    Sauvignon Blanc*

5 tablespoons extra virgin olive oil

2 teaspoons salt

½ teaspoon red pepper flakes

*Four 6-ounce cod fillets,
    preferably Alaskan*

All-purpose flour for dusting

1 tablespoon finely chopped fresh parsley

1. Preheat the oven to 375°F.

2. Combine the onion, garlic, bell pepper, tomatoes, orange zest, thyme, saffron, wine, 2 tablespoons of the olive oil, 1 teaspoon of the salt, and the red pepper flakes in a

Dutch oven. Cover and place in the oven for 30 minutes. Remove the cover and continue to cook for another 15 minutes. Remove from the oven and keep warm. (Leave the oven on.)

3. Meanwhile, pat the cod dry with paper towels. Sprinkle with the remaining 1 teaspoon salt, then dust with flour. Heat the remaining 3 tablespoons olive oil in a large skillet over high heat and cook the cod, turning once, until lightly golden on both sides.

4. Transfer the fish to the Dutch oven and replace in the oven to finish cooking, about 3 to 4 minutes, depending on the thickness of the fish. When the fish is done, arrange on a platter and mound the *Portuguaise* in the center. Sprinkle with the parsley and serve immediately.

Loup de Mer au Fenouil
Striped Bass Fillets with Fennel

MAKES 4 SERVINGS

Usually, the fishmongers in Paris will throw in a few sprigs of parsley with your purchase of fish. Once, though, when I bought some terrific-looking striped bass at the *poissonier* in the new Marché Saint-Germain, he wrapped up some dried fennel stalks for me to take home. Bass with fennel is classic, I think, because the flavor of the fennel matches so nicely with the unique flavor of the fish. One is unlikely to find dried stalks of fennel here, but I've found a combination of fresh fennel bulb and toasted fennel seeds gives the same effect.

2 teaspoons fennel seeds

1 teaspoon cornstarch

1/2 cup fish broth or Homemade Chicken
   Broth (page 237)

1/2 cup dry white wine, such as
   Sauvignon Blanc

1 clove garlic, thinly sliced

3 shallots, thinly sliced

1/2 teaspoon salt

1/2 teaspoon freshly ground black pepper

1 tablespoon unsalted butter

2 small fennel bulbs, trimmed, cored,
   and finely slivered from tip to root

1 tablespoon crème fraîche or 2
   tablespoons heavy cream

Four 7-ounce striped bass fillets

1 tablespoon finely chopped fresh parsley

1. Heat a small skillet over medium heat. Add the fennel seeds and toast until golden. Place the seeds in a spice grinder and grind. Or place in a paper bag and pound with a mallet until crushed to a mealy consistency. Set aside.

2. Dissolve the cornstarch in the broth and set aside.

3. Combine the wine, garlic, shallots, salt, and pepper in a nonreactive saucepan, cover, and bring to a boil. Add the broth mixture, butter, and fresh fennel and simmer, covered, for 5 minutes. Add the créme fraîche and fish fillets and continue to simmer, covered, until the desired doneness, about 3 minutes or more, depending on the thickness. Transfer the fish to a plate.

4. To serve, arrange a bed of the fennel on a platter. Arrange the fish on top, mix the parsley into the sauce, and pour over the fish. Sprinkle the ground fennel seeds over the top.

Astuce : Toasting Seeds

Toasting seeds intensifies their flavor, as well as making them crunchier. The most common candidates for toasting are fennel seed, aniseed, mustard seed, cumin seed, and coriander. Heat a skillet over medium heat and when the skillet is hot, add the seeds. Heat them, constantly shaking the pan until their aroma rises and they begin to take on a bit of color.

Poêlé de Thon au Romarin, Marinade Chaude
Pan-Seared Tuna Served with Its Marinade

MAKES 4 SERVINGS

For this dish, tuna is prepared like a fillet of beef—seared quickly over high heat so the center remains medium-rare to rare. Ask your fishmonger to cut tuna steaks from a small loin so you'll get good thick ones. First marinate the tuna in red wine, then reduce the marinade to a concentrated essence.

Four 6-ounce tuna steaks

1 cup dry red wine, such as Merlot

¼ cup red wine vinegar

1 teaspoon fresh thyme leaves

1 clove

Salt and freshly ground black pepper

All-purpose flour for dusting

2 tablespoons vegetable oil,
*   preferably canola*

2 large shallots, minced

1 teaspoon Dijon mustard

2 tablespoons unsalted butter

1. Place the tuna in a glass dish, cover with the wine and vinegar, and season with the thyme and clove. Cover, place in the refrigerator, and marinate for at least 2 hours and up to 4 hours.

2. Remove the tuna from the marinade, reserving the marinade, and pat dry. Season with salt and pepper and lightly dust with flour.

3. Heat the oil in a large skillet over high heat. When the oil is smoking hot, add the tuna. Cook for 1 to 2 minutes on each side, depending on the thickness. Remove the tuna from the skillet and keep warm. Discard any oil remaining in the skillet.

4. Reduce the heat to medium, add the shallots and mustard, and whisk in the marinade to dissolve the mustard. Boil the liquid until reduced by two thirds. Whisk in the butter and remove from the heat.

5. To serve, arrange the tuna on a serving platter and spoon over the sauce.

Marché Saxe-Breteuil,
looking at the Eiffel Tower,
7th arrondissement

Féra à la Mode de Loing

Broiled Whitefish with White Wine and Shallots

MAKES 4 SERVINGS

This is a recipe from my former cooking professor Roger Lallemand and is adapted from his book of recipes of the Ile-de-France, the region that comprises Paris and its environs. He cooks in the very classic fashion that he was taught, and this dish is a perfect example. The sauce, thickened with a single egg yolk, then enriched with cream and butter, is simple to prepare and the result so rich and satisfying that you're happy with only a little.

Four 6-ounce whitefish or halibut
    fillets with skin
2 tablespoons olive oil
3 tablespoons fresh lemon juice
½ teaspoon dried thyme
1 bay leaf, broken up
Salt and freshly ground black pepper
1 cup dry white wine, preferably
    Chardonnay

2 tablespoons minced shallots
1 large egg yolk
2 tablespoons crème fraîche
    or sour cream
1 tablespoon unsalted butter
1 tablespoon finely chopped
    fresh parsley

1. Place the fish in a dish, skin side down, drizzle with the oil and lemon juice, and season with the thyme, bay leaf, and salt and pepper. Cover and place in the refrigerator to marinate for at least 1 hour and up to 4 hours.

2. About 30 minutes before you cook the fish, place the wine and shallots in a saucepan over medium heat and boil until reduced by half. Pour into the top of a double boiler set over simmering water. Whisk in the yolk and cook, whisking gently but constantly, until the mixture thickens. Turn off the heat and beat in the cream, then the butter. Mix in the parsley and keep the sauce warm over hot water while you cook the fish.

3. Preheat the broiler. Place the fish, skin side up, in a broilerproof baking dish and pour over the marinade. Place under the hot broiler and broil, without turning, until the fish is cooked, 5 to 7 minutes.

4. To serve, arrange the fish skin side up on a platter and pass the sauce separately.

Friture de Limande

Panfried Lemon Sole

MAKES 4 SERVINGS

Lightly battered fish is a popular method for delicate fillets such as sole and flounder. Since only egg whites are used, the result should be crispy; here are a few pointers from Parisian cooks for achieving crispy fillets: Pat the fish dry. When you dust the fillets, shake off all the excess flour and after you've dipped them, allow excess batter to drip off. When you heat the butter, let the butter foam subside before adding the fish. Cook the fish in two batches, or use two skillets, rather than crowding the fish into one. "After all, it's not the métro," one cook told me. The usual accompaniment is boiled potatoes nicely seasoned with salt and pepper and tossed with a fistful of chopped parsley. A little melted butter flavored with cornichon pickles, shallots, and tarragon and a generous squeeze of fresh lemon passes on most tables as sauce.

2 large egg whites

6 tablespoons warm water

½ cup plus 3 tablespoons all-purpose flour

Salt and freshly ground black pepper

2 tablespoons unsalted butter, melted, plus 6 tablespoons

Four 6-ounce lemon sole fillets

6 cornichon pickles

2 shallots, minced

2 teaspoons fresh tarragon leaves, chopped, or 1 teaspoon dried (see note)

2 tablespoons fresh lemon juice

Lemon wedges for serving

1. Beat the egg whites and water together in a small bowl. Place ½ cup of the flour in a work bowl and slowly mix in the egg mixture, stirring to prevent lumps. Add ½ teaspoon salt, then give a few grinds of the peppermill. The batter should have the consistency of a pancake batter. If it is too thick, add a little more water. Beat in the melted butter and set aside.

2. Pat the fish fillets dry, sprinkle with a little salt and pepper, and lightly dust with the remaining 3 tablespoons flour, shaking off the excess. Dip the fish in the batter, then lift out and let excess batter drip off. Set the fillets on two plates.

3. In a skillet large enough to comfortably hold 2 fillets, melt 2 tablespoons of the butter over medium high heat. Add 2 fillets and cook until golden on both sides, turning only once. Transfer the fillets to a plate and keep warm while you repeat this step with 2 more tablespoons butter and the remaining 2 fillets.

4. Wipe the skillet clean, add the remaining 2 tablespoons butter, and melt over medium heat. Add the cornichons, shallots, tarragon, lemon juice, and a pinch each of salt and pepper.

5. To serve, arrange the fillets on a platter, garnish with the lemon wedges, and drizzle with the butter sauce.

NOTE: If using dried tarragon, refresh it in 1 tablespoon of water for 10 minutes, then drain.

Lotte Rôti aux Betteraves Jaunes
Monkfish Roasted with Yellow Beets

MAKES 4 SERVINGS

This irresistible combination of yellow beets and monkfish is a personal creation of a young wine merchant who lives above his shop near the place de la Nation. On market days, he shops just as the market is closing at one o'clock, returns home, and makes a large lunch. His recipe calls for roasting a whole monkfish tail on the bone so the texture of the fish, chewy when sautéed as medallions, softens. He roasts small yellow beets in their jackets, concentrating their sweet earthy flavor. He was very careful to point out that the wine should be crisp—a little acidic, with herbaceous tones, such as a Muscadet or Sancerre from the Loire Valley: "To marry the beets and fish, monsieur, which one would not think should go together." But they do.

1¼ pounds small yellow beets with tops

¼ cup minced shallots

3 tablespoons plus 1 teaspoon unsalted butter

1 or 2 monkfish tails (about 2 pounds)

Salt and freshly ground black pepper

½ cup herbaceous dry white wine, preferably Muscadet or Sancerre

1 tablespoon finely chopped fresh chervil

1. Remove the beet greens and wash them. Remove and discard the stems. Reserve the trimmed leaves. Wash the beets. Place the beets in a small roasting pan, cover tightly, and place in the oven. Turn the oven to 400°F and roast until the beets are tender when poked with a knife, 1 hour or more, depending on their size and age. Remove the beets from the oven, place under cold running water, and slip off the skins. If the beets are the size of golf balls, leave them whole; otherwise, halve or quarter them. Leave the oven on.

2. Meanwhile, in a small skillet over medium heat, cook the shallots in 3 tablespoons of the butter, stirring, until soft but not browned, about 2 minutes. Remove from the heat and set aside.

3. Season the monkfish with salt and pepper, place in a small roasting pan or baking dish, and spoon over the butter/shallot mixture. Pour the wine into the pan, place in the oven, and roast until tender, 30 to 40 minutes, depending on the size of the tail(s). Baste every 10 minutes with the pan juices, and add the beets to the roasting pan for the last 15 minutes of baking.

4. Meanwhile, melt the remaining 1 teaspoon butter in a skillet over medium heat. Sauté the beet greens until wilted, about 1 minute. Season with salt and pepper, remove from the heat, and keep warm.

5. Remove the roasting pan from the oven and transfer the monkfish to a cutting board. Slice down the center of the fish to remove the central bone. You will have 2 long round fillets or 4 if using 2 tails. Slice each fillet into 1-inch rounds and arrange on a platter on a bed of the beet greens. Arrange the beets around the fish and spoon the cooking juices over the fish. Sprinkle with the chervil and serve.

Les Volailles — Le Poulet, la Dinde, le Canard, et le Lapin

Poultry—Chicken, Turkey, Duck, and Rabbit

Ah, My Little Chickadee

One morning as we were entering the market on the boulevard Rochechouart, I was saying to my friend Auguste, "Coming from an American point of view, I don't for a minute think all this fuss the French are making about European food standards is a *canard* (they're not crying duck). If anyone is trying to mislead the public, it's the Euro-unionists. They take you French for *des pigeons* (for dupes). How can you be such a *faisan* (a cockeyed pheasant) when it's a question of *la patrimoine française*?"

"*Tiens! Des volailles,*" cried Auguste, no longer listening to my harangue.

"What a surprise, Auguste, poultry. And in a market, no less. But I'm not looking for poultry this morning."

"No, not that kind of poultry, Michel . . . That!" And he pointed to several rouged (at nine in the morning) young women. "*Chaudes commes des cailles, ces petites dindes.* (They look as warm and cuddly as quails, and dumb as turkeys.)"

"You're incorrigible, Auguste. And a sexist . . . and . . . "

"And you're too serious about my figures of speech. Besides, I love poultry. Don't I call you *ma poule,* my little chickadee, even though you're not my mistress?"

The French language is full of figures of speech and terms of endearment and derision that refer to poultry. Birds represent both free spirit and community. They're carefree and they're also stupid. One can clip their wings, and confine

them to fields or yards, but birds were meant to fly—or at least peck content-
edly, foraging the ground. Or perhaps it's because they're egg layers, obvious
symbols of fertility, that they hold such a special place in the argot of the French
language. And on the table.

Chickens are prepared
for cooking after they
are purchased.

Le Poulet ✦ Chicken

The sight of a chicken farmer arriving at the market to sell his twelve chickens each week is not something you'll see in Paris—poultry is too big a business these days. But Parisians still want to know where their chickens are from, and that the Sunday roast bird was a well-fed and happy lass. In France, people know their chickens by breed. Poulets de Bresse, twice as expensive as other chickens in the market, are a breed of chicken with pale yellow flesh and black feet. Flavorful roasting hens, they come from the Midi, the South of France, where they're raised exclusively on a diet of wheat and milk. Poulets de Périgord are from the Southwest and fed exclusively on corn. Being young, they're best for sautéing. Jaunes des Landes and Noirs des Landes are two breeds originally from the Atlantic coastal region south of Bordeaux, but now raised all over France. Les Jaunes are so called because they have yellow feet; les Noirs have black feet. They're a more all-purpose bird. Here in the States, I buy mostly free-range and kosher chickens, but when I buy supermarket chickens, I choose between young fryers and old roasters.

Astuce : Brining Chickens

In Paris, most fresh poultry is free-range and comes to market plucked but otherwise intact, with a necklace of feathers and shiny yellow or black feet. Since their cavities are not emptied until you buy them, you're assured of freshness—a full cavity doesn't last long before becoming "high." The skins have a matte finish, as if they've been cured or dried. They cook up crisp, giving up their fat, basting the bird, and protecting the flesh. Brining the common American chicken (whole birds only, please) approximates the texture of French chickens, and rids our birds of the excess water in the flesh that's the result of processing: Dissolve $\frac{1}{4}$ cup kosher salt in 1 cup hot water, then add 3 cups cold water. Place the chicken in a deep container and add the salted water. The chicken should be completely submerged; add more water as necessary to cover. Place in the refrigerator for at least 8 hours, and up to 12 hours. Drain the chicken, pat dry, and proceed with the recipe. This is similar to the process of "koshering" a chicken, so if you buy a kosher chicken, this trick is unnecessary.

Poule au Pot

Boiled Chicken

Boiled chicken is a dish that invites guests to relax, to be *comme chez soi,* at home. Use an old hen for this recipe, one that requires long, tempered cooking to soften the sinewy flesh. Begin with cold liquid to draw out flavor into the soup, and don't ever let the kettle boil. Ask your butcher to order chicken feet, a split calf's foot, or a pig's tail and cook it with the chicken, adding richness and body to the broth. This is simple cooking, requiring but patience.

One 5½-pound boiling hen, brined
    (see page 187) if not kosher,
    or large roasting chicken
2 chicken feet, 1 calf's foot, halved,
    or 1 pig's tail
1 lemon, cut in half
1 bottle dry white wine
3 sprigs fresh thyme
6 sprigs fresh parsley
2 bay leaves

6 coriander seeds
12 peppercorns
2 teaspoons salt
2 medium onions, cut in half
2 large carrots, cut in half
3 stalks celery, cut in half
8 small new potatoes, peeled
8 baby carrots, scrubbed
8 baby turnips, peeled
Dijon mustard for serving

1. Rinse the chicken and pat dry. Turn the wings under the chicken and tie the legs together. Place the chicken, giblets, chicken feet, and lemon in a pot and add the white wine and enough cold water to cover the bird. Place on the stove, covered, over high heat. Bring the liquid to a near boil, then remove the cover and immediately reduce the heat so that the liquid is just simmering. Skim the foamy impurities that collect on the surface. Add the thyme, parsley, bay leaves, coriander, peppercorns, salt, onions, halved carrots, and celery. Replace the cover and simmer for $1\frac{1}{2}$ hours. Do not let the liquid boil.

2. Preheat the oven to 200°F.

3. Transfer the hen to an ovenproof dish, cover with a damp towel, and keep warm in the oven. Skim the chicken fat that has collected on the surface of the cooking liquid; save for another use or discard. Strain the liquid and discard the contents of the strainer. Return the liquid to the pot, place over medium heat, and add the potatoes, baby carrots, and turnips. Simmer for 10 to 15 minutes, or until all the vegetables are tender. Remove the vegetables as they become tender, and keep warm.

4. Cut the chicken into serving pieces and arrange on a platter. Surround the bird with the vegetables. Pour the cooking liquid into a soup tureen. Serve the chicken in wide-rimmed soup bowls with the broth and offer mustard on the side.

Poulet Rôti en Cocotte
Casserole-Roasted Chicken

MAKES 4 TO 5 SERVINGS

Casserole-roasting is one of the most common ways of cooking in Paris, where, in years past, the oven had no real thermostat, just a knob that regulated the flow of gas. Roasting in a casserole protected the Sunday chicken from changeable conditions in the oven. And for people with tiny ovens or no ovens at all, a tight-lidded casserole, almost too heavy to lift, became the oven-surrogate.

There are only a few essentials to remember about this cooking method. You must use a heavy pot with a heavy tight-fitting lid. Copper pots are fine, but often their lids are ill-fitting and too thin to reflect heat back into the pot. Cast iron reacts with acids—wine, onions, shallots, even garlic. My preferred vessel is enameled cast iron, which distributes heat evenly across its bottom surface, and whose heavy lid radiates the interior heat back into it.

Whereas roasting occurs, or should occur, in a dry-air oven environment, casserole-roasting occurs under moister, less brutal conditions. Little of the natural moisture escapes the vessel and the result is browned, crisp, well-cooked chicken that is unbelievably moist.

One 4½- to 5-pound roasting chicken
Salt and freshly ground black pepper
3 tablespoons unsalted butter
1 tablespoon vegetable oil,
    preferably canola
5 large shallots, thinly sliced
½ cup dry white wine, such as
    Chardonnay

½ cup Homemade Chicken Broth
    (page 237) or low-sodium
    chicken broth
2 bay leaves
½ teaspoon dried thyme

1. Preheat the oven to 475°F.

2. Rinse the chicken and pat dry. Season the chicken inside and out with salt and pepper. Turn the wings under the bird and tie the legs together.

3. Melt 1 tablespoon of the butter in the oil in a Dutch oven over medium-high heat. Lay the bird on its side, cover, and transfer the casserole to the oven. Reduce the oven temperature to 375°F and roast for 30 minutes. Carefully turn the chicken onto its other breast, cover, and roast for another 20 minutes. Turn the bird on its back, cover, and roast for another 20 to 30 minutes, or until the juices run clear when a thigh is pierced. Transfer the chicken to a platter, cover, and keep warm.

4. Skim the fat from the juices in the casserole. Place the casserole over medium heat and cook the shallots, stirring, until soft but not browned, about 2 minutes. Add the wine, broth, bay leaves, and thyme. Boil the liquid until reduced by half, then remove from the heat and pour in any collected chicken juices. Stir in the remaining 2 tablespoons butter. Pour the sauce into a sauceboat and serve on the side.

Poulet Rôti en Cocotte aux Petits Pois et aux Lardons

Casserole-Roasted Chicken with Peas and Bacon

MAKES 4 TO 5 SERVINGS

The friend who shared this recipe with me is an unabashed Italophile who was inspired to add prosciutto and cream to a French roast chicken. What I like best about his improvisation is the sorrel, which tips the balance away from salty bacon and rich cream, cutting through and lightening the dish. Balance and subtlety is what French cuisine is all about.

One 5-pound boiling hen,
    with feet if possible
Salt and freshly ground black pepper
3 tablespoons, unsalted butter
2 tablespoons olive oil
2 cups fresh or frozen peas
4 shallots, thinly sliced

¼ cup dry vermouth or herbaceous
    dry white wine, such as Muscadet
    or Vouvray
¼ cup crème fraîche or heavy cream
¼ pound prosciutto, finely diced
12 sorrel leaves, center ribs removed and
    leaves chopped

1. Preheat the oven to 475°F.

2. Rinse the chicken and pat dry. Season the chicken inside and out with salt and pepper. Turn the wings under the bird and tie the legs together.

3. Melt 1 tablespoon of the butter in the oil in a Dutch oven. Lay the bird on one breast, cover, and transfer to the oven. Roast for 30 minutes. Carefully turn the chicken onto its other breast, cover, and roast for another 20 minutes. Turn the bird on its back, cover, and roast another 20 to 30 minutes, or until the juices run clear when a thigh is pierced. Transfer the chicken to a platter, cover, and keep warm.

4. Skim the fat from the juices in the casserole and return it to low heat. If using fresh peas, add them now. Add the shallots and cook until soft but not browned, about 2 minutes. Add the vermouth, créme fraîche, and prosciutto, and cook until the liquid is reduced by half, about 4 minutes. Pour any juices that have collected around the bird into the pot. Add the frozen defrosted peas, which only need to warm through, and the sorrel.

5. Remove from the heat, swirl in the remaining 2 tablespoons butter, and pour the sauce into a sauceboat. Serve immediately with the chicken.

Poulet Rôti en Cocotte à l'Ail Nouveau

Casserole-Roasted Chicken with Garlic Cream

MAKES 3 TO 4 SERVINGS

Of the many flavors Parisians give to pot-roasted chicken, one of the most appealing is garlic bathed in a cream sauce. During the few weeks of late spring when it's available, many people use cloves of new garlic to prepare this dish. The cloves are large and the soft skins can be left intact or are easily peeled off, like fava beans. They lack the nuttiness of fully mature cloves and are more volatile when used raw, but they quickly lose their edge when cooked. In the States, elephant garlic gives a similar cooked result.

One 3½- to 4-pound fryer chicken,
   brined (see page 187) if not kosher
Salt and freshly ground black pepper
A couple of sprigs fresh rosemary
2 tablespoons unsalted butter
1 tablespoon oil

3 shallots, minced
8 cloves elephant garlic, peeled
¾ cup dry white wine, such as
   Chardonnay
½ cup heavy cream

1. Preheat the oven to 475°F.

2. Rinse the chicken and pat dry. Season the cavity with salt and pepper and insert the rosemary sprigs into the cavity. Turn the wings under the bird and tie the legs together.

3. Place a Dutch oven on the stove and melt 1 tablespoon of the butter in the oil. Set the chicken in the casserole on its side, cover, and transfer to the oven. Roast for 20 minutes. Carefully turn the chicken onto the other breast, cover, and roast for another 20 minutes. Turn the bird on its back, add the shallots and garlic, cover, and roast for another 15 to 20 minutes, or until the juices run clear when a thigh is pierced. Transfer the chicken to a platter, cover, and keep warm.

4. Skim the fat from the juices in the casserole. Add the wine and boil over high heat, stirring, until the liquid is reduced by half, about 5 minutes. Pour in any collected chicken juices. Add the cream and boil until the sauce is thick enough to coat a spoon, about 5 minutes longer. Whisk in the remaining 1 tablespoon butter and remove from the heat. Pour the sauce into a sauceboat and serve with the chicken.

Me discussing poultry

Poulet en Cocotte au Mirepoix Aromatique

Casserole-Roasted Chicken with Aromatic Vegetables

MAKES 3 TO 4 SERVINGS

Dice onions, carrots, and celery together and you have what's called a *mirepoix,* the flavor foundation of French cooking. In this dish, the fragrance of parsley root, turnip, and parsnip added to the classic trio adds a sweet touch, and the vegetables make this a one-dish main course.

One 3½- to 4-pound fryer chicken

Salt and freshly ground black pepper

1 tablespoon fresh rosemary leaves

1 tablespoon unsalted butter

1 tablespoon vegetable oil, preferably canola

2 medium onions, diced

3 medium carrots, cut into ½-inch dice

2 small turnips, peeled and cut into ¾-inch dice

1 large Yukon Gold potato, peeled and cut into ¾-inch dice

1 large parsnip, peeled and cut into ¾-inch dice

½ medium celery root, peeled and cut into ¾-inch dice

1. Preheat the oven to 350°F.

2. Rinse the chicken and pat dry. Sprinkle the cavity with salt and pepper and the rosemary. Turn under the wings and tie the legs together. Season the chicken with salt and pepper.

3. Place a Dutch oven over medium-high heat and melt the butter in the oil. Set the chicken in the casserole on one breast and cook until browned, about 4 minutes. Carefully turn the chicken onto the other breast and cook until browned, about 4 minutes longer. Lay the chicken on its back, scatter all the vegetables around it, season with salt, and give a few turns of the peppermill. Cover and place in the oven for $1\frac{1}{4}$ hours, or until the juices run clear when a thigh is pierced. Stir the vegetables every 20 minutes during roasting. Transfer the chicken and vegetables to a platter and keep warm.

4. Skim the fat from the juices in the casserole. Boil over high heat, stirring, until the juices are reduced to $\frac{1}{2}$ cup. Pour the sauce over the chicken and serve.

Poulet Rissolé au Beurre

Panfried Chicken

MAKES 2 TO 3 SERVINGS

Chicken pieces cooked in butter with no liquid render their fat and become crisp, and, when done in the time-honored fashion, have the appeal of Southern fried chicken. Of the universals that transcend culture and class, those of a culinary nature are the most comforting. Cook a nice rice pilaf to go with this simple dish.

3 to 3 1/2 pounds chicken pieces
Salt and freshly ground black pepper
2 tablespoons unsalted butter
2 shallots, minced
1 clove garlic, minced
1 tablespoon all-purpose flour
1/2 cup dry vermouth or herbaceous
    dry white wine, such as Muscadet
    or Vouvray

1 tablespoon chopped fresh tarragon
    or 2 teaspoons dried,
    refreshed in water
1/2 teaspoon dried thyme
1 tablespoon chopped fresh chervil
1 tablespoon chopped fresh parsley

1. Rinse the chicken pieces, pat dry, and season with salt and pepper. In a heavy lidded skillet large enough to comfortably hold the chicken in a single layer, melt the butter over medium-low heat. Add the chicken skin side down and cook, turning only once, for about 30 minutes or until cooked through. Shake the pan occasionally to avoid sticking. Transfer the pieces to a plate as they are done, cover, and keep warm.

2. Discard all but 1 tablespoon of the fat from the pan and add the shallots and garlic. Cook for 1 minute, without browning, then stir in the flour. Add the vermouth and any collected chicken juices. If using dried tarragon, add it now. Cook, stirring, until the liquid thickens and becomes saucelike. Replace the chicken in the pan, add the thyme, cover, and heat through. Mix in the fresh tarragon, if using, and the chervil and remove from the heat.

3. Transfer the contents of the pot to a serving dish, scraping up all the sauce, and serve immediately.

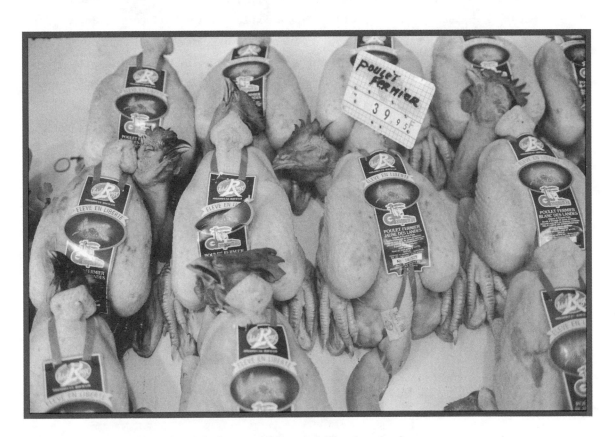

Farm-raised chickens, the white-footed Blanc des Landes from southwest France

Poulet Sauté au Verjus
Chicken Sauté with Green Grape Juice

MAKES 2 TO 3 SERVINGS

If you've never cooked with verjus, juice from unripened grapes, you're in for a treat. The juice is green on the palate, tart and fruity. Traditionally used by home cooks in the wine-producing regions of France, it's part of a more erudite culinary vocabulary in Paris. My first introduction to it was in the Marché Saint-Quentin, where an *épicier,* a purveyor of dry goods and spices, was giving away introductory tastes. The effect that it has on this chicken is mesmerizing—adding a fruity tartness without the acidity of wine. In America you can buy verjus in some specialty food markets. Serve with a bowl of mashed potatoes and apples (page 290) for a truly magnificent meal, honest and plain in its perfection.

3 to 3 1/2 pounds chicken pieces

Salt and freshly ground black pepper

2 tablespoons olive oil

4 shallots, thinly sliced (about 1/2 cup)

1 cup verjus

1/2 teaspoon dried savory

2 bay leaves

1 tablespoon finely chopped fresh parsley

1 tablespoon unsalted butter

1. Rinse the chicken, pat dry, and season on both sides with salt and pepper. Heat the oil in a large skillet over medium heat. Add the chicken, without crowding the pan. Cook in batches if necessary and brown the chicken on both sides, about 7 minutes per side. Remove the chicken pieces when they are nicely golden, and pour off all but 1 tablespoon of the fat from the pan.

2. Add the shallots to the pan and cook, stirring, to soften. Replace the thigh and drumstick pieces, skin side up, pour in the verjus, and add the savory and bay leaves. Cover the skillet, reduce the heat to low, and cook for 5 minutes. Return the breasts to the skillet, along with any collected chicken juices, cover, and continue to cook for another 10 minutes, or until the chicken is cooked through. Remove the chicken, arrange on a platter, cover, and keep warm.

3. Continue cooking the liquid until it has reduced by about one third. Remove the pan from the heat and remove the bay leaves. Add the parsley and whisk in the butter. Pour the sauce over the chicken and serve.

Poulet Sauté à l'Estragon
Tarragon Chicken

Tarragon chicken is one of the best-known dishes in the French repertoire. I was thrilled to get this variation, with a *soupçon* (a suspicion) of vinegar added to wake up the flavors. Cooked together with mushrooms, this chicken needs no other accompaniment.

3 to 3 ½ pounds chicken pieces

Salt and freshly ground black pepper

4 tablespoons (½ stick) unsalted butter

4 large shallots, minced (about ½ cup)

1 clove garlic, minced

¼ pound white mushrooms,
 thinly sliced

1 tablespoon chopped fresh tarragon or
 1 teaspoon dried, refreshed in water

1 tablespoon all-purpose flour

½ cup dry vermouth or herbaceous
 dry white wine, such as Muscadet
 or Vouvray

2 tablespoons white wine vinegar

1 tablespoon chopped fresh parsley

1. Rinse the chicken pieces, pat dry, and season with salt and pepper. In a heavy non-reactive lidded pan large enough to hold the chicken in a single layer, melt the butter over medium-low heat. Add the chicken skin side down, cover, and cook, turning once, for about 30 minutes, or until cooked through. Remove the pieces as they are done and set aside on a plate.

2. Discard all but 1 tablespoon of the fat from the pan and add the shallots, garlic, mushrooms, and dried tarragon. Cook for about 4 minutes, stirring, then stir in the flour. Add the vermouth and cook, stirring, until the liquid thickens and reduces to a thin saucelike consistency.

3. Replace the chicken in the pan, cover, and heat through. Mix in the fresh tarragon, if using, and parsley and remove from the heat. Transfer the contents of the pan to a serving dish, scraping up all the sauce, and serve immediately.

Poulet Sauté aux Olives Vertes
Chicken Sauté with Green Olives

MAKES 2 TO 3 SERVINGS

Salty and sour balance each other in this delightfully aromatic dish. It was served at lunch one Sunday afternoon after a morning tour of the flea market with friends. We ate it with potatoes *en salade* (page 287).

3 to 3½ pounds chicken pieces
Salt and freshly ground black pepper
2 tablespoons extra virgin olive oil
4 shallots, thinly sliced (about ½ cup)
2 cloves garlic, thinly sliced
¼ teaspoon dried thyme
½ cup dry vermouth or herbaceous
    dry white wine, such as Muscadet
    or Vouvray

½ cup Homemade Chicken Broth
    (page 237) or low-sodium
    chicken broth
½ cup small green olives,
    such as Picholines
2 tablespoons unsalted butter

1. Rinse the chicken, pat dry, and season on both sides with salt and pepper. Heat the oil in a large skillet over medium heat. Add the chicken, without crowding the pan—cook in batches if necessary—and brown on both sides, about 7 minutes per side. Remove the chicken pieces and set aside. Pour off all but 1 tablespoon fat.

2. Add the shallots and garlic to the pan and cook, stirring, to soften, about 5 minutes. Replace the thigh and drumstick pieces, skin side up, sprinkle with half of the thyme, and add the vermouth, broth, and olives. Cover the skillet, reduce the heat to low, and cook for 7 minutes. Return the breasts to the skillet, sprinkle with the remaining thyme, and continue to cook for another 10 minutes, or until the chicken is cooked through. Remove the chicken from the skillet and keep warm on a plate.

3. Continue cooking the liquid until it has reduced by about half. Add any collected chicken juices, then whisk in the butter. Arrange the chicken on a serving platter, pour over the sauce, and serve.

Poule au Vinaigre à l'Ancienne

Chicken in Aged Red Wine Vinegar

MAKES 4 TO 5 SERVINGS

Parisians are particular about the quality of their ingredients, especially pungent ones like vinegar, which should be aged in wooden casks to mellow its tang. "Flavors should marry, not fight," said the *épicier*, or dry goods grocer, who was telling me about good cooking vinegar. "If you use a rough vinegar to cook with, it will stand out like a thumb." I tried this dish with ordinary vinegar and the chicken tasted pickled; with a nice aged wine vinegar, the flavor was rich with wine undertones.

One 5-pounds boiling hen, cut up, or
   about 4½ pounds chicken pieces
1 onion, peeled
2 cloves
2 carrots
2 stalks celery
1 bunch fresh parsley
4 sprigs fresh thyme
   or 2 teaspoons dried
2 bay leaves
1 teaspoon peppercorns
2 chicken feet, ½ calf's foot,
   or 1 pig's tail

Salt
1 cup robust red wine,
   such as Zinfandel
½ cup aged red wine vinegar
2 cups Homemade Chicken Broth
   (page 237) or low-sodium
   chicken broth
Freshly ground black pepper
1 tablespoon cornstarch
2 tablespoons cold water
2 tablespoons unsalted butter

1. Rinse the chicken pieces and pat dry. Halve the onion and stick 1 clove in each half. Make a bed of the carrots, celery, onion, parsley, thyme, bay leaves, peppercorns, and chicken feet in a large deep casserole and sprinkle with salt. Arrange the thigh and drumstick pieces, skin side up, on the bed and pour in the wine and vinegar. Cover the pot, place over high heat, and cook for 5 minutes. Reduce the heat to medium, add the broth, cover, and simmer (do not boil) for 20 minutes.

2. Add the chicken breasts, season the chicken pieces with salt and pepper, and continue simmering for another 20 minutes, or until the chicken is tender. Remove the chicken from the pot, cover, and keep warm while you finish the sauce.

3. Pour the cooking liquid through a strainer and discard the contents of the strainer. Skim and discard any fat from the surface of the liquid, then pour the liquid back into the pot. Dissolve the cornstarch in the cold water and add to the pot. Turn the heat to medium and reduce the liquid until it has a saucelike consistency. Skim the liquid as impurities rise to the surface. When you like the consistency of the sauce, remove the pot from the heat and whisk in the butter. Pour any collected chicken juices into the sauce. Transfer the chicken to a warm serving platter and spoon a little sauce over all the pieces. Serve the remaining sauce in a sauceboat.

Blanc de Dinde aux Oignons Confits

Pan-Roasted Turkey Breast with Onion Marmalade

MAKES 3 TO 4 SERVINGS

Turkey is extremely popular in Parisian homes, but since it's not a traditional holiday feast, you rarely ever see a whole bird for sale. Often Parisians buy boneless breasts that the butcher has seasoned and tied into roasts. This turkey breast absorbs the flavor of the caramelized onions with which it's cooked, and becomes lusciously sweet.

4 small sprigs fresh rosemary

*One 1 1/2- to 2-pound boneless
   turkey breast*

Salt and freshly ground black pepper

4 tablespoons (1/2 stick) unsalted butter

*5 medium onions, finely chopped
   (about 2 1/2 cups)*

1/8 teaspoon freshly grated nutmeg

*1 cup dry white wine, such as
   Chardonnay*

*1 cup Homemade Chicken Broth
   (page 237) or low-sodium
   chicken broth*

1. Insert the sprigs of rosemary under the skin of the turkey, then lay it skin side down and season with salt and pepper. Tie the breast with butcher's twine to form a compact cylinder and season the skin with salt and pepper.

2. Melt 2 tablespoons of the butter in a large skillet over medium heat. Add the turkey and cook until light golden on all sides, 8 to 10 minutes. Transfer the turkey to a plate and set aside.

3. Reduce the heat to medium-low, add the onions, nutmeg, and salt as desired, and cook, stirring occasionally, until the onions dry out and darken, 30 to 35 minutes.

4. Place the turkey on top of the onions and pour in the wine and broth. Cover and cook until the breast is tender, about 30 minutes. Transfer the breast to a work surface.

5. Increase the heat to medium and cook until the cooking liquid reduces and thickens, about 5 minutes. Turn off the heat and swirl in the remaining 2 tablespoons butter.

6. Untie the breast and slice into serving pieces. Pour any collected juices into the onions. Scrape the onions onto a platter, arrange the sliced turkey on top, and serve.

Paillards de Dinde à l'Anglaise
Turkey Cutlets in Batter
with Sage and Lemon Butter

MAKES 4 SERVINGS

Preparing something *à l'anglaise* (in the English style) is perfect for a low-fat item such as turkey cutlets, because the light batter keeps the meat moist. Nowadays, many Parisians prefer a turkey cutlet to a traditional veal cutlet both for health and affordability. Accompany these turkey cutlets with Warm Lentils (page 281).

2 large eggs

3 tablespoons canola or corn oil

2 tablespoons water

Salt and freshly ground black pepper

All-purpose flour for dusting

Four 5-ounce turkey cutlets

4 tablespoons (½ stick) unsalted butter

2 tablespoons fresh lemon juice

*1 tablespoon finely chopped fresh sage
  or dried*

1. Using a fork or small whisk, lightly beat together the eggs, 1 tablespoon of the oil, and the water in a wide-rimmed shallow bowl. Season with salt and pepper. Place the flour in another bowl. Season the turkey with salt and pepper. Dust lightly with flour, shaking off the excess. Dip the cutlets in the egg mixture and let the excess egg run off.

2. Heat the remaining 2 tablespoons oil and 2 tablespoons of the butter in a large skillet over medium heat until the butter foams and then subsides. Add the cutlets one at a time, without crowding (in two batches, if necessary), and cook until golden on both sides, 6 to 7 minutes total. As they are done, remove the cutlets to a serving platter and keep warm in a 200°F oven.

3. Melt the remaining 2 tablespoons butter in the skillet, add the lemon juice and sage, season with a pinch of salt, and give a grind of the peppermill. Add any juices that may have collected around the turkey. Pour the sauce over the cutlets and serve immediately.

Astuce: Cooking à l'Anglaise

In France, anything dipped first in flour and then in beaten egg is called *à l'anglaise*, or in the English style. Of course in England and the States, it's called *à la française*, in the French style. Whatever you call it, though, it's a wonderful way of cooking thin cutlets of fish and poultry. Here are the tricks I learned in Paris: When you dust with flour, shake off all the excess, and let all the excess egg drip off. You don't need a lot. Heat the oil over medium heat until hot but not smoking. If the oil doesn't immediately bubble when the food is introduced, the oil's not hot enough. Maintain a constant temperature by increasing the heat slightly when adding food to the pan. A mixture of oil and butter gives better flavor than straight oil and can be heated to a higher temperature than straight butter. If the skillet is crowded, you'll lose bits of batter and your food will come out greasy and soggy.

Poêlé de Cuisses de Dindeaux, Endives, et Champignons

Pot-Roasted Turkey Thighs, Endive, and Mushrooms

MAKES 4 SERVINGS

French turkeys are relatively small, for the ones that come to Parisian markets are generally free-range. For many, the favored morsel is the thigh, for its unctuous texture. The poultrymen tell me that it's nearly always bought on the bone, because it adds its special richness to the meat during cooking. I find this one-dish main course fascinating for the way the bitter endive and woodsy mushroom flavors intensify the gamy quality of the dark meat. American turkeys will benefit from the same flavor enhancing. One poultryman said it perfectly. "We like to think that all dark-fleshed birds have been shot out of the sky. Of course, there are no wild turkeys in France to shoot out of the sky. In fact, turkeys don't even really fly, do they? But the fantastic thing for us is to imagine where things on our plates came from, for it increases our appreciation."

2 turkey thighs

Salt and freshly ground black pepper

2 tablespoons vegetable oil, preferably canola

1 teaspoon dried thyme

4 heads Belgian endive, halved lengthwise

1 pound white mushrooms

1 tablespoon grainy mustard

1/2 cup Homemade Chicken Broth (page 237) or low-sodium chicken broth

2 tablespoons unsalted butter

1 tablespoon chopped fresh chervil

1. Season the turkey thighs with salt and pepper. Heat the oil in a Dutch oven over medium heat. Add the thighs, skin side down, cover, reduce the heat to low, and cook for 20 minutes. Turn the thighs, sprinkle with the thyme, and cook for another 20 minutes.

2. Remove the thighs and arrange the endive, cut side up, in the pot. Return the thighs to the pot, placing them skin side up on top of the endive. Season with salt and pepper, cover, and cook for 20 minutes. Add the mushrooms and continue to cook for another 15 minutes.

3. Transfer the contents of the pot to a serving platter, arrange everything nicely, and keep warm in a 200°F oven.

4. Stir the mustard into the pot, then stir in the broth, increase the heat to medium-high, and boil until reduced to a saucelike consistency, about 5 minutes. Remove from the heat and stir in the butter and chervil. Spoon the sauce over the turkey and serve.

One of Paris's best bakers, on rue de Turenne in the Marais, uses wild yeast.

Le Canard ◆ Duck

*W*hen Parisians are in the mood for a nice bird, duck is second in popularity to chicken. The famous Rouen ducklings have the richest meat, for they are not bled. (Unlike other ducks and poultry, these birds are smothered.) They're the most prized. During the summer months, Barbary ducks abound in the markets. They're closest to Long Island ducks. During the month of October, many merchants have canard sauvage—wild duck. They're not exactly wild, though; they're more free-range. But the range of a duck is in flight, not pecking the ground like a chicken. The farmers clip the birds' wings so they can't fly too far from the roost. Then, when it's the season, they shoot them out of the air, pluck them, and bring them to market. Here in the States, look in the shops for fresh ducks and you'll see how differently they cook from the average supermarket duck. I always buy my ducks in Chinese markets, because they are the freshest you can find. They render their fat easily and have the gamy flavor that I like.

Canard Rôti aux Navets
Roasted Duck and Turnips

MAKES 2 TO 3 SERVINGS

This trick of cooking duck in a pressure cooker is something that I picked up years ago, when I was a student in Paris. Cooked in a moist environment, the meat tends to remain more succulent than when roasted in the dry heat of an oven. And most of the duck's fat is rendered in the pressure cooker, making for a much less messy kitchen. Finishing the bird in a hot oven crisps and browns the skin. This garnish of turnips is most traditional. The cabbagelike flavor of turnips enhances the gamy flavor of the bird and contrasts with the slightly sweet-and-sour character of the sauce, with the result that the sauce is neither cloying nor sour but simply rich-tasting.

One 4½- to 5-pound duckling
Salt and freshly ground black pepper
3 medium turnips, peeled and quartered
2 tablespoons dark brown sugar

3 tablespoons red wine vinegar
1 cup low-sodium beef broth
1 tablespoon all-purpose flour
1 tablespoon unsalted butter

1. Rinse the duckling and pat dry. Sprinkle the cavity with salt and pepper. Tie the wings together under the bird and tie the legs together. Fill a pressure cooker with a 1½-inch depth of water and place the duck, standing or lying flat, on a rack in the pressure cooker. Secure the lid, place over medium-high heat, and, once the pressure is achieved, cook the duck for 30 minutes.

2. Meanwhile, preheat the oven to 375°F.

3. Remove the pressure cooker from the heat and let the pressure drop naturally. When the pressure has subsided, open the pressure cooker and transfer the bird, breast up, to a roasting pan large enough to hold the duck and (eventually) the turnips. Place in the oven for 20 minutes.

4. Meanwhile, place the turnips in a pot, cover with salted cold water, cover the pot, bring to a boil over high heat, and immediately drain.

5. Remove the duck from the oven and drain off all the fat that has collected in the roasting pan. Arrange the turnips around the duck, season with salt and pepper, replace in the oven, and roast for 35 to 40 minutes, basting the turnips with the duck drippings that collect in the roasting pan, until the duck is crisp and the turnips are tender and golden.

6. While the duck is cooking, combine the sugar and vinegar in a saucepan, place over medium heat, and cook until the mixture boils and reduces to a thick syrup, 5 to 7 minutes. Stir in the broth and remove from the heat.

7. Arrange the duck and turnips on a platter and keep warm in the turned-off oven. Pour off all but 1 tablespoon of fat from the roasting pan and place over medium heat. Stir in the flour, then whisk in the vinegar/broth mixture. Cook until the liquid thickens and becomes saucelike. Whisk in the butter, taste for seasoning, and add salt and pepper to taste.

8. Pour the sauce through a strainer into a sauceboat. Remove the duck and turnips from the oven and, using poultry shears, cut the duck into serving pieces. Arrange on the platter, surrounded by the turnips, and serve immediately with the sauce.

Canard en Cocotte au Poivre Vert

Casserole-Roasted Duck with Green Peppercorn Sauce

MAKES 2 TO 3 SERVINGS

Parisians are fond of re-creating dishes savored in restaurants, but they adapt them for ease of home cooking. This is a rendition of the famous duck dish served at one time at the Tour d'Argent. Don't think you'll need a sterling silver duck press to serve this bird—it's well cooked in a casserole, not rare-roasted in the oven like the original. But do expect a famously conceived combination of flavors.

One 4½- to 5-pound duckling
Salt and freshly ground black pepper
2 cups water
1 cup Homemade Chicken Broth
    (page 237) or low-sodium
    chicken broth
4 bay leaves
1 tablespoon dried thyme

1 tablespoon dried savory
1 tablespoon all-purpose flour
1 teaspoon chopped fresh tarragon
    or dried
½ cup dry red wine, such as Pinot Noir
½ cup heavy cream
1 tablespoon green peppercorns
    in water, drained

1. Rinse the duckling and pat dry. Season the cavity with salt and pepper. Tie the wings together under the bird and tie the legs together. Prick the skin all over with a meat fork.

2. Place the duck, breast up, in a large pot. Add the water, broth, bay leaves, thyme, and savory. Cover, place over high heat, and bring to a boil. Reduce the heat to medium-low and simmer, covered, for 1¼ hours. Remove the duck from the pot and when cool enough to handle, use poultry shears to cut the duck into serving pieces. Set the pieces aside. Strain the cooking juices. Skim off the fat and reserve the liquid and fat separately.

3. Place the flour in the pot and stir in 1 tablespoon of the reserved duck fat. (Save the remaining fat for another use.) Stir the reserved liquid into the pot and place over medium heat. If using dried tarragon, add it now. Add the wine and simmer for 5 minutes. Add the cream and peppercorns and continue to simmer until the mixture has a saucelike consistency, about another 5 minutes. Add the fresh tarragon, if using, and remove from the heat.

4. Meanwhile, preheat the broiler. Place the duck in a shallow roasting pan and place under the broiler, turning once, until the skin is crisp and golden on both sides. Remove the duck from the broiler and, using poultry shears, cut up the duck.

5. Arrange the pieces on a serving platter, pour the sauce into a sauceboat, and serve.

Cuisses de Canard à l'Ail
Duck Legs in Garlic Cream

MAKES 4 SERVINGS

I was going to prepare dinner for eight in the minuscule kitchen of my friend Philippe Gautier's loft and I needed to cook something special yet easy. So I went down the street to the Marché Secrétan, one of only a dozen covered markets that still exist in Paris. One of the poultry vendors was displaying some large, plump duck legs. They looked yummy and the price was right. I asked the vendor for a recipe, and this is the one she shared with me. My only change was to cook the legs in Philippe's pressure cooker, as it was getting late. If you want to cook this dish using a regular pot, choose a heavy casserole and count on cooking the legs for about one and a quarter hours.

1 onion, peeled

2 cloves

2 stalks celery

1 carrot

*3 cups Homemade Chicken Broth
  (page 237) or low-sodium
  chicken broth*

16 cloves garlic, peeled

8 duck legs

Salt and freshly ground black pepper

1 tablespoon dried savory

3 bay leaves

½ cup heavy cream

1 tablespoon chopped fresh chervil

1. Halve the onion and stick 1 clove in each half. Place the onion halves in a pressure cooker along with the celery, carrot, and garlic. Lay the duck legs on top, add the broth, and sprinkle with salt and pepper, the savory, and bay leaves. Secure the lid and place over medium-high heat until the pressure is achieved. Lower the heat to medium and cook for 35 minutes.

2. Release the pressure with the quick-release method, remove the lid, and transfer the duck legs to a shallow roasting pan. Remove and discard the onion, celery, and carrot; reserve the garlic. Pour the liquid into a container, let the fat rise to the top, and remove it. (Save the duck fat for other cooking uses.)

3. Pour the liquid into a saucepan, add the garlic, place over medium-high heat, and boil down until reduced by half, about 10 minutes. Add the cream and continue to boil until reduced to a saucelike consistency, about 8 minutes longer. Pour the sauce into a blender and blend until smooth. Strain the sauce back into the saucepan and keep warm.

4. Preheat the broiler. Place the duck legs under the heat and cook, turning once, until crisp on both sides, about 5 minutes.

5. Spoon some sauce onto a serving platter and pour the remaining sauce into a sauceboat. Arrange the legs on the platter, sprinkle with the chervil, and serve immediately.

My friend Philippe Gautier, in whose tiny kitchen I learned to use a pressure cooker

Cuisses de Canard "Confit" aux Pommes

Preserved Duck Legs with Apples

MAKES 4 SERVINGS

Ducks that have been fattened for their livers are used for making confit—a preparation where the duck is slowly cooked and stored in its own fat. Traditionally, it was a way of preserving ducks in a cool cellar for several months, where their flavor would develop. It's not exactly the kind of procedure one attempts in an apartment kitchen, and most people in Paris buy confit in jars. This mock confit, which is made in a pressure cooker, is infinitely simpler to prepare than the farm recipe, and its flavor, if not really comparable, is very, very delicious. If, however, you want to prepare a somewhat more authentic confit, place the legs in a storage container just large enough to hold them, pour the cooking fat over them, and place in the fridge for two weeks before using. Either way, this recipe gives a bonus—the delicious fat, which may be used for sautéing chicken or potatoes.

8 duck legs

Coarse salt

6 cloves garlic, peeled

1 onion, chopped

12 peppercorns

6 sprigs fresh thyme

6 bay leaves

3 cloves

1 cup Homemade Chicken Broth (page 237) or low-sodium chicken broth

½ cup canola or peanut oil

1 tablespoon unsalted butter

3 Granny Smith apples, peeled, cored, and cut into ¾-inch wedges

Salt and freshly ground black pepper

1. The night before serving, place the duck legs in a nonaluminum dish, sprinkle all over with coarse salt, and place in the refrigerator, uncovered.

2. The next day, rinse the legs. Place the legs in a pressure cooker along with the garlic, onion, peppercorns, thyme, bay leaves, and cloves. Pour in the broth and oil. Secure the lid and place over high heat. When full pressure is reached, reduce the heat to low and cook for 35 minutes.

3. Remove from the heat and let the pressure subside naturally. Carefully remove the lid and remove the duck from the pressure cooker. Pour the liquid into a container, let the fat rise to the top, and remove it. (Save the duck fat for other cooking uses.)

4. Pour the liquid into a saucepan and boil over medium heat until reduced to a sauce-like consistency. Set aside.

5. Preheat the broiler. Place the duck legs under the heat and cook, turning once, until crisp on both sides, about 5 minutes.

6. Meanwhile, melt the butter in a skillet over medium heat. Add the apples and salt and pepper and cook, stirring, until the apples are tender and golden around the edges, about 5 minutes.

7. To serve, arrange the apples and duck on a platter and spoon over the sauce.

Astuce : Sautéing

Sauté comes from the word for "to jump." To properly sauté, you need just enough butter or oil in your pan to prevent food from sticking, in order to allow what you're cooking to be flipped, or to jump in the pan. The sauté ingredients should be patted dry and seasoned with salt and pepper. The pan should be moderately hot, but the oil should not be smoking.

Foie de Canard aux Raisins Secs
Foie Gras with Sultanas

MAKES 2 SERVINGS

It's rare that people cook foie gras (specially fattened duck or goose liver) at home, but I did meet an avid Parisian cook who prepared this dish from time to time. It's not at all a family dinner, but rather a sophisticated, sumptuous, and, yes, expensive dish to prepare. But, what heavenly joy to be able to eat foie gras until you can't eat any more. So, prepare this as the centerpiece of a dinner *à deux.* You'll probably only need a salad after gorging yourself on this extravagance, but do serve toasted slabs of a good country loaf with walnuts. You could also serve this as a starter for six to eight people.

1 fresh duck foie gras
 (about 1¼ pounds)
Salt
2 cups Homemade Chicken Broth
 (page 237) or low-sodium
 chicken broth

1 cup semi-sweet white wine, such as
 Sauternes or Gewürztraminer
2 bay leaves
2 sprigs fresh thyme
8 peppercorns
½ cup sultanas (golden raisins)

1. Carefully separate the two large lobes of the liver and with your fingers remove the center vein as well as you can without destroying the liver. Sprinkle with salt and set aside.

2. Combine the broth, wine, bay leaves, thyme, and peppercorns in a heavy pot just large enough to hold the liver, cover, bring to a boil, and reduce the heat to low. Add the liver to the pot. It should be completely submerged in the liquid. Replace the lid and poach for 10 minutes. The liquid should barely simmer. The liver will be lightly springy to the touch when done; it should be medium, slightly pink at the center.

3. Remove the liver from the pot, cover, and keep warm. Strain the liquid and skim off the fat. (Save the fat to use in other cooking.) Return the cooking liquid to the pot, add the sultanas, and simmer until reduced to a glaze.

4. To serve, slice the foie gras into ¾-inch-thick slabs, arrange on a warm platter, and spoon over the sauce.

Ragoût de Lapin Moutardé et Flambé au Calvados

Braised Rabbit with Mustard and Calvados

MAKES 3 TO 4 SERVINGS

Béatrice the cheese vendor gave me her favorite recipe for rabbit, which she serves with buttered egg noodles. Flamed with Calvados, then simmered in white wine without any other liquid, the rabbit is rich in flavor. Use a heavy tight-lidded casserole to prepare this ragout. You don't want any juices to escape during cooking. I once prepared this recipe using verjus instead of wine and the result was terrific, with a softer, fruitier tang.

One 2½-pound rabbit, cut up

Salt and freshly ground black pepper

All-purpose flour for dusting

3 tablespoons unsalted butter
    or extra virgin olive oil

¼ cup Calvados or applejack

1 medium onion, finely chopped

4 cloves garlic, thinly sliced

2 cups slightly fruity white wine, such
    as Gewürztztraminer or Riesling

3 tablespoons grainy mustard

1 tablespoon mustard seeds

1 tablespoon dried sage

¼ cup crème fraîche or heavy cream

1. Preheat the oven to 425°F.

2. Rinse the rabbit in cold water, pat dry, and generously sprinkle with salt and pepper. Lightly dust the pieces with flour, shaking off the excess. Heat the butter or oil in a large deep ovenproof skillet over medium-high heat. Brown the rabbit on both sides, turning once, 10 to 12 minutes. Pour in the Calvados and let it cook for 30 seconds—be careful, as the Calvados may flame briefly until the alcohol burns off. When any flames have subsided, remove the rabbit pieces and set aside.

3. Reduce the heat to medium, add the onion and garlic, and cook until the onion softens but doesn't brown, about 7 minutes. Pour in the wine, stir in the mustard, and add the mustard seeds and sage. Replace the rabbit in the pan. As soon as the liquid comes to a simmering boil, cover the pan, transfer it to the oven, and cook for 40 to 45 minutes, or until the rabbit is tender.

4. Transfer the skillet to the stovetop and transfer the rabbit to a serving platter. Add the crème fraîche to the cooking liquid and boil until it becomes saucelike; this will take anywhere from 5 to 15 minutes, depending on how much liquid the rabbit has given up. Pour the sauce over the rabbit and serve immediately.

Ragoût de Lapin Provençal
Pot-Roasted Rabbit with Tomatoes, Fennel, and Tarragon

MAKES 3 TO 4 SERVINGS

Rabbits easily give up moisture during cooking, sometimes becoming dry. The gentle heat of a moderately slow oven coaxes out the natural juices, the meat absorbing the flavors of the ragout like a sponge. My friend Corinne Megy, who cooked this dish for me, serves it with Saffron Rice and Onions (page 279).

One 2½-pound rabbit, cut up
Salt and freshly ground black pepper
2 tablespoons extra virgin olive oil
6 ripe Roma (plum) tomatoes, peeled, seeded (see page 52), and chopped, or one 14½-ounce can whole tomatoes, drained and quartered
2 medium fennel bulbs, trimmed, cored, and thinly sliced

1 medium onion, finely chopped
6 cloves garlic, thinly sliced
2 fresh or dried bay leaves
1 tablespoon chopped fresh tarragon or 2 teaspoons dried
½ cup dry white table wine
1 tablespoon Pernod
3 tablespoons unsalted butter

1. Preheat the oven to 375°F.

2. Rinse the rabbit in cold water, pat dry, and generously sprinkle with salt and pepper. Heat the oil in a Dutch oven over medium heat, add the tomatoes, fennel, onion, garlic, and bay leaves, and cook, stirring, for 5 minutes. If using dried tarragon, add it now. Bury the rabbit in the fennel mixture and pour in the wine and Pernod. Cover, bring to a simmer, and transfer to the oven. Cook for 50 to 60 minutes.

3. Replace the pot on the stovetop. Transfer the rabbit to a serving platter and keep warm. Boil down the cooking liquid over high heat until reduced by about one third. Remove from the heat, beat in the butter, and add the fresh tarragon, if using. Pour the ragout onto the center of the platter, arrange the rabbit pieces on top, and serve immediately.

Corinne Megy

Les Viandes —
Le Veau, le Boeuf, l'Agneau, et le Porc

Meats — Veal, Beef, Lamb, and Pork

People cook what their parents cooked. Of course they prepare certain *modernités* (modern dishes), but even so they stay with their traditions." So Patrick Hayée, the butcher in the Marché Beauveau-Antoine, was telling me. "Everyone prefers to eat the foods that they grew up with, *n'est-ce pas*? It's our traditions and our culinary birthright that keeps us French." I've heard this said by so many Parisians that it's become an anthem.

Meat, once a bit of a luxury, is still a special *plat*, although the real luxury today is having the time to prepare a traditional *ragoût* or *daube*. These rustic meat stews connect many Parisians with their *pays*, their ancestral region. Today they also serve to connect a new generation of Parisians with their parents' generation, for not so many years ago, most ovens in Parisian apartments were little more than hot boxes with adjustable levers that controlled the gas, lacking temperature controls. There was usually a single burner on top. Nearly all home cooking consisted of meat or poultry roasted in a *cocotte,* or casserole, like a pot roast, or cooked in sauce, or gratinéed.

Times have changed faster than people's tastes for certain foods, though, and the trick today is preparing a dignified stew in under two hours. The traditional stews require a day's marinating, a couple of hours in the oven, and then a day in the refrigerator to develop flavor before serving. That's the ideal. But Parisians are not ready to give up their favorites and they have adapted recipes to fit their hectic schedules. During the week they may take shortcuts, or rely on the pressure cooker to get a meal on the table. Or, they prepare quick recipes for minute steaks, veal cutlets, pork chops, and the like, saving the traditional cooking for weekends and holidays.

Happily, today's kitchens are equipped with modern ranges and the average Parisian's repertoire of meat cookery is much expanded from that of a generation ago. When we Americans want the luxury of an expensive steak for dinner, we cook it outside or go out to a steakhouse. In Paris, luxury is being able to take a homely second-quality cut of meat and prepare it in the traditional style.

Patrick Hayée, the butcher in the covered Marché Beauveau-Antoine, 12th arrondissement

Jarrets de Veau, Sauce Panade
Veal Shanks with Bread Sauce

MAKES 4 SERVINGS

This is a lovely way to prepare veal shanks, which, as every cook knows, are the most flavorful meat of the animal. Shanks need patient braising, though, and this is more a weekend meal than a midweek one. Using bread crumbs to thicken a full-flavored braising liquid is another technique I picked up in Paris and I use it a lot now in my cooking.

1 tablespoon olive oil

1 tablespoon unsalted butter

Four 12-ounce center-cut veal shanks

Salt and freshly ground black pepper

1 medium onion, chopped

1 stalk celery, chopped

1 medium carrot, chopped

1 cup dry white wine, such as Sauvignon Blanc

2 cups Homemade Chicken Broth (page 237) or low-sodium broth

1 sprig fresh thyme

1 teaspoon fresh rosemary leaves

2 bay leaves

¼ cup fine fresh bread crumbs

2 tablespoons chopped fresh parsley

1. Heat the oil and butter in a Dutch oven over medium-high heat. Season the meat on both sides with salt and pepper and add to the pot. Brown the shanks well on both sides, 8 to 10 minutes total. Remove the shanks to a plate and degrease the pot by pouring off the fat.

2. Add the onion, celery, and carrot to the pot and cook, stirring, to dissolve any residue that remains on the bottom of the pan. Return the meat to the pot, add the wine, and cook for a minute to burn off the alcohol. Add the broth, thyme, rosemary, and bay leaves, cover tightly, and bring to a boil. Reduce the heat to low and simmer until meat is tender but not falling apart, about 1¼ hours.

3. Carefully remove the shanks and keep warm, covered, on a platter. Strain the cooking liquid and discard the contents of the strainer. Skim the fat from the surface and return the liquid to the pot. Stir in the bread crumbs and cook, stirring, over medium heat until the mixture thickens, about 5 minutes. Add any juices that collect around the shanks. Add the parsley to the sauce, taste for salt and pepper, and add as desired.

4. Pour the sauce around the veal shanks and serve.

Making sausages at Boucherie Hayée in the covered Marché Beauveau-Antoine, 12th arrondissement

Poitrine de Veau Farcie

Stuffed Breast of Veal

MAKES 4 TO 5 SERVINGS

The French really know how to turn the poorer cuts of meat, such as veal breast, into magnificent pot roasts by stuffing them with tasty mixtures of ground meat and vegetables. As the breast cooks, its somewhat stringy texture relaxes and seems to dissolve, becoming tender but not dry. The *liaison* of bread crumbs, milk, and eggs absorbs the juices of the roast like a sponge.

The marketer who explained the workings of her recipe braises the breast with milk in order to, as she says, "whiten the meat." I've adapted her method and found that using evaporated milk gives a tastier sauce with a richer texture. Don't panic when the braising liquid curdles, because that's what it will do. A few pulses of a blender or food processor will bring it back.

4 tablespoons (½ stick) unsalted butter

¾ pound celeriac, peeled and
    finely diced

1 medium carrot, finely diced

1 medium leek, white part only, thinly
    sliced and well washed

1 teaspoon dried thyme

2 teaspoons chopped fresh sage leaves,
    or 1 teaspoon dried

⅛ teaspoon allspice

2 teaspoons salt

1 teaspoon freshly ground white pepper

6 ounces pork sausage, removed
    from casings

⅓ cup fresh bread crumbs

¼ cup milk

2 large eggs

1 breast of veal, boned (about
    1½ pounds), or a shoulder clod
    (boneless shoulder), butterflied
    (have the butcher do this)

Freshly ground black pepper

1 cup dry vermouth or herbaceous
    dry white wine, such as Sancerre
    or Vouvray

1 cup Homemade Chicken Broth
    (page 237) or low-sodium
    chicken broth

1 cup evaporated milk

1. Melt 2 tablespoons of the butter in a heavy pot over medium heat Add the celeriac, carrot, leek, thyme, sage, allspice, salt, and the white pepper. Cover and cook, stirring occasionally, until the vegetables are tender, about 25 minutes. Remove from the heat and transfer to a mixing bowl to cool.

2. Add the sausage meat to the vegetables and mix well. Mix in the bread crumbs, milk, and eggs.

3. Lay the veal breast on a work surface and, using kitchen twine, fold over and sew up two sides to form a pocket. Fill the pocket with the sausage/vegetable mixture and sew it closed. Tie up the breast with kitchen twine to form a compact cylinder. Or, if using a butterflied shoulder, instead of sewing up the pocket, lay it flat on a piece of cheesecloth 6 inches larger than the breast on all sides. Spread with the vegetable/sausage mixture, roll it up in the cheesecloth, and secure it with butcher's twine. Season the veal with salt and black pepper.

4. Melt the remaining 2 tablespoons butter in a Dutch oven over medium heat. Add the veal and cook, turning occasionally, until golden on all sides, about 10 minutes. Pour in the wine and broth, cover, and braise for 30 minutes, basting occasionally.

5. Add the evaporated milk and continue to cook, basting, until the meat is very tender, 1 to $1\frac{1}{4}$ hours more.

6. Remove the veal from the pot, untie it, and keep warm. Pour the contents of the pot into a blender or use a small hand blender and blend until smooth. Strain the liquid and keep warm.

7. Carefully slice the veal and lay the slices on a serving platter. Spoon some sauce around and pass the remaining sauce separately in a sauceboat.

Blanquette de Veau, Sauce Poulette

Creamy Veal Stew with Mushrooms and Pearl Onions

MAKES 5 TO 6 SERVINGS

Blanquette de veau literally means "white of veal," named for the beautiful white sauce of this dish. Think "blanket," though, for the sauce seems to protect the mixture of veal, onion, and mushrooms and keep everything cozy. Everyone in Paris prepares this, the most venerable of veal stews. In the ideal *blanquette,* the flavor of the rich clear broth, heavy with vegetable overtones, shines through the nutty flavor of the crème fraîche. Since cream tends to mask these flavors, the broth needs to be double strength. Roger Feuilly of the *Guide Pudlowski* explains that celery gives a particular "color and expression" to a *blanquette.* I especially like my friend Pierre's mother Eve Piacentini's *blanquette,* which I've been making for years. A halved lemon and the slightest hint of freshly grated nutmeg give the bouillon a subtle tang and is especially useful if you're not using crème fraîche. I find that with American veal, shin meat is as rich in flavor as the French veal and has a forgiving texture that plumps up with the creamy sauce. The secret to cooking the meat is never to let the contents of the pot come to a boil.

3 cups pearl onions

1 onion, peeled

2 cloves

2 ½ pounds boneless veal shin meat or
    shoulder clod roast, cut into
    2-inch pieces

1 bouquet garni: 2 bay leaves,
    1 teaspoon peppercorns, 4 sprigs fresh
    parsley, and 4 sprigs fresh thyme (or
    1 teaspoon dried), tied together in a
    square of cheesecloth

2 stalks celery, cut up

1 carrot, cut up

2 teaspoons salt, or to taste

¼ teaspoon freshly grated nutmeg

2 tablespoons fresh lemon juice

2 cups Homemade Chicken Broth
    (page 237) or low-sodium
    chicken broth

2 tablespoons unsalted butter

1 tablespoon all-purpose flour

1 teaspoon sugar

½ cup crème fraîche or heavy cream

¾ pound small white mushrooms

1. Place the pearl onions in warm water and set aside for at least 30 minutes and up to 2 hours. Stick the onion with the cloves.

2. Place the veal, onion, bouquet garni, celery, carrot, salt, peppercorns, and nutmeg in a heavy casserole. Add the lemon juice, chicken broth, and enough water to cover. Place over high heat, cover, and bring to a boil. Immediately reduce the heat to low and simmer, skimming from time to time, for 1 hour, or until the veal is tender.

3. While the veal is cooking, cream together 1 tablespoon of the butter and the flour in a small bowl and set aside.

4. Drain and peel the pearl onions and place in a saucepan just large enough to hold them in one layer. Add water to barely cover, then add the remaining 1 tablespoon butter and the sugar. Place over medium heat and boil until all the liquid evaporates. Continue cooking an additional minute or two until the onions become shiny. Remove from the heat and set aside.

5. When the veal is tender, remove the meat from the cooking liquid and set aside on a plate, covered with a damp towel. Strain the liquid and discard the solids. Return the liquid to the pot, stir in the butter mixture, and whisk in the cream. Place over medium heat and cook for 15 minutes, skimming occasionally. Add the mushrooms and cook for another 5 minutes.

6. Add the onions and veal and heat through. Pour the stew into a serving bowl or tureen. Serve immediately, accompanied by rice pilaf.

Astuce: Peeling Onions and Shallots

Soak onions and shallots in tepid water for at least 30 minutes, and up to 2 hours, to soften the skins. Peel the skins from the top to the base.

Pierre Piacentini and his tiny kitchen. His mother's *blanquette de veau* is my favorite.

Homemade Chicken Broth
or All-Purpose Broth

MAKES 1 QUART

For all the recipes in this book, the preferred broth is homemade chicken broth and the second choice is low-sodium canned chicken broth. If using a chicken bouillon cube, add any salt after your recipe is prepared so that you don't oversalt.

Parisian cooks are thrifty cooks, and the idea of discarding vegetable trimmings and chicken feet, what we might call the detritus of a recipe, would be shocking to their sense of home economy—not to mention that excellent flavors can be extracted from what, at first glance, may seem like scraps. This recipe for homemade broth is really only a guide, for the ingredient list depends on what meals have been prepared over the course of several days. The broth might include some chicken necks and feet, maybe the giblets, even perhaps a piece of bone from a steak or pork roast. The meat is really not important, or rather, not as important as the base of aromatic vegetables that gives most of the flavor to the broth. Use onion skins and leek, carrot, celery, and turnip. Parsley stems are always welcome. Add a small amount of whole peppercorns, a couple of bay leaves, and a few sprigs of thyme. Do avoid starches such as potato peelings; they add texture to the liquid.

1 to 2 handfuls any combination chicken bones, necks, or feet; beef, veal, or pork bones; or other meat trimmings, cooked or not

2 to 3 cups mixed celery, onion, leek, carrot, and tomato trimmings

Up to 1 bunch parsley stems

12 peppercorns

2 bay leaves

A few branches fresh thyme

6 cups cold water

1. Combine all the ingredients in a pot, place over high heat, and bring to a boil. Reduce the heat to medium-low and simmer for 1½ hours.

2. Strain the liquid and discard the contents of the strainer. Let the broth cool completely. Refrigerate or freeze. The broth will keep for up to a week in the refrigerator, or up to 3 months in the freezer. Skim off the fat before using.

Making Sauce at Home

"*Non, non, non.* I don't really know how to make sauces," Madame Perrier was telling me. "Chefs make sauces. I find that most things, if you cook them properly, make their own little sauce. Of course, Cédric would not agree." Her son Cédric is studying for his C.A.P. at Ferrandi, the Paris cooking school. For him, sauces are the apotheosis of French cooking.

Madame Perrier continued, "I said to Cédric: 'So, you've now decided that you haven't eaten well these last seventeen years? Now my cooking isn't good enough for your trained palate?'

"He tells me: 'At school, we cook with lots of heat. When we sear a piece of meat, it takes on a rich color, the flavor changes. It becomes *digne* [worthy].'

"At home," Madame Perrier said, "the neighbors would call the *pompiers* [the firemen] if I tried that. At school, they reduce stocks and wine to next to nothing, then replace the lost liquid with crème fraîche and butter. Can you imagine if people cooked like that at home? We'd all be dead, or so fat that we wouldn't be able to climb the stairs in the métro.

"Anyway, I said to him, and this really got him angry, I said, '*Mon très cher fils* [my dear son], where do you think all you *grandes toques* [tall hats] get your ideas? I'll tell you where. From your mothers. And if you learned a little common sense and kitchen economy, more of us would be able to afford to eat out more often.' *Il allait s'exploser* [he was going to explode], Michel.

"You see, we cook more gently on our small ranges and more patiently, probably, than you Americans, with your fancy stoves. We tease the juices, the essences, out of our ingredients. My salmon steaks, cooked in butter, give up a wonderful *jus.* I add a scant quarter cup of wine, a tablespoon of crème fraîche, let it boil for a minute, and there's my sauce. If I'm garnishing fish with anchovies, I pour some of the oil from the can into the sauce. Or the oil or brine from the olives that I buy in the market. I use the liquid in the jar of capers or green peppercorns. All these things have flavor. Why throw them out?

"I don't have the luxury of spending all day making a *fond* [stock] so we can make a sauce. I don't have room on the stove for a large pot, I don't have room in the refrigerator to keep it. And I don't need it.

"A pan-grilled piece of meat leaves a nice residue in the bottom of the skillet. A little wine dissolves it, and a little butter gives it texture. It's enough.

"Stewed dishes cook in liquid and make their own sauce. And I use bouillon cubes, but just a small amount, which of course Cédric says makes me unfit to be a Frenchwoman. But, everyone uses cubes. I add a pig's tail, or a calf's foot, to a stew or a *pot-au-feu* (boiled dinner) for richness. Or, I may moisten the pot entirely with wine.

"So, to answer your question. Well, you tell me. Do I make sauces? I suppose I do, after a fashion. I wouldn't really call them sauces, though, it's just what we make. We can't sit down to a plate of dry food, Michel. We're French."

Rôti de Veau Poêlé aux Anchois et aux Capres

Pot-Roasted Veal with Anchovies and Capers

MAKES 5 TO 6 SERVINGS

There's no mistaking the Provençal nature of this veal roast, which Jean-François Ferrandiz remembers his mother preparing. She would finish the sauce with olive oil, the butter of Provence. Use a good French oil for this dish, as it is the foundation that tames the flavors of anchovy, garlic, and herbes de Provence. Madame Ferrandiz would not have had the use of a blender or food processor, but I find that using one to incorporate the oil results in a silky smooth sauce.

Freshly ground black pepper

4 shallots, minced (about ½ cup)

3 cloves garlic, minced

1 cup dry white wine, such as Chardonnay

1 teaspoon herbes de Provence with lavender

2 bay leaves

½ teaspoon salt

¼ teaspoon freshly ground white pepper

8 anchovy fillets, plus oil from the tin to taste

2 tablespoons fresh lemon juice

2 tablespoons drained capers

One 2½-pound veal top round roast

½ cup extra virgin olive oil

2 tablespoons chopped fresh chervil

1. Place all the ingredients except the veal, olive oil, and chervil in a Dutch oven, cover, and quickly bring to a boil over high heat. Add the veal, reduce the heat to medium-low, and simmer for 35 minutes, turning once.

2. Transfer the veal to a plate, cover, and keep warm in the turned-off oven. Increase the heat to high and boil down the cooking liquid by half, or until it has the consistency of heavy cream. Pour the liquid into a blender and turn the power to medium. With the blender running, slowly add the olive oil until incorporated.

3. Remove the veal from the oven and pour any juices that have collected on the plate into the sauce. Thinly slice the veal and arrange on a serving platter. Spoon the sauce over the meat, sprinkle with the chervil, and serve immediately.

Astuce: Tender, Moist Veal

When braising, stewing, or pot-roasting veal, whether in chunks or as a whole cut, never let the liquid in the pot cook at hotter than a simmer. Any temperature above 200°F will change the texture of the meat and make it chalky.

Poêlé de Veau au Persil

Parsleyed Veal

MAKES 5 TO 6 SERVINGS

Large chunks of nicely browned veal, cooked with only enough liquid to keep the meat from burning, give up their juices to make a rich, meaty sauce. Prepare this dish in a heavy tightly lidded casserole just large enough so that the chunks of veal are a bit crowded. I learned that cleansing flavors—in this case lemon, white wine, and parsley—lighten the effect that rich cuts of meat have on the palate. When I prepared this dish in the States, I blended the parsley into the sauce rather than simply mixing it in. I obtained a fresher, more highly pronounced parsley flavor and the sauce turned an appealing green.

4 tablespoons (½ stick) unsalted butter

2½ pounds boneless veal shin or
    shank meat, cut into 12 pieces

1 small onion, minced

1 small carrot, finely diced

1 stalk celery, finely diced

½ teaspoon salt

Freshly ground black pepper

1 tablespoon chopped fresh rosemary

½ cup dry white wine, such as
    Sauvignon Blanc

1 lemon, cut in half

⅓ cup finely chopped fresh parsley

1. Preheat the oven to 325°F.

2. Melt 2 tablespoons of the butter in a heavy pot or Dutch oven over medium heat. Add the veal, in batches if necessary so as not to crowd the pan, and cook, turning the pieces, until lightly golden, about 10 minutes. If you cooked it in batches, return

all the veal to the pot. Add the onion, carrot, and celery and season with the salt, pepper, and rosemary. Add the wine and bury the lemon halves in the meat. Cover the casserole and place in the oven for 1½ hours, or until the meat is very tender. Check the casserole periodically and stir the contents; if necessary, add a tablespoon or two of water to prevent scorching.

3. Remove the casserole from the oven and remove and discard the lemon. Strain the contents of the pot and transfer the veal and vegetables to a serving bowl. Place the cooking liquid in a blender, add the remaining 2 tablespoons butter and the parsley, and blend until incorporated. Pour the sauce into the serving bowl and serve immediately.

The Tripe Butcher/Philosopher

Like an ancient seer who could see the future in the blood of a sacrificed ram, the tripe butcher is a philosopher. "People deny themselves many things. But they're mistaken. You have to make your organs work. The less they are made to work, the less they are capable of working. Okay, you have high cholesterol. So you have to cut out fat. But you must continue to eat at least some so that the organs will continue to work to eliminate it from the system."

Rissolé de Riz de Veau aux Artichauts, Petits Pois, et Pommes Nouveaux

Veal Sweetbreads with Artichokes, Peas, and Potatoes

MAKES 4 SERVINGS

"You know, men do a better job in the kitchen with things that require patience and persistence, like sweetbreads. Women, they are better everyday cooks, but men, they are artists." This bit of "men's club" wisdom was imparted by Jean-Pierre Ducotte, a butcher in the covered market in Passy, a swank neighborhood abutting the Bois de Boulogne. Preparing sweetbreads is not an everyday affair, but Monsieur Ducotte sometimes prepares this dish for the special *repas de dimanche,* or Sunday dinner. Cleaning them requires a bit of patience, but otherwise this is not difficult to prepare.

Sweetbreads are the most subtle of the variety meats, white and creamy-textured. Jean-Pierre cooks them in butter until they're golden and serves them in *vol-au-vents,* puff pastry shells that he buys at the bakery. I serve them on toasted brioche.

1 ½ pounds calf's sweatbreads

8 tiny new potatoes (about ½ pound)

2 tablespoons fresh lemon juice

6 baby artichokes

1 tablespoon extra virgin olive oil

3 tablespoons unsalted butter

2 ounces Bayonne ham or prosciutto, finely diced

1 medium onion, finely diced

1 teaspoon dried marjoram

1 teaspoon salt

Freshly ground black pepper

½ fresh or frozen peas

½ cup dry vermouth or herbaceous dry white wine, such as Sancerre or Vourvay

1 tablespoon chopped fresh chervil

1. Place the sweetbreads in a pot, cover with cold water, place over high heat, and bring to a boil. Immediately drain the sweetbreads and place under running water to cool. Peel off as much of the outer membranes as possible and remove any interior veins. Pull apart or cut the sweetbreads into pieces the size of pecans and dry on kitchen towels.

2. Peel the potatoes. If they are larger than the size of a walnut, halve them. Set aside in a bowl of water.

3. Place the lemon juice in a small bowl and fill halfway with water. Trim and discard the outer layers of leaves from each artichoke until the light green leaves are exposed. Trim and discard any dark bits from the base. Trim and discard the top $\frac{1}{4}$ inch. Halve the artichokes from top to stem and place them in the lemon water.

4. Heat the oil and 1 tablespoon of the butter in a Dutch oven over medium heat. When the butter foam subsides, add the sweetbreads and ham. Cover and cook for 5 minutes, stirring once or twice. Drain the potatoes and artichokes and add the onion, potatoes, and artichokes to the pot. Season with the marjoram, salt, and pepper. Replace the cover and cook, stirring occasionally, for 20 minutes. Add the peas and continue to cook for another 5 minutes, or until the potatoes are tender. Transfer the contents of the casserole to a platter and keep warm in a 200°F oven.

5. Return the casserole to the stove, pour in the vermouth, and cook for 5 minutes, stirring to scrape up any bits that have stuck to the bottom of the pot. Remove from the heat and stir in the remaining 2 tablespoons butter and the chervil.

6. Remove the platter from the oven and pour the sauce around the sweetbreads. Serve immediately.

Onglet aux Échalotes
Skirt Steak with Shallots

MAKES 4 SERVINGS

Onglet is a cut of meat considered something between meat and organ, partly because it's diaphragm and partly because its taste is so rich, with a hint of liver. In the States, ask the butcher to sell you the plump end of the skirt steak. This striated morsel, prized for its texture as well as for its rich flavor, is much sought after in Paris for this traditional dish of steak bathed in butter and shallots. French cooks know when to leave well enough alone. No sauce needed here, only an accompaniment of heady Dijon mustard.

$3/4$ cup minced shallots

3 tablespoons unsalted butter

Coarse salt and freshly ground
    black pepper

1 tablespoon chopped fresh parsley

Four 6-ounce strips skirt steak

$1/4$ cup dry white wine, such as
    Chardonnay

1. Cook the shallots in the butter in a large heavy skillet over medium heat until soft but not browned, about 5 minutes. Season with coarse salt and pepper, mix in the parsley, and transfer to a small bowl. Keep warm.

2. Return the skillet to the stove over high heat. When the skillet is smoking hot, add the steaks. Season with pepper and cook for 3 minutes. Turn the steaks over and season with salt and pepper. Cook for another 3 minutes for rare, up to 5 minutes for medium. Transfer the steaks to a platter.

3. Return the skillet to the stovetop over low heat, add the wine, and stir with a wooden spoon to scrape up any brown bits that have stuck to the bottom of the skillet. Cook until the liquid in the skillet is reduced to a mere tablespoon, then mix the *déglaçage* into the shallots. Spoon the shallots over the steaks and serve immediately.

Astuce : Steaks on the Stove

There's no better way to cook steaks at home than by searing them over high heat. Use a heavy skillet or saucepan made of cast iron, lined copper, or stainless steel with a copper wedge. Don't crowd the skillet, and expect a fair amount of smoke in your kitchen.

Waiting their turns at the greengrocer

Tournedos au Roquefort

Beef Tenderloin Steaks with Roquefort Sauce

MAKES 4 SERVINGS

This dish is in the repertoire of all Parisian cooks. It's totally simple and quick to prepare and the sauce tastes as if it spent hours simmering on the stove. I like it for the way the salty, heady blue cheese flavors enhance the richness of the meat. Most Parisians use only wine to make the sauce, or may add a quarter cube of beef bouillon, but I use a mixture of wine and broth to achieve a truer meat flavor. Parisians serve potatoes with the steak and follow this dish with salad and cheese (it wouldn't be dinner without salad and cheese!), but most Americans will find that a simple green salad and good bread to sop up the sauce are plenty of accompaniment.

Four 6-ounce filets mignons
Vegetable oil, preferably canola
Freshly ground black pepper
Coarse salt
¹/₄ cup dry red wine, such as
    Cabernet Sauvignon

¹/₄ cup low-sodium beef broth or
    Homemade Chicken Broth
    (page 237)
¹/₄ cup heavy cream
¹/₄ cup crumbled Roquefort cheese
1 tablespoon chopped fresh parsley

1. Heat a heavy-bottomed skillet over high heat until very hot. Lightly brush the steaks with oil, place in the pan, season generously with pepper, and cook for 3 minutes. Turn the steaks, season with salt and pepper, and cook for 4 minutes for rare. If you prefer your steaks more well done, reduce the heat to medium and continue to cook to the desired doneness, up to 7 minutes for medium-well. Transfer the steaks to a plate and keep warm.

2. Return the skillet to the stove over medium heat, add the wine, and stir with a wooden spoon to scrape up the browned bits that have stuck to the bottom of the skillet. Add the broth and cream and continue to simmer until the liquid becomes saucelike, about 3 minutes. Stir in the cheese and remove from the heat.

3. Pour any juices that have collected around the steaks into the sauce, ladle the sauce around the steaks, sprinkle with the parsley, and serve.

Faux-Filet, Beurre d'Anchois
Sirloin Steak with Anchovy Butter

MAKES 4 SERVINGS

Don't let the name of this dish alarm you. Anchovies are used as a condiment, their complex salty and fishy flavor actually enhancing the meaty flavor rather than, as you might assume, fighting with it. If you're a fan of anchovies, though, add a little oil from the tin to adjust the anchovy flavor to your liking.

Four 7-ounce boneless sirloin steaks

Vegetable oil, preferably canola

Freshly ground black pepper

Coarse salt

$\frac{1}{4}$ cup dry white wine, such as
   Sauvignon Blanc

2 tablespoons minced shallots

4 anchovy fillets, chopped, plus some
   of the oil from the tin if desired

$\frac{1}{4}$ cup low-sodium beef broth or
   Homemade Chicken Broth
   (page 237)

3 tablespoons unsalted butter

1 tablespoon chopped fresh parsley

1 tablespoon chopped fresh chervil

1. Heat a heavy-bottomed skillet over high heat until very hot. Lightly brush the steaks with oil, place them in the pan, season generously with pepper, and cook for 4 minutes. Turn the steaks, season with salt and pepper, and cook for 5 minutes for rare. If you prefer your steaks more well done, reduce the heat to medium and continue to cook to the desired doneness, up to 7 minutes for medium-well. Transfer the steaks to a plate and keep warm.

2. Return the skillet to the stove over medium heat, add the wine, shallots, and anchovies, and stir with a wooden spoon to scrape up the browned bits that have stuck to the bottom of the skillet. Add the broth and continue to cook until the liquid reduces to a glaze, about 2 minutes. Whisk in the butter, remove from the heat, and mix in the parsley and chervil.

3. Pour any juices that have collected around the steaks into the sauce, ladle the sauce around the steaks, and serve.

The whole family shops
on Sundays.

Bifteks à la Minute, Sauce à l'Estragon
Minute Steaks with Tarragon

MAKES 4 SERVINGS

You can't really sear minute steaks as you can others, because they're so thin. Better to coddle them with butter in a moderately hot skillet. Ask your butcher to pound the steaks to tenderize them and prevent shrinkage. Season them with salt and press liberal amounts of crushed or coarsely ground black pepper into one side of the steaks. Add more pepper and you have a home version of steak *au poivre*.

Four 6-ounce minute steaks
Salt and coarsely ground black pepper
2 tablespoons unsalted butter
2 tablespoons dry white wine, such as
    Sauvignon Blanc

1 tablespoon white wine vinegar
1 tablespoon Dijon mustard
1 tablespoon chopped fresh tarragon

1. Season the steaks on both sides with salt and pepper as described in the headnote. Melt the butter in a large nonreactive skillet over medium heat. Cook the steaks for about 2 minutes on each side. Remove from the skillet.

2. Add the wine and vinegar to the skillet and whisk in the mustard. Replace the steaks and cook for a minute or until the sauce smooths and thickens. Add the tarragon and remove from the heat.

3. Arrange the steaks on a platter and scrape the sauce over the top. Serve immediately.

Daube de Boeuf | Beef Stewed in Wine

MAKES 5 TO 6 SERVINGS

In Paris, much lore about cooking relates to rustic traditions from the provinces. *Daube,* which some say is the mother of all stews, cooks in a *daubière,* a heavy pot with a concave lid that, in years past, was filled with water so the heat of a wood fire radiated all around the stew. Today's ovens make this special pot unnecessary, yet many people still use *daubières* for this much-beloved beef stew. As a result, Parisians tend to call anything cooked in this pot a *daube.*

What differentiates a true *daube* from other stews and gives it its rich complex flavor, however, is the fact that it's moistened entirely with wine. A proper *daube* requires three days: The meat must marinate overnight before cooking, and after the *daube* cooks, you should refrigerate it for a day for the flavors to develop. *Joues de boeuf,* or beef cheeks, are without question the best morsel to use; as a stewed cut, their fine texture is unequalled. Special-order them from a superior butcher (and pray). Happily, boneless short ribs of beef run a very close second and are more easily available. Cook this *daube* in a heavy lidded ceramic or glazed cast-iron casserole.

2 ½ pounds beef cheeks, trimmed, or boneless beef short ribs, cut into 3-inch pieces

1 onion, quartered

2 stalks celery, halved

2 bay leaves

2 sprigs fresh thyme

1 small sprig fresh rosemary

1 bottle red wine, such as Côtes du Rhône or Côteaux d'Aix-en-Provence

2 tablespoons olive oil

½ calf's foot or a pig's foot or tail (optional)

¼ bunch fresh parsley, stems trimmed and tied in a bundle, leaves finely chopped

1 teaspoon salt

12 peppercorns

2 medium carrots, sliced on the bias into ¼-inch ovals

2 tablespoons unsalted butter

1. Place the beef, onion, celery, bay leaves, thyme, and rosemary in a dish, pour in the wine, cover, and place in the refrigerator overnight, or up to 24 hours.

2. The next day, strain the ingredients and reserve the wine and solids separately.

3. Preheat the oven to 250°F.

4. Melt the oil in a heavy casserole or Dutch oven over medium heat. Add the beef and vegetables and cook, stirring occasionally, until the vegetables soften, 12 to 15 minutes. Pour in the reserved wine, add the calf's foot and parsley bundle, and season with the salt and peppercorns. Cover, transfer the pot to the oven, and cook for 3 hours, or until the meat is very tender.

5. Remove the meat and set aside. Strain the liquid and discard the contents of the strainer. Pour the liquid back into the pot, place over medium heat, add the sliced carrots, and simmer until the carrots are tender, 12 to 15 minutes. Replace the meat and cook to heat through. Remove from the heat and stir in the butter.

6. Pour the stew into a serving bowl and serve immediately, accompanied with buttered noodles.

Astuce: Cooking with Red Wine

For ordinary stews and sauces, the ones that don't specify a particular wine, use a thick, fruity red wine, the kind the French call *corsé*, with an alcohol content of 11 or 12 percent. In France, these wines are reasonably priced. In the States, they may be an extravagance. Although I can't raise the alcohol content of the wine I use, I open a bottle of modest red wine, recork it, and let it sit for a day or two before cooking with it. The oxidation that occurs in the wine will take away some of the forward fruit freshness and give a more winey, full-bodied aspect to your cooked dish.

Boeuf aux Carottes à l'Ancienne
Beef with Carrots Prepared the Traditional Way

MAKES 5 TO 6 SERVINGS

This is one of those venerable dishes for which every cook in Paris (and even some non-cooks) seems to have his or her own "true" recipe, *la véritable*. I've seen Parisians discuss at length various renditions of this dish as if, by revealing its manner of preparation, a hitherto-unknown secret of the cook leaked out into the sauce. Personally, I cook this dish a lot, and here's what I've found to be helpful: Use toasted flour when thickening the broth for its nutty, caramel flavor. Use a fruitwood-smoked bacon rather than the usual hickory-flavored type—it tastes closer to the French *lardons*. Most important, use young, sweet, organic carrots. For after all is said, this is but a simple dish of beef and carrots. Parsleyed buttered egg noodles always accompany it.

3 bay leaves

1 bunch fresh parsley

3 sprigs fresh thyme

12 peppercorns

2 tablespoons vegetable oil, preferably canola

2 1/2 pounds boneless chuck roast, cut into 2 1/2-inch cubes

1/4 pound slab bacon, cut into 3/8-inch cubes

3 medium onions, roughly diced (about 2 1/2 cups)

1 tablespoon toasted flour (see page 257)

1/4 cup brandy

3 cups dry white wine, such as Chardonnay

1 teaspoon salt, or more to taste

1 cup cold water, or to cover

1 1/2 pounds small organic carrots, scrubbed

Freshly ground black pepper

1. Tie up the bay leaves, parsley, thyme, and peppercorns in a piece of cheesecloth and set aside. Heat the oil in a Dutch oven or heavy nonreactive casserole over medium-high heat. Add the beef and bacon, without crowding (add the beef in batches if nec-

256 PARISIAN HOME COOKING

essary), and brown the beef on all sides, 12 to 15 minutes. Remove the beef and bacon and set aside.

2. Pour off all but 1 tablespoon of the fat from the pot, add the onions, and cook, stirring, until soft but not browned, about 5 minutes. Mix in the flour and cook for another minute, stirring. Replace the meat, add the brandy, and cook for a minute or so to burn off the alcohol. Add the wine, salt, and the herb bundle. Add enough of the cold water to barely cover the meat, reduce the heat to low, cover, and simmer for 1¼ hours.

3. Add the carrots and cook until tender, another 25 to 35 minutes, depending on their age and size.

4. Remove the stew from the heat, and remove and discard the herb packet. Taste for salt and pepper and add as needed. Pour the stew into a serving dish and serve.

Astuce : BROWN ROUX

To get the special flavor that French stews have, use lightly toasted flour for thickening. Place 1 cup flour in a shallow baking dish, place in a 375°F oven, and cook, stirring every 10 minutes to ensure that all the flour toasts evenly and to break up the chunks that form. The flour is ready when it's a light honey color. Remove from the oven, let cool, and store in an airtight container as you would any flour. The flour will darken threefold when you add butter or oil to it to make a roux. Since toasting reduces the thickening ability of the gluten, increase the amount of flour by about 25 percent in recipes that call for using flour to thicken a liquid.

Côtes d'Agneau aux Poireaux
Lamb Chops with Leeks

MAKES 4 SERVINGS

"When I cook lamb chops, there's an odor of sizzling fat that fills the kitchen and makes me feel so . . . so . . . like such a good cook," said Odile Bernard-Schröder, a friend who, by her fastidiousness, limits her cooking to pan-grilled meats or poultry, baked potatoes, steamed vegetables, and green salads. Anything more complicated, she buys at the *traiteur* (caterer) or orders in restaurants.

I've been to the market with her, and she'll spend fifteen minutes choosing the perfect tomato or mushroom. She'll travel across Paris for cheese. She'll go to Berthillon's original shop in the Ile St-Louis because she insists the ice cream is fresher there than the Berthillon that you buy in the shops. When I remarked once that she spent more time shopping than cooking, she took it as a compliment of her good taste. "For most things, I am *incapable. Merci* for having noticed, Michel. You're so *sensible.*"

For these simple lamb chops, she claims as her secret ingredients the finest flake salt from Brittany, freshly ground pepper, a liberal bath of really good Normandy butter, and a squeeze of fresh lemon juice. Her butcher cuts double-thick rib chops for her, because it's the only way to get the thin covering of fat crisply rendered and still manage rare to medium-rare meat. This is a dish that, by its simplicity and reliance on a few perfect ingredients, is probably better *chez* Odile than in most restaurants in Paris.

¼ *pound slab bacon, finely diced*
2 *large leeks, light green part only,*
    finely diced and washed well
3 *tablespoons unsalted butter*
Flake or coarse sea salt and freshly
    ground black pepper

1 *tablespoon Pernod*
8 *center-cut double rib lamb chops*
    (about 1¾ pounds total)
1 *tablespoon chopped fresh chervil*
Fresh lemon juice

1. Place the bacon and leeks in a heavy skillet with 1 tablespoon of the butter and season with salt and pepper. Add the Pernod, cover, place over medium heat, and cook, stirring occasionally, until the leeks are soft, about 7 minutes. Scrape the contents of the skillet onto a serving platter and keep warm.

2. Return the skillet to the stove over medium-high heat, add the lamb chops, and season with salt and pepper. Cook for about 2 minutes, then turn the chops and season the second side. Cook for another 3 to 4 minutes for medium-rare. Remove from the heat, swirl in the remaining 2 tablespoons butter, and add the chervil.

3. To serve, arrange the lamb on the leeks, pour over the pan sauce, and squeeze a few drops of lemon juice over the chops.

Astuce: Salt and Pepper

Season steaks, chops, and cutlets of meat, fish, and poultry with coarse salt and coarsely ground pepper. The larger particle size makes the seasoning more prominent, giving more flavor to each bite. The French don't always use more salt and pepper, they just want to taste it more clearly.

Gigot à Sept Heures
Seven-Hour Leg of Lamb

MAKES 8 TO 10 SERVINGS

When Sylvain, a friend who's prone to exaggeration, invited me for his leg of lamb, which he said cooked for seven hours, I figured it was a typical *gasconnade* on his part. But this method of slow-cooking the leg was a revelation—succulent, moist, gamy, and full of garlic and rosemary flavors. And it was obvious to me that the lamb had indeed cooked for seven hours, or close to it, for it was falling-off-the-bone tender, yet not stringy.

In the States, I make this dish for company. The lamb needs little attention as it cooks in the oven, and I can prepare the platter for serving before we sit down to our first course. When you make this dish, use young, corn-fed American lamb, the smaller the animal, the better. (If you're lucky enough to know a butcher who sells milk-fed lamb around Easter or Passover, don't waste it in this recipe.) The meat of today's farm-raised lamb does not require the traditional seven hours, rather more like four or five; you'll know when the roast is ready when the meat is loose from the bone. When you remove the leg from the oven, let it rest for ten minutes to allow the meat to firm. If you've eschewed bone-in legs of lamb for their clumsiness of carving, this recipe will change your mind.

One 6- to 7-pound bone-in leg
   of young lamb
4 to 6 cloves garlic, sliced
Olive oil
Coarse salt and freshly ground black
   pepper
1 tablespoon fresh rosemary leaves,
   chopped
2 teaspoons dried thyme
2 onions, chopped

3 carrots, chopped
3 stalks celery, chopped
3 tablespoons tomato paste
2 cups Homemade Chicken Broth
   (page 237) or low-sodium
   chicken broth
2 cups red wine
3/4 cup aged red wine vinegar
4 bay leaves
2 tablespoons unsalted butter

1. Preheat the oven to 425°F.

2. Make small incisions all over the leg and stuff them with the slices of garlic. Rub the lamb with oil and season well with salt and pepper, the rosemary, and thyme. Make a bed of the onions, carrots, and celery in a large roasting pan, lay the lamb on top, and place in the oven, fat side down, for 20 minutes. Turn the lamb over, give a stir to the vegetables, and roast for another 20 minutes. Reduce the oven temperature to 325°F, tightly cover the roasting pan, and roast for $2\frac{1}{2}$ hours.

3. Meanwhile, dissolve the tomato paste in the broth, wine, and vinegar and set aside.

4. After the lamb has roasted for $2\frac{1}{2}$ hours, remove the cover, add the bay leaves, and begin basting the lamb using all the liquid. Cook with the broth mixture for another 1 to 2 hours, basting from time to time. The lamb is ready when it is falling apart.

5. Remove the roasting pan from the oven, carefully transfer the roast to a work surface, and let it sit, tightly covered, for 10 to 15 minutes before removing the bone and slicing the meat. Scrape the vegetables and cooking juices into a large strainer and press well to extract all the juices. Pour these juices into a saucepan, add the butter, and place over medium heat until the butter is melted.

6. To serve, pour some of the cooking liquid onto a platter and arrange the sliced lamb on top. Pass the remaining juices separately.

Épaule d'Agneau à la Boulangère
Rolled Shoulder of Lamb with Potatoes and Onions

SERVES 5 TO 6

No one has been able to tell me why a garnish of potatoes and onions is called "in the manner of the baker." My hypothesis is that, in the years before people had home ovens, the baker cooked this one-dish *plat* for the housewives of the *quartier* who would bring him their casseroles after he had finished baking bread for the day. That no longer being the case, here's what Parisians do at home. They crowd lamb, potatoes, and onions into an oval or rectangular oven-to-table roasting pan. The potatoes and onion diminish in volume during roasting, and when the lamb is done, they remove it from the roasting pan, spread out the potato mixture, which now fits the pan perfectly, moisten it with white wine, and top it with cheese. The potatoes are returned to the oven to gratinée, the lamb is sliced, and the two are served separately.

1 boneless shoulder of lamb,
   3 to 3 1/2 pounds
Salt and freshly ground black pepper
2 cloves garlic, thinly sliced
1 teaspoon dried thyme
8 tablespoons (1 stick) unsalted
   butter, melted
2 medium onions, halved from top
   to stem and thinly sliced
2 pounds waxy potatoes, peeled
   and thinly sliced

1 teaspoon dried savory
1/4 cup dry white wine, such as
   Chardonnay
1/4 cup Homemade Chicken Broth
   (page 237) or low-sodium
   chicken broth
1/4 to 1/2 cup grated Gruyère cheese
2 tablespoons minced fresh parsley
Dijon mustard for serving

1. Preheat the oven to 475°F.

2. Season the lamb with salt and pepper, the garlic, and thyme and, using kitchen twine, tie it into a compact roast. Place in an oven-to-table roasting pan large enough to hold the lamb, potatos, and onions, drizzle with ¼ cup of the butter, and place in the oven for 1 hour, turning once.

3. Meanwhile, cook the onions, stirring, in the remaining ¼ cup butter in a skillet over medium heat to soften, about 5 minutes. Remove from the heat, mix in the potatoes, and season with salt, pepper, and savory.

4. Lower the oven temperature to 375°F. Arrange the onions and potatoes around the lamb and continue to roast for another 45 minutes.

5. Remove the roasting pan from the oven and transfer the lamb to a cutting board. Let the roast rest while you finish the onions and potatoes. Spread out the vegetables in the roasting pan, pour in the wine and broth, and sprinkle with the cheese. Return the potatoes to the oven and cook until bubbling, about 12 to 15 minutes.

6. To serve, untie the roast and thinly slice it. Arrange on a serving dish and sprinkle with the parsley. Serve the potatoes and onions from the roasting pan and serve mustard on the side.

Pot-au-Feu d'Agneau Farci aux Blettes

Boiled Dinner of Lamb Shoulder Stuffed with Chard

MAKES 4 TO 5 SERVINGS

This recipe is from Madame Beltrans, the concierge in the building where my friend Philippe Gautier lives. She puts this boiled dinner on the stove to simmer all morning while she works to keep the building spick-and-span, polishing stairs and cleaning hall-

Waiting my turn at the pork butcher

ways. The hardest chores of the day accomplished, she and Monsieur take a two-hour break for their main meal. When Madame Beltrans shops, she buys small vegetables for this dish and adds them to the pot all at the same time. Here in the States, if baby vegetables are not available, cut larger vegetables to the proper size and add them separately so that they'll all be done at the same time. She serves the broth in wide-rimmed soup plates, to which they each add their vegetables and lamb.

4 tablespoons (½ stick) unsalted butter

1 onion, finely diced

2 cloves garlic, minced

1 bunch green Swiss chard, ribs removed and leaves roughly chopped

2 large eggs

¼ cup milk

⅛ teaspoon allspice

½ teaspoon fresh marjoram leaves or ¼ teaspoon dried

2 teaspoons salt, or more to taste

1 teaspoon freshly ground black pepper

¾ cup fresh bread crumbs

2 pounds boneless lamb shoulder, trimmed of fat

1 quart Homemade Chicken Broth (page 237) or low-sodium chicken broth

2 bay leaves

3 large carrots, quartered

½ large celeriac bulb, peeled and cut into eighths

2 large White Rose potatoes, peeled and quartered

3 large leeks, white part only, halved lengthwise and washed well

Flake or coarse salt, mustard, and horseradish for serving

1. Melt 2 tablespoons of the butter in a large skillet over medium heat. Cook the onion until soft but not browned, about 3 minutes. Add the garlic and chard and cook for another 5 minutes, or until the chard is wilted and somewhat dry. Transfer the contents of the skillet to a mixing bowl and mix in the eggs and milk. Season with the allspice, marjoram, 1 teaspoon of the salt, and ½ teaspoon of the pepper. Add the bread crumbs and mix well.

continued

2. Season the lamb with the remaining 1 teaspoon salt and ½ teaspoon pepper and lay it on a piece of cheesecloth that extends beyond it on all sides. Spread the stuffing evenly over the lamb. Roll the lamb up tightly in the cheesecloth and secure both ends and the middle with kitchen string.

3. Bring the broth to a boil in a large lidded pot over high heat. Reduce the heat, add the lamb and bay leaves, cover, and simmer for 40 minutes.

4. Taste the broth and add salt as desired. Add the carrots and celeriac to the pot and cook for 10 minutes. Add the potatoes and continue to cook for 10 minutes. Add the leeks to the pot and continue simmering for 5 minutes. Remove the vegetables as they become tender, and keep warm. Remove the lamb from the pot, increase the heat to high, and boil the cooking liquid until it reduces to about 3 cups. Remove from the heat, and stir in the remaining 2 tablespoons butter; strain.

5. To serve, unwrap and untie the lamb, slice into serving slices, and arrange on a platter. Arrange the vegetables around the meat. Pour the cooking liquid into soup bowls and serve separately. Accompany with small bowls of flake or coarse salt, mustard, and horseradish.

Jarrets d'Agneau
aux Pruneaux d'Agen
Braised Lamb Shanks with Prunes

MAKES 4 SERVINGS

When sweet ingredients are used in savory French dishes, they're always combined with a strong opposite flavor—vinegar, wine, or brandy—to mitigate the sweetness. They're best in balance with game, dark poultry, and even calf's liver, as they marry their sweetness with the gamy flavor of the meat. Prunes from the town of Agen, in the Southwest of France, are famous all over the country for their plumpness and their distinct flavor of faded plums. For this recipe, buy prunes that are soft to the touch, shiny, and still with their pits. Cook them with large, meaty shanks—smaller ones have too much gristle in proportion to meat. Momo, an acquaintance of mine whose family is from Morocco—and the donor of this recipe—serves this braise with steamed couscous. I like it as well with rice.

Four 14-ounce lamb shanks
Salt and freshly ground black pepper
2 tablespoons vegetable oil,
    preferably canola
1 medium onion, finely chopped
1 cup dry white wine, such as
    Sauvignon Blanc
2 cups low-sodium beef broth

1 teaspoon dried thyme
2 bay leaves
3/4 cup unpitted prunes
1 teaspoon cornstarch
1/4 cup brandy
2 tablespoons unsalted butter
2 tablespoons chopped fresh parsley

1. Season the lamb with salt and pepper. Heat the oil in a Dutch oven over medium-high heat. Sear the lamb well on all sides, about 15 minutes. Remove the lamb from the pot and pour out any fat.

continued

2. Add the onion to the pot and cook, stirring, until soft but not browned, about 3 minutes. Replace the lamb in the pot, add the wine, and let cook for a minute or two to burn off the alcohol. Add the broth, thyme, and bay leaves, cover, reduce the heat, and simmer for 1½ hours or until the lamb is tender. Add the prunes and continue simmering another 10 to 15 minutes.

3. Remove the lamb and arrange on a serving platter. Strain the cooking liquid, arrange the prunes with the lamb, and keep warm. Skim all of the fat from the surface of the braising liquid and place the liquid in a saucepan. Dissolve the cornstarch in the brandy, add it to the cooking liquid, and place over medium heat. Cook until thickened, about 2 minutes. Remove from the heat and stir in the butter and parsley.

4. Spoon the sauce over the lamb and prunes and serve.

Le Marché Saxe Breteuil, 7th arrondissement

Tournedos de Porc à la Charcutière
Pork in the Style of the Butcher's Wife

MAKES 4 SERVINGS

This classic pork is sauced with an herbed mustard cream sauce and garnished with a salty, sour dice of capers and cornichons, the little tart tarragon-flavored pickles of France. The combination is as comfortable to a Parisian as tartar sauce on fried fish is to an American. If you use butter pickles, sweet dills, or even kosher sour dills, the flavor of this dish will be completely different. Still delicious, but different.

Four 6- to 7-ounce boneless pork
    loin steaks
Freshly ground black pepper and
    coarse or flake sea salt
1 tablespoon Dijon mustard
1/4 cup dry white wine, such as
    Sauvignon Blanc
1/2 teaspoon minced fresh savory
    or 1/4 teaspoon dried

1/2 teaspoon minced fresh tarragon
    or 1/4 teaspoon dried
2 tablespoons unsalted butter
3 tablespoons heavy cream
1 teaspoon capers, finely chopped
6 cornichons, finely chopped
    (about 2 tablespoons)
1 teaspoon finely chopped fresh chervil

1. Generously season the pork with pepper and sprinkle with salt. Dissolve the mustard in the wine and, if using dried herbs, add the savory and tarragon now. Set aside.

2. Melt the butter in a large nonreactive skillet over medium-low heat. Cook the chops on both sides until lightly golden, about 2 minutes per side. Add the wine mixture and cook for another 3 to 5 minutes, or until the pork seems springy to the touch. Transfer the pork to a platter and keep warm.

3. Add the cream, capers, and cornichons to the skillet and cook until the liquid is reduced to a saucelike consistency, about 2 minutes. Add any juices that have collected around the pork to the skillet, along with the fresh savory and tarragon, if using, and the chervil.

4. Arrange the pork chops on a platter, pour over the sauce, and serve immediately.

Côtes de Porc à l'Aneth
Dilled Pork Chops

MAKES 4 SERVINGS

Gently cooking pork in a mixture of cream and stock plumps the meat and keeps it from becoming tough. The butcher admonished me against "seizing" the meat, meaning that it should neither be browned nor cooked at a high temperature. This method is especially good for cooking today's lean American pork.

4 thick-cut rib pork chops

Salt and freshly ground black pepper

*½ cup Homemade Chicken Broth
(page 237) or low-sodium
chicken broth*

¼ cup heavy cream

2 tablespoons Pernod

1 teaspoon dried dillweed

1 teaspoon minced garlic

2 tablespoons unsalted butter

1 teaspoon finely chopped fresh dill

1. Season the pork on both sides with salt and pepper and place it in a skillet with the broth, cream, Pernod, dillweed, and garlic. Cover, place over medium heat, and simmer, turning the chops once, until the pork is springy to the touch, 15 to 18 minutes, depending on the thickness of the chops.

2. Transfer the pork to a plate and keep warm. Boil down the cooking liquid for a minute or two, until it has a thin saucelike consistency. Remove from the heat, add any liquid that has collected around the chops, and whisk in the butter.

3. Add the fresh dill, pour the sauce over the chops, and serve.

La Choucroute | Pork Braised in Sauerkraut

Because such a variety of pork products goes into the pot, this feast of Alsatian origin needs a crowd to enjoy it. If you've never braised sauerkraut with brined and smoked pork, you're in for a special moment. The sauerkraut loses its sour taste, soaks up the meat drippings with which it cooks, and becomes translucent and golden as an orange peel in marmalade. In turn, the juice from the sauerkraut tempers the salt-and-smoke aspect of the various meats. Here in the States, you'll find the half-brined pork products needed for this dish in Latino markets and at some German butchers. You also need smoked pork loin and Toulouse or a kielbasa-type sausage.

If the pot becomes too dry during cooking, add a couple of spoonfuls of wine and broth. If, on the other hand, it remains too soupy after the meats are cooked, place the pot on the stove and quickly boil down the liquid. There are few meals as sumptuous as a large platter piled high with glistening honey-colored sauerkraut topped with a variety of pork and sausages. Accompany the *choucroute* with hot mustard.

*1 tablespoon juniper berries
  or ¼ cup gin*

2 teaspoons coriander seeds

2 cloves

*2 tablespoons lard or vegetable
  shortening*

4 cloves garlic, thinly sliced

1 onion, roughly chopped

3 large carrots, sliced

6 cups drained sauerkraut

*3 cups Homemade Chicken Broth
  (page 237) or low-sodium
  chicken broth*

*2 cups Gewürztraminer or other fruity
  white wine, such as Riesling*

¾ pound slab bacon, in one piece

1 pound pork shoulder roast

1 pound smoked pork loin

1 pound ham

1 pound Toulouse or kielbasa sausage

Dijon mustard for serving

1. Preheat the oven to 325°F.

2. Tie the juniper berries, if using, the coriander, and cloves in a square of cheesecloth. Heat the lard in a large heavy nonreactive pot over medium heat. Add the garlic and onion and cook briefly, without browning. Add the carrots, sauerkraut, broth, wine, and the gin, if using. Bury the spice packet, bacon, and pork shoulder roast in the sauerkraut. Cover the pot and place in the oven for 1 hour.

3. Stir the sauerkraut to prevent sticking to the bottom of the pot, add the pork loin and ham, cover, and continue to cook for 45 minutes. Remove the lid, stir the contents of the pot, add the sausage, and cook, uncovered, for another 45 minutes. If the pot is too dry, add a few tablespoons wine or broth.

4. Remove the pot from the oven. Transfer the meat to a cutting board. Remove and discard the spice packet. If the sauerkraut is very moist, place the pot over medium heat and boil off most of the liquid. Cut the sausage into 1½-inch rounds. Slice the pork roast, pork loin, and ham into serving pieces.

5. Pile the sauerkraut on a large platter, arrange the meat on top, and serve immediately. Accompany with Dijon mustard.

Les Accompagnements

Androuët, the famous cheese restaurant near the Gare Saint-Lazare, has opened cheese shops around the city.

Side Dishes

*I*n France, the *plat principal* is rarely served with a vegetable accompaniment, for the vegetables have already been served as their own course. The accompaniment to the second course, if it's a *plat principal,* is almost always a starch—potatoes, rice, or beans. Sometimes the starch is actually not a starch at all, but is a puréed vegetable that seems, at least to a Frenchman, like a starch—puréed vegetables such as peas or carrots, roasted or puréed root vegetables such as celery or parsley root, or even puréed chestnuts, a popular accompaniment for game and red meat poultry.

There are, naturally, some traditions and commonsense rules that help the cook decide on an appropriate side dish. For instance, never serve two sauces on the same plate. If your *plat* is cooked in sauce, the accompaniment should not be. Stews, for instance, are served with nothing more than buttered and parsleyed noodles. Cream stews, say a blanquette, will be served with rice. Boiled potatoes go with fish, while meat and poultry get a crispy potato concoction. The French think of their starch as another bread, something to soak up sauce, a somewhat neutral but tasty accompaniment that enhances the main dish and may give it more weight. But in the French tradition, rules are to be tested, interpreted, and broken, when need be. With a plainly cooked morsel of meat, poultry, or fish, why not serve a Provençal ratatouille (a compote of eggplant, zucchini, and tomatoes)? Or put an artichoke bottom under a beef tournedo? Yes, you may serve a vegetable gratin with the *plat,* if it goes.

But think French, when you organize your dinner. Simplify. Remember variety is the key. And we've not had our starchy food yet.

Purée de Carottes | Carrot Purée

This is a lovely accompaniment to poultry, especially game birds, as well as to beef and lamb. People especially enjoy a naturally sweet vegetable with full-flavored meats and dark poultry, such as squab, duck, and goose.

1½ pounds carrots, cut into
    ½-inch rounds
1 medium onion
1 tablespoon unsalted butter
¼ cup Homemade Chicken Broth
    (page 237) or low-sodium
    chicken broth, vegetable broth,
    or water

1 teaspoon salt
¼ teaspoon freshly ground
    white pepper
2 bay leaves
1 sprig fresh thyme or
    ¼ teaspoon dried

1. Preheat the oven to 375°F.

2. Combine all the ingredients in a small heavy lidded pot and place in the oven for 1¼ hours, until the carrots are falling apart.

3. Remove the pot from the oven and retrieve and discard the bay leaves and the thyme sprig, if using. Pour the contents of the pot into a food processor and purée until smooth. Or place the contents in a mixing bowl and mash well. Keep warm until ready to serve.

Purée de Céleri-Rave | Celeriac Purée

This purée has an intense celery flavor. It's often served with venison and other game. Use small bulbs of celeriac for the purée. It's tedious to peel four or five small bulbs, but the larger ones are usually too fibrous to make a nice purée. Either way, use a sharp knife and peel until you've removed all the mottled surface. As you work, place each peeled bulb in water into which you've squeezed a lemon, then drain and cut up.

2 pounds celeriac, peeled and cut into
  $\frac{1}{2}$-inch cubes
1 medium onion
1 tablespoon unsalted butter

$\frac{1}{2}$ cup milk
1 teaspoon salt
$\frac{1}{4}$ teaspoon freshly ground white pepper
2 bay leaves

1. Preheat the oven to 375°F.

2. Combine all the ingredients in a small heavy lidded pot and place in the oven for $1\frac{1}{4}$ hours, until falling apart.

3. Remove the pot from the oven and retrieve and discard the bay leaves. Pour the contents of the pot into a food processor and purée until smooth. Or place the contents in a mixing bowl and mash well. Keep warm until ready to serve.

La Soubise | Onion and Rice Purée

This classic purée is a wonderful porridgy, creamy mass of sweet cooked onions bound with rice. Cook it long and slow to develop the sweetness of the onions and the nutty flavor of the rice. Serve to accompany roasted white meats and poultry.

1¾ pounds yellow onions,
   cut into eighths

¼ cup long-grain white rice

½ cup water

¼ cup heavy cream

1 tablespoon unsalted butter

1 teaspoon salt

¼ teaspoon freshly ground
   white pepper

Pinch of allspice

1. Preheat the oven to 375°F.

2. Combine all the ingredients in a small heavy lidded pot and place in the oven for 1¼ hours, until the rice is falling to bits.

3. Remove from the oven, transfer the contents of the pot to a food processor, and purée until smooth. Or run the mixture through a food mill. Keep warm until ready to serve.

Riz et Oignons Safranés
Saffron Rice and Onions

MAKES 4 SERVINGS

This beautifully shiny rice, Iberian in spirit with its orange color and saffron flavor, accompanies chicken, rabbit, or seafood cooked with tomatoes or peppers.

¾ cup Homemade Chicken Broth
  (page 237) or low-sodium broth,
  or water
4 teaspoons butter or
  extra-virgin olive oil
1 large onion, roughly diced

1 teaspoon minced garlic
½ cup long-grain rice
¼ teaspoon saffron threads
¼ teaspoon grated orange peel
¼ teaspoon salt, or as desired
Pinch cayenne pepper

Preheat the oven to 350°F. Place the broth in a small pot, cover, and bring to a boil. Set aside. Melt butter or oil in a small ovenproof pot over medium heat, add onion and garlic, and cook until the onion softens slightly, about 2 minutes. Add the rice and cook, stirring to coat all the grains, until the rice becomes aromatic, about 3 minutes. Add the broth, saffron, orange peel, and salt and pepper and stir once. Cover, transfer the pot to the oven, and cook for 12 minutes.

Navets au Four

Roasted Turnips with Sage

MAKES 4 SERVINGS

For years I've been blanching turnips prior to roasting them in order to achieve a golden outside and a creamy inside. Here's a better way that I discovered poking around a pal's kitchen. Start the turnips in the oven, in a tightly lidded vessel, so they steam in their own juices. After a bit, uncover the baking dish and let them brown and crisp.

*1 ½ pounds turnips, peeled and
   cut into 1 ½-inch wedges*

*2 tablespoons unsalted butter,
   cut into 6 pieces*

½ teaspoon salt

Freshly ground black pepper

2 pinches of allspice

*4 sprigs fresh sage or
   1 tablespoon dried*

3 tablespoons water

1. Preheat the oven to 375°F.

2. Place the turnips in a baking dish just large enough to hold them without crowding, dot with the butter, and sprinkle with the salt, pepper to taste, and the allspice. Bury the sage sprigs in the turnips or sprinkle with the dried leaves. Pour in the water, cover tightly, and place in the oven for 30 minutes, or until the turnips are just becoming tender.

3. Baste the turnips well with the cooking juices, increase the oven temperature to 425°F, and roast, uncovered, until tender and browned, about another 30 minutes. Pour the contents of the baking dish into a serving bowl and serve immediately.

Lentilles Tièdes | Warm Lentils

This is the potato salad of France, delicious served at any temperature. Parisians eat it as a side with roast pork or ham or as a dinner first course or light lunch, garnished with smoked fish. Here's the secret to its flavor—cook the lentils with only enough liquid to keep them moist, and let cool in their cooking liquid. The cooking liquid will have a good flavor, especially when the vinaigrette is added, and will keep the salad moist.

$1^{1}/_{4}$ cups small French du Puy *lentils*

4 cups vegetable broth, Homemade Chicken Broth (page 237), or low-sodium chicken or vegetable broth, or water

$^{1}/_{2}$ teaspoon salt

Freshly ground black pepper

2 sprigs fresh thyme or 1 teaspoon dried

2 bay leaves

3 tablespoons vegetable oil, preferably canola

2 medium onions, coarsely diced

2 medium carrots, thinly sliced

3 stalks celery, thinly sliced

$^{1}/_{2}$ cup red wine vinegar

2 tablespoons Dijon mustard

$^{1}/_{4}$ cup finely chopped fresh flat-leaf parsley

1. Combine the lentils, broth, salt, pepper to taste, thyme, and bay leaves in a pot, cover, place over medium heat, and simmer until the lentils are tender, about an hour. Remove from the heat, transfer the contents of the pot to a mixing bowl, and let cool, unrefrigerated, to room temperature.

2. Meanwhile, heat the oil in a large skillet over medium heat. Add the onions, carrots, and celery and cook until the carrots are soft, about 12 minutes. Do not allow the onions to brown.

3. Add the contents of the skillet to the warm lentils and gently mix together. Stir in the vinegar and mustard and mix in the parsley. Serve immediately, or chill and serve.

Flageolets au Pissenlit
Flageolet Beans with Dandelion Greens

MAKES 5 TO 6 SERVINGS

Flageolets, the favorite French bean, is the dried bean of a late-harvest green bean. They're pale green in color and, I think, have the creamiest texture of any bean. They invite butter, so much so that you wouldn't think of preparing them with anything else. Flageolets dislike being boiled in generous amounts of water. Add only enough to cover the beans by about an inch and simmer them gently, adding more water as necessary during cooking to just keep the pot moist. Once the beans are tender, the remaining cooking liquid with, of course, the addition of butter makes the most delicious background moistening.

This variation, with the addition of chopped dandelion greens, gives the beans an intriguing bitter edge, and goes well with their most traditional accompaniment, a roast leg of lamb. Other greens, such as sorrel, collard greens, and Swiss chard, also go well with flageolets.

*1 pound dried flageolets, soaked in
  warm water for 2 hours and drained*
1 onion, minced
1 medium carrot, finely chopped
2 cloves garlic, crushed
½ teaspoon dried thyme

½ teaspoon dried savory
1½ cups chopped dandelion greens
2 tablespoons unsalted butter
2 teaspoons salt
Freshly ground black pepper

1. Place the beans in a flameproof casserole with the onion, carrot, garlic, thyme, and savory and add enough water to cover the beans by 1 inch. Cover, place over medium heat, and bring to a bare boil, then reduce the heat and simmer for 1 hour. When the water level drops to that of the beans, add additional water as necessary just to cover the beans so they don't dry out during cooking. There should always be only enough water to cover the beans.

2. Add the dandelion greens and continue to cook for another 30 minutes, or until the beans are creamy.

3. Remove from the heat, swirl in the butter, and add the salt and pepper to taste. Serve immediately.

The variety of dried beans is enormous.

Tomates à la Crème | Creamed Tomatoes

MAKES 4 SERVINGS

Sauced side dishes like this are best served with plainly grilled or roasted fish, poultry, or meat—Parisians never serve two sauces on the same plate. The juice of the tomato bleeds into the skillet and, with the addition of cream, creates a few tablespoons of rich sauce.

8 ripe but firm vine-ripened Roma
　(plum) tomatoes
1 tablespoon olive oil
1 tablespoon unsalted butter
1/4 teaspoon dried marjoram

Salt and freshly ground black pepper
1/4 cup heavy cream
2 teaspoons minced fresh chervil
　or chives

1. Cut out the cores from the tomatoes. Drop them into boiling salted water, and leave until the skins crack, 1½ to 3 minutes. Drain, and when cool enough to handle, slip off and discard the skins. Cut a large X in the tip of each tomato and gently squeeze out the seeds.

2. Heat the oil and butter in a skillet over medium heat. Add the tomatoes, season with the marjoram and salt and pepper, and cook, tossing gently, for 7 to 8 minutes. Add the cream, cover the skillet, and continue to cook another 2 minutes. Remove the lid and continue to cook until the cream and the tomato juices reduce and thicken enough to coat the tomatoes.

3. Transfer the tomatoes to a serving bowl, spooning the sauce over them, sprinkle with the chervil, and serve.

Haricots Blancs à la Tomate
White Beans and Tomatoes

These white beans flavored with tomatoes are a delight. Serve them with roasted lamb or goat, ham, or grilled sausages. When you extend the time that it takes for dried beans to metamorphose from hard and dry to soft and cooked, you're bound to end up with a bean that's creamy and smooth and full of flavor. Many people claim that cooking beans with summer savory mitigates their *ventosité,* or windiness. This claim I cannot vouch for.

2 medium onions, peeled

2 cloves

1 pound dried white navy beans, soaked in warm water for 2 hours and drained

1 teaspoon dried summer savory

1 teaspoon freshly ground black pepper

1 pound Roma (plum) tomatoes

2 tablespoons unsalted butter

2 teaspoons salt

1. Stick each onion with a clove and place them in a casserole. Add the beans, savory, pepper, and enough cold water to cover the beans by about 2 inches. Cover, place over medium heat, and slowly bring to a boil, then reduce the heat and simmer for 1½ to 1¾ hours, or until the beans are tender. When the level of the water drops to that of the beans, begin adding just enough water to keep the beans from drying out during cooking. When the beans are creamy tender, remove the onions. Remove and discard the cloves. Roughly cut up the onions and return them to the beans.

2. Meanwhile, bring a pot of water to a boil, add the tomatoes, a few at a time, and leave until their skins crack, 1 to 2 minutes. Remove the tomatoes and peel, halve crosswise, and gently squeeze out the seeds. Chop the tomato pulp and set aside.

3. Once they are tender, drain the beans, reserving the liquid.

4. Melt the butter in a large skillet. Add the tomatoes and salt and cook, stirring, until the tomatoes are soft, 3 to 5 minutes. Add the contents of the skillet to the beans and add enough reserved cooking liquid to moisten. Serve hot.

Salade de Pommes de Terre

Potato Salad

This is one Parisian's take on a classic *pommes à l'huile,* a simple mix of potatoes and olive oil that she tosses with lettuce and serves with a platter of charcuterie. Although it's perfect on its own, you'll also want to make this the base of many salads.

2 tablespoons Dijon mustard

¼ cup white wine vinegar

6 tablespoons olive oil

¾ pound tiny new potatoes, left whole
 and peeled, or new potatoes,
 peeled and quartered
 into 2-inch pieces

2 cups roughly chopped lettuce,
 such as Bibb or Boston

Freshly ground black pepper

1. To make the vinaigrette, place the mustard in a medium mixing bowl, mix in the vinegar, and slowly beat in the oil. Set aside.

2. Cook the potatoes in boiling water until tender. Drain and toss with the vinaigrette in the bowl. Allow the potatoes to cool to room temperature; then add the lettuce and mix. Add a few grinds of pepper over the top. Mound the salad on a plate and serve.

**Monsieur Zamba,
the *patatologue***

Primeurs au Vinaigre

Fingerling Potatoes in White Wine and Vinegar

MAKES 4 SERVINGS

When I prepared this dish in Paris, I was so taken by it that I forwent the main course and ate only a big plate of the potatoes, followed by cheese and salad. *Primeurs* are the first potatoes of spring, dug out of the ground when they're the size of your thumb. They're sweet, not starchy, and have a firm texture. They're also just about the only potato that Parisians eat without peeling.

These potatoes are so fine that it's a shame to waste even the liquid in which they're cooked, which accounts for cooking them in wine and vinegar here. Prick the potatoes so that what little starch there is bleeds into the cooking liquid. The cooking liquid should reduce and thicken during cooking, making a potato "gravy."

Here in the States, I've picked through bushels of White Rose potatoes at the supermarket, choosing only the smallest ones (the grocery store manager never seems to mind), but I've come closest to re-creating the magic of this dish using fingerling potatoes that I buy at the greenmarket, or with tiny Yellow Finns when they're available during the winter and early spring.

1 1/2 pounds fingerling or Yellow
   Finnish potatoes
1/2 cup minced shallots
1 1/2 cups dry white wine, such as
   Sauvignon Blanc

1/4 cup white wine vinegar
2 tablespoons unsalted butter
1 teaspoon salt
Freshly ground black pepper
2 tablespoons chopped fresh parsley

1. Wash the potatoes and prick each one twice with a fork. Place the potatoes in a deep saucepan or skillet, along with the remaining ingredients except the parsley, cover, place over medium heat, and simmer for 20 minutes, or until the potatoes are tender. Using a slotted spoon, transfer the potatoes to a serving bowl.

2. Replace the skillet over medium heat, uncovered, and reduce the liquid until it has the consistency of heavy cream. Add the parsley to the liquid, pour over the potatoes, and serve.

Purée de Deux Pommes
Mashed Potatoes and Apples

MAKES 4 SERVINGS

Both potatoes and apples are called *pommes* in French. *Pommes de terre,* of the ground, are potatoes, and *pommes à l'air,* of the sky, are apples. For traditional mashed potatoes, most people use waxy ones that don't absorb a lot of water during cooking. French mashed potatoes are not meant to be fluffy, but rather smooth and sticky. But Charlotte, an apple merchant/specialist who gave me this recipe, was very specific about the varieties of apple and potato she uses for this light purée. Both must be mealy and fall apart during cooking. I use large russet potatoes and Red Delicious apples. This dish accompanies all varieties of sausages, as well as roast duckling or goose.

$^{3}/_{4}$ pound russet potatoes, peeled and
   cut into 2-inch pieces

3 tablespoons unsalted butter

3 large Red Delicious apples, peeled,
   cored, and roughly chopped

$^{1}/_{2}$ cup milk

1 teaspoon salt

$^{1}/_{4}$ teaspoon freshly ground white pepper

$^{1}/_{8}$ teaspoon ground coriander

1. Place the potatoes in a pot and cover with salted water. Cover, place over high heat, bring to a vigorous simmer, and cook until tender, 12 to 15 minutes. Drain the potatoes and place in a large bowl.

2. Meanwhile, melt the butter in a large skillet over medium heat and add the apples. Cover and cook, stirring occasionally, until the apples are soft, about 8 minutes. Add the apples to the potatoes.

3. Combine the milk, salt, pepper, and coriander in a small pot, place over medium heat, bring to a boil, and immediately remove from the heat. Using a potato masher, mash the potatoes and apples together while adding the milk a little at a time. Pour the purée into a pan and gently reheat before serving.

Pommes de Terre
et Oignons Sautés au Cru
Home-Fried Potatoes and Onions

MAKES 4 SERVINGS

The woman who gave me this recipe described it as a *ruine,* a "rubble" of potatoes and onions. If you've ever visited the Cluny Museum or the ruins of the Roman arena, you'll know what the dish is supposed to look like—chunks of potatoes and limp slivers of onion in a sludge of moist potato "dust." These are French-style home fries, redolent of butter and rosemary and perfect with baked fish, chicken, or pork. Parisians prepare them in a well-seasoned heavy cast-iron or enameled skillet. The potatoes brown in parts but don't stick. Use mealy baking potatoes.

1 pound russet potatoes	½ teaspoon salt
1 medium onion	Freshly ground black pepper
2 tablespoons oil	1 tablespoon unsalted butter
2 teaspoons chopped fresh rosemary	2 tablespoons crème fraîche
or 1 teaspoon dried	or sour cream

1. Peel the potatoes, halve lengthwise, cut each half into ½-inch pieces, and place in cold water. Peel the onion and halve it from tip to stem. Lay the halves cut side down and thinly slice each from tip to stem.

2. Heat the oil in a heavy skillet over medium-high heat. Add the potatoes and onion, sprinkle with the rosemary and salt, and give a few turns of the peppermill. Cover and cook for 5 minutes without touching. Remove the cover and shake the skillet vigorously. Continue to cook, shaking the skillet every couple of minutes, until the potatoes are tender, another 10 to 12 minutes.

3. Remove from the heat and mix in the butter and crème fraîche. Transfer the contents of the skillet to a serving bowl, scraping up any bits that have stuck to the bottom of the skillet, and serve immediately.

Pommes Rissolées

Panfried Potatoes

Rissoler, in cooking terms, means to expose an ingredient to high temperatures, resulting in a golden crust. In slang, it means to get sunburned. How perfectly it describes these potatoes, the hissing of steam escaping from the little cubes as they bubble in oil. Then, as they start to soften, the surfaces turn golden, and they're done.

The woman who gave me this recipe was emphatic that the potatoes be cooked in goose fat. Although the flavor of rendered fat—goose, duck, or chicken—is delicious, you can also use vegetable oil with the addition of some butter for flavor. Most important, though, are the cooking temperature and the size of the skillet. Test the temperature of the oil by dropping a potato cube into the skillet. It should immediately begin to bubble. If not, the oil's not hot enough. And don't crowd these potatoes as they cook, or the escaping steam will cause them to fall to pieces. Better to cook them in two batches. These potato gems don't stay crisp for very long, so serve them immediately.

3 pounds large russet potatoes

2 tablespoons unsalted butter
  (if not using goose fat)

Canola, peanut, or grapeseed oil
  or rendered goose fat

1 teaspoon salt

Freshly ground black pepper

1 tablespoon chopped fresh chives

1. Trim each potato into a brick shape by slicing off the two ends and the rounded parts of the other four surfaces. Cut each potato lengthwise into ⅜-inch-thick slabs. Pile up two or three slabs and cut them lengthwise into ⅜-inch-wide sticks, then cut the sticks into ⅜-inch cubes. As you go along, place the potato cubes into a pot with cold salted water to cover. When all the potatoes are cut, place the pot over high heat, bring to a boil, and immediately drain the potatoes. Place on a kitchen towel and pat dry.

2. Preheat the oven to 200°F.

3. Place a large skillet over medium heat and melt the butter with enough oil so you have a ½-inch depth of melted fat. (Or use all rendered goose or chicken fat instead of butter and oil.) When hot, add half of the potatoes, or enough to fill the skillet without crowding, and cook for 5 minutes, gently shaking the skillet from time to time. When the potatoes begin to turn golden, use a slotted spoon to turn them, so that all the surfaces color equally, and cook for another 7 to 10 minutes, or until golden on all sides and tender. Remove the potatoes. Place on a kitchen towel on a baking sheet and keep warm in the oven while you cook the remaining batch.

4. To serve, toss the potatoes with the salt, pepper to taste, and chives.

*E*VERYONE KNOWS THAT POTATOES ARE BEST WHEN COOKED IN GOOSE FAT," SAID THE SHORT WHITE-HAIRED WOMAN NEXT TO ME IN LINE AT THE GREENGROCER. (NO, CREAM, I THOUGHT.) "BUT, *tant pis* FOR US, WE PARISIANS DON'T COOK GOOSE VERY OFTEN, SO WE DON'T OFTEN HAVE GOOSE FAT ON HAND. TRADITIONAL PEOPLE, PEOPLE IN THE COUNTRY, WOULD FALL INTO AN APOPLECTIC FIT IF THEY KNEW WHAT WE'RE WILLING TO SPEND AT FAUCHON FOR A JAR OF GOOSE FAT IN WHICH TO COOK POTATOES. BUT, MONSIEUR, PARIS HAS OTHER CHARMS AND THE ADVANTAGES OF LIVING HERE FAR OUTWEIGH THE EXTRA COST OF GOOSE FAT, *n'est-ce pas?"*

Galette de Pommes de Terre

Potato Cake

MAKES 6 TO 8 SERVINGS

On my visits to the Parisian food markets, I was given perhaps a dozen recipes for potato *galettes*. Some cooks insisted on using a nonstick skillet, others made theirs in cast iron. Some were like potato crêpes, with cream and eggs; some were more like *rösti* potatoes, crispy and flavored with lard. One was like *pommes Anna*, a tall layered cake of potatoes rich with butter and a bit pretentious.

My favorite is a large *galette* that Deborah Irmas, an American friend living in the Marais, made one night to go with Barbary duck with cherries. It was about eleven inches in diameter and about one and a half inches thick, crispy on the outside and creamy inside. Deborah had quite a time flipping the cake and ended up sliding it onto a plate, then putting the skillet over the plate and turning everything upside down so the cake landed back in the skillet. To ensure success, use a nonstick skillet.

1 ½ pounds large White Rose potatoes

2 teaspoons white wine vinegar

½ cup minced shallots

2 tablespoons all-purpose flour

1 teaspoon salt

½ teaspoon freshly ground black pepper

4 tablespoons (½ stick) unsalted butter
or a combination of unsalted butter
and oil

1. Peel the potatoes, shred in a food processor, or grate using a coarse grater, and immediately toss with the vinegar to keep from discoloring. Transfer them to a bowl. Mix the potatoes with the shallots, flour, salt, and pepper.

2. Melt 2 tablespoons of the butter in an 11-inch nonstick skillet over medium heat. When the foam has subsided, pour in the potato mixture. Using a spatula, press down on the surface of the *galette*. Then, going around the perimeter of the cake, press the sides toward the center to compact and shape it. Cover the skillet and cook for 10 minutes. Shake the skillet in a circular motion to dislodge the cake, which has probably begun to stick.

3. Remove the skillet from the heat and invert a plate over it. Grab the handle of the skillet with the inside of your wrist facing up, place your other hand on the plate, and turn the skillet and plate over in one confident motion to turn out the *galette*. Replace the skillet on the heat. Add the remaining 2 tablespoons butter to the skillet and slide in the *galette.* Cover the skillet and cook for 5 minutes. Remove the cover and continue to cook the *galette* until the potatoes are cooked in the center, about 7 minutes more. Slide the *galette* onto a plate and serve immediately.

Deborah Irmas getting ready to flip her potato *galette*

Manqué de Pommes de Terre au Gruyère

Mashed Potato Cake with Gruyère Cheese

MAKES 8 SERVINGS

This lumpy mashed potato fantasy, attributed to a nineteenth-century Parisian chef, is baked in a ring mold called a *manqué,* which means missed, after a failed sponge cake attempt. Inside the herb-and-crumb crust, which does, in fact, resemble an unfrosted sponge cake, is a creamy, buttery, lumpy mass of mashed potatoes flavored with onions. I've also made this using leeks instead of onions and adding some finely diced ham. Another nice thing to do is cook up some diced bacon to use in addition to the butter.

4 large russet potatoes

6 tablespoons unsalted butter

¼ cup dry bread crumbs

3 tablespoons finely chopped
   fresh parsley

3 tablespoons minced fresh chives

1 medium onion, finely chopped,
   or 1 large leek, white part only,
   thinly sliced and washed well

1¾ cups milk

Pinch of freshly grated nutmeg

2 large eggs

2 large egg yolks

¾ cup grated Gruyère cheese

¾ teaspoon salt

Freshly ground black pepper

1. Preheat the oven to 400°F.

2. Bake the potatoes until tender, about 1 hour. Remove from the oven and scoop the flesh into a mixing bowl. Reduce the oven temperature to 375°F.

3. Meanwhile, generously butter a 2-quart ring mold 7 or 8 inches in diameter with 1 tablespoon of the butter. Mix the bread crumbs, parsley, and chives together in a small bowl and sprinkle evenly over the inside of the mold. Set the mold aside.

4. Melt the remaining 5 tablespoons butter in a small saucepan. Cook the onion until soft but not browned, about 3 minutes. Add the milk and nutmeg. Pour this mixture into the potatoes, then add the eggs and yolks. Using a large fork, lightly mash the potatoes, incorporating the milk and eggs but leaving many lumps. Mix in the cheese. Add the salt and pepper to taste.

5. Scoop the potato mixture evenly into the prepared mold. Place in the oven and bake for 45 minutes, or until the sides turn golden and begin to pull away from the mold. Remove from the oven, run a knife around the potatoes to loosen the cake from the mold, and turn out onto a serving plate. Serve immediately.

Timbale de Pommes de Terre et de Poireaux

Leek and Potato Timbale

MAKES 6 SERVINGS

The recipe for these little haystacks of shredded potato and leeks comes from a customer of Monsieur Zamba, a self-proclaimed *patatologue* in the rue Monge market. Although she tops the stacks with fillets of smoked herring, garnishes them with crème fraîche, and serves them as starters, they are too delicious on their own not to serve them as is with a chicken in sauce or plainly cooked meat. If you don't own Teflon-coated ramekins or large nonstick muffin tins, cut circles of parchment paper to line the bottoms of your molds; if you can't buy parchment paper, brown paper supermarket bags will also work nicely. This is to ensure that your timbales don't stick to the bottom. The timbales can be made in advance and easily rewarmed in a 350°F oven.

6 tablespoons unsalted butter	½ teaspoon salt
1 pound russet potatoes	¼ teaspoon freshly ground black pepper
1 large leek, white part only, chopped and washed well	⅛ teaspoon freshly grated nutmeg

1. Preheat the oven to 425°F. Generously butter four nonstick 6-ounce ramekins or muffin tins. If you don't have nonstick molds, cut out circles the size of the ramekin bottoms using parchment paper or brown paper bags and fit them into the bottom of the ramekins. Then butter the paper and molds.

2. Peel the potatoes and grate by hand or with a food processor fitted with the shredding blade. Combine the potatoes and leek in a bowl and season with the salt, pepper, and nutmeg. Pack the mixture into the ramekins and place in the oven.

3. Melt the remaining butter. About every 10 minutes or so as the timbales bake, press each one down using a large spoon and pour in a little butter. Repeat three or four times during baking. The potatoes are done when they easily pull away from the sides of the molds, about 35 minutes. They should be nicely browned and crispy on the outside. Remove from the oven, run a knife around the perimeter of each mold, and unmold onto plates.

Monsieur Zamba, the self-described *patatologue,* with his assistant

Pommes Boulangère
Potato and Onion Gratin Cooked with Broth

MAKES 4 TO 5 SERVINGS

These potatoes are really best cooked in a large roasting pan along with a roast of beef, lamb (see Epaule d'Agneau à la Boulangère, page 262), or chicken. However, they're so delicious that there are bound to be times when you'll want to cook them on their own. Here's the all-purpose recipe that most Parisians use, and which I've seen them improvise on by using equal parts potatoes and turnips or potatoes and celeriac.

2 pounds large waxy potatoes, such as
   White or Red Rose, peeled and
   thinly sliced
2 medium onions, halved from top to
   stem and thinly sliced
3 tablespoons unsalted butter
¾ cup Homemade Chicken Broth
   (page 237) or low-sodium
   chicken or vegetable broth

¼ cup dry white wine, such as
   Chardonnay
1 teaspoon dried savory
Pinch of freshly grated nutmeg
1 teaspoon salt
½ teaspoon freshly ground black pepper
¾ cup grated Gruyère cheese

1. Preheat the oven to 375°F.

2. Mix the potatoes and onions together and place in an 8- by 11-inch baking dish. Combine the butter, broth, wine, savory, nutmeg, salt, and pepper in a small pan, bring to a simmering boil, and pour over the potatoes. Cover and place in the oven until the potatoes are just tender, about 45 minutes.

3. Uncover the potatoes and sprinkle with the cheese. Return to the oven and continue to bake until the cheese is melted and golden, another 10 to 15 minutes. Serve immediately.

Gratin Dauphinois | Scalloped Potatoes

These sinfully rich potatoes are simple to prepare, and not really as rich as they taste. I side with those Parisians who cook the potatoes in a mixture of cream and milk (please don't use 2 percent milk; it will curdle) instead of pure cream. I eschew eggs as a means of tightening the whole, because I like a moister gratin. Remember also that the cheese in the recipe is a flavor enhancement, so seek out a really fine, aged semi-firm cheese, with an intense cheese flavor.

2 tablespoons unsalted butter, melted

2 pounds waxy large new potatoes, such as White or Red Rose, peeled and thinly sliced

1/2 cup grated Gruyère, Emmenthaler, Cantal, or Beaufort cheese

1 tablespoon minced garlic

Pinch of freshly grated nutmeg

1 teaspoon salt

1/2 teaspoon freshly ground black pepper

3/4 cup heavy cream

2 cups whole milk

1. Preheat the oven to 375°F.

2. Mix together the butter, potatoes, cheese, garlic, nutmeg, salt, and pepper and arrange in a 9-inch round oven-to-table baking dish, about 3 inches deep. Pour over the cream and milk, cover, and place in the oven for 45 minutes.

3. Remove the cover and continue to cook until the potatoes are tender and the top becomes golden, another 20 minutes or so. Serve immediately.

Les Desserts

Desserts

I'm not much of a sweets person, but when I'm in Paris, the pastries are my weakness. Well, actually my second weakness, after cheese. In the pastry shops, there are freshly baked cakes, petits fours, and cookies, all detailed with fantastical decorations in icing or piped buttercream, as perfect as architectural models or dollhouse furnishings.

As you might guess, it's the rare Parisian who tries to compete with the *pâtissier*. It's simply not worth it. The desserts Parisians prepare at home are less elaborate. Their repertoire includes flans and puddings, crêpes, fresh fruit compotes, and a few simple cakes. They may purchase pastry dough—puff pastry and sweet tart dough—from the *pâtisserie* to bring home for baking a fruit tart or a fruit turnover. People who make desserts at home approach their preparation more like cooks than like pastry chefs. They're not too worried about exact, intricate concoctions, but concentrate on how the dessert tastes. These recipes are easy to make and, although not too long to prepare, they still add time to meal preparation. So, although most meals at home finish with cheese and perhaps a cooked fruit, here are some recipes I collected for deliciously rustic full-flavored concoctions that will wow you with their unassuming comfortability.

Wild berries, delicate and perishable

Charlotte aux Pommes | Apple Charlotte

An apple charlotte, not to be confused with other charlottes that are chilled creams set in ladyfingers, is a warm dessert of apples sautéed in butter and then baked in a bread crust, a French apple brown Betty, if you will. Apples and butter are the magical combination here, and there are few apple desserts as pleasing as this one. Many Parisians own a *moule à charlotte,* a deep tinned copper mold six or seven inches in diameter. The copper distributes the heat of the oven so that the butter-soaked bread that forms the outside of the charlotte browns and crisps but doesn't burn during baking. I don't own one, so I bake my charlottes in a heavy copper saucepan six and a half inches in diameter and three and a half inches deep. A similar size ceramic-glazed steel or cast-iron pot will also do the trick. If you have to prepare a charlotte that's a bit wider and less tall, well, don't worry about it. But do check the cooking time, for it will be done in less time than in a deep mold.

3 tablespoons fresh lemon juice	⅛ teaspoon vanilla extract
2½ pounds Golden Delicious apples (about 10)	¼ cup applejack, Calvados, or apple juice
12 tablespoons (1½ sticks) unsalted butter	¼ cup fresh bread crumbs
3 tablespoons sugar	One 1-pound Pullman loaf brioche or white bread, preferably unsliced or cut into ¾-inch slices
⅛ teaspoon salt	Crème fraîche or sour cream for serving
⅛ teaspoon ground cinnamon	
2 pinches freshly grated nutmeg	

1. Pour the lemon juice into a large mixing bowl. Peel and core the apples and halve them lengthwise. Lay each half cut side down and thinly slice them, placing the slices in the lemon juice as you work.

2. Melt 2 tablespoons of the butter in a large pot over medium heat. Add the apples, sugar, salt, cinnamon, nutmeg, vanilla, and applejack. Cook the apples until soft but not falling apart, about 25 minutes. Remove from the heat, mix in the bread crumbs, and set aside.

3. Preheat the oven to 400°F.

4. Melt the remaining 10 tablespoons butter. Remove the crust from the bread. If the loaf is unsliced, cut three ¾-inch slices and halve each slice diagonally. Fit the triangles in an overlapping rose pattern in the bottom of the mold, trimming the tips if necessary to make them fit. Cut 4 more ¾-inch slices of bread and fit them around the sides of the mold, overlapping the edges and trimming as necessary. Remove all the bread from the mold and set aside.

5. Grease the mold generously with butter and sprinkle with sugar. Beginning with the bread triangles, lightly dip the sliced bread into the melted butter, turning to coat both sides, and return the triangles to the mold to create the original rose pattern. Dip the rectangular slices in the butter, turning to coat both sides, and line the sides of the mold. Tightly pack the mold with the sautéed apples. If the mold is slightly overfilled, don't worry about it.

6. Place in the oven for 30 to 35 minutes, or until the apples are bubbling. To check for doneness, use the tip of a knife to pull back a little of the bread from the side of the mold. The charlotte is done when the bread is uniformly deep golden. Remove from the oven and let cool for 10 minutes before unmolding.

7. To serve, invert the charlotte onto a serving platter. Tap the bottom of the mold and carefully lift it off. Serve the charlotte warm and offer crème fraîche on the side.

Pêches Pochées aux Épices

Spiced Poached Peaches

MAKES 4 SERVINGS

During the summer, the peaches in Parisian markets are astoundingly delicious—large, white, and aromatic. Parisians agree that the less done with them, the better. The brilliance of this dish of poached peaches is its flavor balance. The syrup should be neither too sweet nor too thick. The aromatic spices should be just present enough to change how we taste the peaches; they shouldn't flavor them. When I was served these peaches, on a lazy summer afternoon in the garden of my friends Corinne and Babette, it was almost like tasting an old bottle of Château d'Yquem. When truly fine peaches aren't in the market, you'll want to reduce the poaching liquid to a stronger syrup. Poached peaches can be served on their own or with a slice of Pound Cake (page 328) or Gâteau Breton (page 323).

¹/₄ cup sugar

3 cups water

6 peppercorns

¹/₂ teaspoon cumin seeds

¹/₂ teaspoon coriander seeds

¹/₄ teaspoon fennel seeds

2 cloves

1 teaspoon ground cardamom

4 large white or yellow peaches

1 teaspoon orange flower water
(optional) (available at specialty
stores and North African, Middle
Eastern, and Sephardic markets)

4 sprigs fresh mint

1. Combine all the ingredients except the peaches, orange flower water, and mint in a pot that's just large enough to hold the peaches, cover, and bring to a boil over high heat. Add the peaches, lower the heat to medium, and simmer, uncovered, for 8 minutes. Turn the peaches over and continue to simmer for another 5 minutes. Transfer the peaches to a plate and continue to cook the liquid until it is reduced by about half, to a thin syrup. Remove from the heat, pour through a strainer into a 2-quart container, and add the orange flower water.

2. Slip the skins off the peaches while they are still warm. Halve them from tip to stem, remove the stone, and place the peach halves in the syrup. Chill in the refrigerator.

3. To serve, place the peach halves and syrup in bowls and garnish with the mint.

On a *rue commerçante*

Coupe aux Fraises | Strawberry Trifle

French strawberries, commonly from the Périgord region or the Loire Valley, are marketed from April to September but are at their peak in June. They are never refrigerated, and are extremely perishable. I've bought them in the morning market only to find them covered with mold by that afternoon. But they are the essence of strawberries—remarkably fragrant and sweet as sugar. They require very little adornment, and this *coupe*—call it a trifle, call it strawberry shortcake in a glass—is the fanciest you'll want to get.

In the States, buy berries in the greenmarket if you can. Choose smaller berries, which are less watery and more concentrated in flavor. Smell them, and if they're really fragrant, then you can be certain they taste good. I like to use kirsch, an unsweetened cherry-flavored alcohol, for soaking the pound cake, but many people prefer the sweeter orange-flavored Grand Marnier or Cointreau. Once you've assembled these *coupes,* you'll need to place them in the refrigerator for at least three hours, or up to five hours, for the ingredients to macerate. Remove them from the refrigerator thirty minutes before serving.

1 pint small strawberries,
  rinsed and hulled
2 tablespoons sugar
3/4 cup heavy cream
2 tablespoons sour cream
2 tablespoons confectioners' sugar

6 thin slices (about 3/8 inch)
  Pound Cake (page 328)
1/2 to 3/4 cup kirsch, Grand Marnier,
  or Cointreau
4 sprigs fresh mint

1. Slice the strawberries from tip to stem into 4 to 6 slices, depending on the size of the berry. Place the berries in a bowl, toss with the sugar, and set aside.

2. Whip the cream in a chilled bowl until stiff, then fold in the sour cream and confectioners' sugar.

3. To assemble the *coupes,* place a tablespoon of whipped cream in the bottom of each of four martini glasses or wineglasses. Cut four circles of cake the diameter of the glass, place one over the whipped cream in each glass, and then spoon over a tablespoon of kirsch. Repeat until you've used all the berries, ending with a layer of whipped cream. Place in the refrigerator for at least 3, and up to 5, hours.

4. Thirty minutes before serving, remove the coupes from the refrigerator. To serve, garnish each one with a sprig of mint.

Clafoutis aux Cerises

Cherry Custard Flan

MAKES 4 TO 6 SERVINGS

Clafoutis is a strange hybrid. It's not quite a flan, and it's thicker than a custard, more like a really thick crêpe. The batter cooks up a little chewy and a little dry, but the cherries melt, forming little pockets of thick cherry syrup. Curiously, you never find clafoutis made with pitted cherries.

1 large egg

1 large egg yolk

⅓ cup sugar

½ cup tablespoon all-purpose flour

1 cup heavy cream

3 tablespoons kirsch

4 tablespoons (½ stick) unsalted
  butter, melted

4 cups cherries, stems removed

Confectioners' sugar for dusting

Crème fraîche or sour cream for serving

1. Preheat the oven to 400°F. Butter and flour a 9-inch flan ring or round baking dish and set aside on a baking sheet.

2. In a bowl, beat the egg and egg yolk together, then beat in the sugar. Add the flour and mix until incorporated. Stir in the cream, kirsch, and melted butter. Pour the mixture into the flan ring and distribute the cherries evenly over it.

3. Place in the oven until puffed and golden, about 30 minutes. Let cool, then turn the clafoutis upside down onto a wire rack or plate. Turn right side up onto a serving plate, sprinkle with confectioners' sugar, and serve, accompanied by crème fraîche or sour cream.

Prunes au Marzipan

Plums Baked with Marzipan

MAKES 4 SERVINGS

I like to prepare these plums in individual ramekins or soufflé dishes. The plums are not macerated in sugar, but go straight into the baking dishes, resulting in a sour contrast to the sweet, intense marzipan batter. They puff up quite a bit in the oven and look tantalizingly rustic—the plums with their wrinkled skins and the marzipan filling with its golden crust. When I had these in Paris, they were accompanied with crème fraîche, but I served them back in Los Angeles with plain buttermilk, which was, I decided, more delicious.

Unsalted butter and all-purpose flour
   for preparing the molds
4 large red plums
3 ounces almond paste
2 large eggs

1 cup whole milk
3 tablespoons sugar
Pinch of salt
Buttermilk, crème fraîche,
   or sour cream for serving

1. Preheat the oven to 375°F. Generously butter four 4-ounce ramekins or soufflé dishes and dust with flour, shaking out the excess.

2. Halve the plums lengthwise and remove the stones.

3. Combine the almond paste, eggs, milk, sugar, and salt in a blender and pulse until smooth.

4. Place 2 plum halves, skin side up, in each ramekin and pour in the almond paste mixture. Place the ramekins in the oven and bake for 25 minutes until well puffed and the plums are soft.

5. Serve the plums hot or at room temperature and accompany with buttermilk, crème fraîche, or sour cream.

Frangipane aux Fruits
Almond Cake with Berries

MAKES 6 TO 8 SERVINGS

This all-purpose almond cake is a favorite. People serve it plain, with a sprinkling of confectioners' sugar, frosted with mocha buttercream, or served with berries, as here. It can be baked in a pastry shell, or decorated with various fresh fruits that have been macerated in sugar and liqueur.

Unsalted butter and all-purpose flour
    for preparing the molds
7 ounces almond paste, crumbled into
    small pieces
¼ cup sugar
8 tablespoons (1 stick) unsalted butter,
    at room temperature
¼ cup Madeira or dry sherry

3 large eggs, separated
½ cup cake flour
¼ teaspoon salt
1 pint strawberries, raspberries,
    mulberries, blueberries, or
    blackberries, or a combination
¼ cup Grand Marnier
Crème fraîche or sour cream for serving

1. Preheat the oven to 350°F. Butter and flour an 8-inch round cake pan.

2. Combine the almond paste, sugar, butter, Madeira, and egg yolks in a mixer bowl and beat until smooth. Transfer the contents of the mixer bowl to another bowl and fold in the flour.

3. Beat the egg whites and salt until stiff peaks form. Mix one third of the whites into the almond batter, then gently fold in the remainder. Scrape the batter into the prepared cake pan and smooth the top.

4. Place in the middle of the oven and bake for 30 to 35 minutes, or until a knife inserted into the center of the cake comes out clean. Remove the cake from the oven and let cool. Turn the cake upside down onto a serving plate.

5. Clean the berries. If using strawberries, halve or quarter them, depending on their size. Mix the berries with the Grand Marnier in a mixing bowl, and transfer to a serving bowl. Offer the berries with the cake, and pass the crème fraîche.

Tarte Bourdaloue | Pear and Almond Tart

This tart of fresh pears and almond-flavored custard is a regional classic, a housewife's dessert. Use firm pears such as Anjou that won't fall to bits during cooking. The tart will look a bit like a bather out for the first trip to the beach—white and pasty—but will come alive when glazed with apricot jelly.

$^1\!/_2$ *cup sugar*

1 cup plus 2 tablespoons
all-purpose flour

$^1\!/_8$ *teaspoon salt*

5 tablespoons chilled unsalted butter,
cut into teaspoon-sized bits

3 large eggs

1 tablespoon ice water

$^1\!/_3$ *cup crème fraîche or heavy cream*

$^1\!/_4$ *cup finely ground almonds*
(almond meal)

$^1\!/_2$ *teaspoon almond extract*

2 firm pears, such as Anjou

2 tablespoons apricot jelly

2 tablespoons water

1. Place $^1\!/_4$ cup of the sugar, the flour, and salt in a mixer bowl, add the butter, and beat at medium speed until the mixture resembles grainy meal. Add 1 egg and the ice water and mix until the mixture begins to form a mass. Remove from the bowl, wrap in plastic wrap, and chill in the refrigerator for 45 minutes before using.

2. Meanwhile, in a medium bowl, beat the remaining $^1\!/_2$ cup sugar with the remaining 2 eggs. Stir in the cream, then mix in the ground almonds and almond extract and set aside.

3. Peel the pears, halve lengthwise, and remove and discard the stems and cores. Lay the pear halves cut side down on a work surface and cut them crosswise into $^1\!/_4$-inch slices, keeping the shape of the pears intact. Set the pears aside.

4. Preheat the oven to 375°F.

continued

5. Flour a work surface and roll the pastry into a 10-inch circle. Line a 9-inch tart ring or fluted tart pan with the pastry. Prick the bottom of the pastry in a few places with a fork and place in the freezer for 5 minutes.

6. When the dough is well chilled, line it with aluminum foil, making sure to work the foil into the corners. Place the tart crust on the bottom rack of the oven and bake for 12 minutes. Remove the tart shell from the oven and remove the foil. Leave the oven on.

7. Slide a frosting spatula or a long slender knife under one pear half and press down on the top to spread and fan the slices. Carefully transfer the fanned pear half to the tart ring. Repeat with the remaining halves, so that they are positioned with the stem end in the center of the tart shell at 12 o'clock, 3 o'clock, 6 o'clock, and 9 o'clock.

8. Place the tart on the middle rack of the oven and carefully pour in the almond mixture. Bake for 25 to 30 minutes, or until the filling is set and the pastry turns golden around the edges. Transfer the tart to a rack and let cool completely before removing it from the tart ring.

9. Combine the jelly and water in a small saucepan, place over medium heat, and dissolve the jelly in the water. Remove from the heat and generously brush over the entire surface of the tart. Serve the tart at room temperature. (This can be made a day in advance and kept tightly wrapped at room temperature; do not refrigerate.)

Tarte au Citron | Lemon Tart

My favorite lemon tart in Paris comes from the renowned Christian Constant. I'd never succeeded in duplicating his version until I tried the following recipe. The crust is almost a big shortbread cookie, not the easiest to work with, but worth the bother. If it tears when you roll it out, don't despair. Do the best you can to line your tart pan and piece together bits where necessary. Be certain that the pastry is well chilled before you bake it.

1 cup plus 2 tablespoons all-purpose flour

¼ teaspoon salt

½ cup sugar

5 tablespoons chilled unsalted butter, cut into teaspoon-sized pieces, plus 1 tablespoon unsalted butter, melted

1 tablespoon ice water

3 large egg yolks

2 large eggs

Juice of 3 lemons (about ⅓ cup)

¼ cup crème fraîche or heavy cream

1. Place the flour, salt, and ¼ cup of the sugar in a mixer bowl. Add the chilled butter and mix at medium speed until the mixture resembles grainy meal. Add the ice water and 1 of the egg yolks and mix just until a mass begins to form. Remove from the bowl, roll into a disk, wrap in plastic wrap, and chill in the refrigerator for 45 minutes before using.

2. Meanwhile, in a medium bowl, beat together the remaining 2 yolks with the eggs. Beat in the remaining ¼ cup sugar, the lemon juice, and the crème fraîche. Stir in the tablespoon of melted butter. Set the mixture aside.

3. Preheat the oven to 375°F.

4. Flour a work surface and roll the pastry into a 10-inch circle. Line a 9-inch tart ring with the pastry. Prick the bottom of the pastry in a few places with a fork and place in the freezer for 5 minutes.

continued

5. When the dough is well chilled, line it with aluminum foil, making sure to work the foil into the corners. Place the piecrust in the freezer to chill for 5 minutes, then transfer to the bottom rack of the oven and bake for 10 minutes.

6. Remove the tart pan from the oven and remove the foil. Place the tart shell on the middle rack of the oven and pour in the lemon mixture. Bake for 20 to 25 minutes, or until the lemon mixture is set. Remove the tart from the oven and cool completely before unmolding. (This can be made a day in advance and kept tightly wrapped at room temperature; do not refrigerate.)

Didier Bertrand sells his cakes at the Port-Royal market, 5th arrondissement.

Flan aux Marrons | Chestnut Cake

MAKES 6 SERVINGS

During late fall, Parisians fall into *marron* mania. Chestnuts appear everywhere—in soups, in vegetable dishes, in sauces for game, and, naturally, in desserts. When I was given this recipe for chestnut cake, I was told to use fresh roasted chestnuts. There's nothing like the aroma of chestnuts roasting at home, but quite frankly, removing chestnuts from their thin shells and skins is an enormous task to undertake. I use sweetened chestnut purée. The flan consists of a thin, flaky outer crust and a dense chestnut filling.

1 cup all-purpose flour

¼ cup sugar

⅛ teaspoon salt, plus a pinch

5 tablespoons chilled unsalted butter, cut into bits

4 large eggs

2 tablespoons heavy cream

One 8¾-ounce can sweetened puréed chestnuts

1¼ cups whole milk

Crème fraîche or sour cream for serving

1. Combine the flour, sugar, ⅛ teaspoon salt, and the butter in a mixer bowl and mix at medium speed until the mixture resembles coarse meal. Add 1 of the eggs and the cream and mix until the dough begins to form a mass. Remove the dough from the mixer and roll into a disk. Cover and chill in the refrigerator for 45 minutes.

2. When the dough is chilled, roll it out on a floured surface to a 12-inch circle. Line a 9-inch springform mold or cake pan with the pastry; it should come about 2 inches up the side of the pan. Replace in the freezer while you make the filling.

3. Preheat the oven to 375°F.

4. Separate the remaining 3 eggs. In a large mixing bowl, mix the chestnut purée with the yolks, then stir in the milk. Set the mixture aside. In another bowl, add the pinch of salt to the egg whites and whisk them until stiff peaks form. Scrape the egg whites onto the chestnut mixture, then gently fold together.

continued

5. Remove the dough-lined pan from the freezer and pour the chestnut filling into it. Using the tip of a small knife, gently pull the excess pastry (higher than the depth of the filling) away from the sides of the pan. This excess pastry will then naturally fall onto the chestnut filling during baking.

6. Place the cake pan on the middle rack of the oven and bake for 30 to 35 minutes, or until the center of the cake is firm and the pastry is golden. Remove the flan from the oven and let cool completely before unmolding. Serve crème fraîche on the side.

LES CAKES

Crème fraîche

FABRICATION

Gâteau de Crêpes au Chocolat Amer

Bitter Chocolate Crêpe Cake

MAKES 8 TO 10 SERVINGS

This is an astonishingly dense confection, a cake of sixteen thin layers of yeast-risen crêpes and chocolate truffle filling. The preparation is a bit time-consuming, but the cake can be prepared in stages. The crêpes can be made up to a day in advance and stored, wrapped in plastic wrap, at room temperature. The cake should be assembled at least eight hours, or up to a day, in advance of serving. I used a $7\frac{1}{2}$-inch skillet for my crêpes and assembled the layers in an 8-inch round cake pan. The reserved chocolate filled the perimeter gap. If it turns out that you have to assemble the layers in a cake pan that's exactly the size of the crêpes, you can cover the sides with chocolate once you have unmolded the cake from the mold.

8 ounces bittersweet chocolate

8 ounces semisweet chocolate, chopped

1 cup heavy cream

8 tablespoons (1 stick) unsalted butter

1 $\frac{1}{2}$ cups whole milk

$\frac{1}{4}$ cup unsweetened cocoa powder

2 tablespoons instant coffee, preferably espresso powder

$\frac{1}{4}$ cup sugar

1 package active dry yeast

1 cup all-purpose flour

2 large eggs, beaten

Crème fraîche for serving

1. Place both chocolates, the cream, and 6 tablespoons of the butter in the top of a double boiler over simmering water and melt the chocolate and butter. Mix the contents of the double boiler well, remove from the heat, and set aside.

2. Combine the milk, cocoa, instant coffee, sugar, and the remaining 2 tablespoons butter in a pan, bring to a boil, and immediately remove from the heat. Let the milk cool until it's comfortable to poke your finger in it, and dissolve the yeast in the milk mixture. Place the flour in a large mixing bowl and slowly pour in the warm milk, stirring constantly to form a batter. Cover and set in a warm place for 30 minutes, or until the batter is bubbling.

3. Mix the beaten eggs into the batter. Heat a 7½-inch skillet over medium heat. Pour in 3 tablespoons of the batter and tilt the skillet in a circular motion to distribute the batter evenly. Cook the crêpe until the surface is dry and the edges detach from the rim of the skillet, a minute or less. Flip the crêpe, let cook for about 30 seconds more, and quickly remove it from the skillet to a plate. Repeat until all the batter is used, stacking the crêpes. You should have 8 crêpes.

4. Line an 8-inch round cake pan with plastic wrap. Remove ½ cup of the chocolate mixture and reserve in the refrigerator. Ladle 6 tablespoons of the warm chocolate mixture into the cake pan and tilt to cover the bottom evenly. Place a crêpe on the chocolate. Continue layering the chocolate and the remaining crêpes, but do not cover the last crêpe with chocolate. Place the pan in the refrigerator until the chocolate is set, at least 6 hours.

5. Turn the cake out onto a cake plate and remove the cake pan and plastic wrap. Rewarm the reserved chocolate in a double boiler. If the sides of the cake are not completely covered with chocolate, pour the melted chocolate down the sides to cover them; otherwise, pour the chocolate over the top and tilt the cake to distribute it evenly. Replace in the refrigerator to set the new layer of chocolate, about 30 minutes.

6. Remove the cake from the refrigerator 1 hour before serving. Accompany with crème fraîche.

Gâteau "Pouding" au Chocolat
Flourless Chocolate Cake

This cake has a truly puddinglike texture, and the most intense chocolate flavor of any chocolate cake I've tasted. It's completely easy to prepare and is one of the most forgiving cake recipes I've come across. The only advice I need to give you is to beat the eggs until they are an airy light yellow cloud.

*Unsalted butter and all-purpose flour
for preparing the cake pan*
*10 ounces unsweetened chocolate,
chopped into bits*
1 cup brewed espresso

8 tablespoons (1 stick) unsalted butter
½ cup sugar
4 large eggs
Cocoa powder for dusting

1. Preheat the oven to 350°F. Butter and flour a deep 7-inch fluted tube pan and set aside.

2. Place the chocolate, espresso, butter, and sugar in the top of a double boiler over simmering water and heat until the chocolate and butter are melted, stirring a few times, about 10 minutes. Remove from the heat and keep the chocolate mixture warm in the top of the double boiler.

3. Meanwhile, in a large bowl, beat the eggs at medium-high speed until they are thick and pale and have quadrupled in volume. (If you have one, use a mixer fitted with a balloon whisk.)

4. Turn the speed to medium-low, pour in the melted chocolate, and mix until incorporated.

5. Pour the batter into the prepared pan, place in the center of the oven, and bake for 40 to 45 minutes, or until the top cracks. The cake should be slightly undercooked in the center, so a toothpick inserted in the center should come out slightly moist.

6. Let the cake cool for 30 minutes before unmolding; then let cool completely. Sprinkle with cocoa powder before serving.

Gâteau Breton | Brittany-Style Cake

The simple charm of this plain cake may be lost on anyone looking for a sumptuous frosted cake. But for those people who prefer the richness of butter and eggs to the cloying sweetness of sugar icings, this cake will become a standard.

Unsalted butter and all-purpose flour
   for preparing the pan
1 tablespoon active dry yeast
1/4 cup milk
1/3 cup hazelnuts, toasted
   and skinned
1 1/2 cups all-purpose flour
1 tablespoon cornstarch
1/2 teaspoon ground mace

1/4 teaspoon salt
1 cup sugar
1/2 pound (2 sticks) unsalted butter,
   at room temperature
2 large eggs
2 large egg yolks
1/4 cup dark rum or Madeira
1 tablespoon grated lemon zest
1/2 teaspoon vanilla extract

1. Preheat the oven to 350°F. Butter and flour a 9-inch round cake pan with 1½-inch-high sides and set aside.

2. Dissolve the yeast in 2 tablespoons of the milk and set aside.

3. Finely grind the nuts in a food processor. Place the flour, cornstarch, ground nuts, mace, salt, sugar, and butter in a mixer bowl and mix until smooth. One by one, add the whole eggs, 1 of the yolks, the rum, yeast mixture, lemon zest, and vanilla, mixing on low speed until blended. Transfer the batter to the prepared pan, smoothing the top with a spatula.

4. Mix the remaining 2 tablespoons milk with the remaining egg yolk and brush the surface of the batter with this glaze. Draw the tines of a fork across the top of the cake in a crisscross pattern. Place the cake on the middle rack of the oven and bake until just firm to the touch, about 20 minutes. Remove the cake from the oven and cool for 30 minutes before unrolling. (This can be made a day in advance and kept tightly wrapped at room temperature; do not refrigerate.)

Gâteau de Riz au Lait

Rice Pudding Cake

MAKES 8 TO 10 SERVINGS

Personally, I'm used to a messy rice pudding, a pile of warm rice custard served in a bowl with heavy cream. So, I was surprised to find that in this recipe, the rice pudding keeps a form. You see, when the partially cooked rice is baked with warm milk and eggs, it sinks to the bottom of the cake pan and forms a cakelike layer. The caramelized sugar bubbles up around the sides, staining the outside of this gâteau a beautiful mahogany color.

2 tablespoons plus 1 teaspoon
   unsalted butter

²/₃ cup Arborio rice

1 quart whole milk

½ teaspoon freshly grated nutmeg

⅛ teaspoon ground cinnamon

½ teaspoon vanilla extract

Grated zest of 3 lemons

¾ cup sugar

3 large eggs, beaten

3 tablespoons water

Crème fraîche or whipped cream
   for serving

1. Preheat the oven to 350°F. Butter a 7- to 8-inch 2-inch-deep round cake pan with 1 teaspoon of the butter and set aside.

2. Combine the remaining 2 tablespoons butter, the rice, milk, nutmeg, cinnamon, vanilla, lemon zest, and ½ cup of the sugar in a 2-quart pot, place over medium heat, and cook for 15 minutes. (If the contents of the pot come to a full boil, lower the heat to keep the milk at a low simmer.) Remove from the heat and let the mixture cool for 10 minutes. Beat in the eggs and set the mixture aside.

3. Combine the remaining ¼ cup sugar and the water in a small saucepan, place over medium-high heat, and cook until the sugar melts and turns a dark caramel color. Immediately pour the caramel into the center of the prepared cake pan. Do not worry if it doesn't cover the bottom of the pan, as it will dissolve and spread during baking.

4. Pour the rice mixture into the cake pan and give it a few gentle shakes to distribute the rice evenly. Carefully transfer the cake pan to the top rack of the oven and bake for 35 to 40 minutes, or until the surface shows some golden areas and the center is just set. Remove the cake pan from the oven and let cool to room temperature.

5. To unmold, place a plate over the cake pan and invert the plate and pan. Give a few gentle taps to the bottom of the cake pan and carefully remove it from the cake. Place another plate over the cake and invert the plates to turn the cake right side up again. Serve the cake warm or at room temperature and accompany with crème fraîche.

Giselle Rummel in her kitchen

Choux Chantilly | Cream Puffs

The idea of cream puffs always evokes feelings in me of decadence, indulgence, and somehow furtive pleasures. Perhaps it's because they are so innocent in appearance, white as a bride, that the pleasure of eating them seems like an act of violation. I love them for these reasons and also because they are not iced or frosted—not gilded in any way whatsoever. There's simply the crusty, eggy *choux* and the ever-so-slightly sweet whipped cream that, invariably, squishes out when you're hoping to seem sophisticated and polite.

1 cup water	*4 large eggs*
⅛ teaspoon salt	*1 cup heavy cream*
2 tablespoons sugar	*½ teaspoon vanilla extract*
5 tablespoons unsalted butter	*3 tablespoons confectioners' sugar*
1 cup all-purpose flour	*3 tablespoons sour cream*

1. Preheat the oven to 400°F. Very lightly grease 2 cookie sheets with unsalted butter.

2. Bring the water, salt, sugar and butter to a boil in a deep saucepan. When the butter is melted, immediately remove from the heat. Pour in the flour all at once and mix well with a wooden spoon. Return the saucepan to medium heat and cook, stirring, to dry the mixture, about 2 minutes. The mixture is ready when it begins to form a ball and pulls away from the sides of the saucepan. Remove from the heat. Add 1 of the eggs and mix to incorporate completely. Repeat until all the eggs are incorporated. (You can accomplish this in a mixer.)

3. Drop generous tablespoons of the batter onto the cookie sheets, making 16 mounds and leaving about 2 inches between each one. If the mounds are not smooth, use a damp pastry brush or wet the back of a spoon to smooth the tops and gather in any unwanted drips of batter. Place the cookie sheets in the oven and turn the oven down to 350°F. Bake until the *choux* are puffed and dark golden on all surfaces, about 20 to 25 minutes. Turn off the oven, prop the door open with a wooden spoon, and let the *choux* dry for 5 minutes before removing from the oven. Place the *choux* on a rack to cool. When the *choux* have cooled, halve each one crosswise and gently remove and discard any damp center dough.

4. No more than 2 hours before serving, place the cream in a chilled bowl with the vanilla and whip until stiff. Gently mix in 2 tablespoons of the confectioners' sugar and the sour cream. Keep the whipped cream covered and chilled in the refrigerator.

5. No more than 20 minutes before serving, generously fill the bottom halves of the *choux* with the whipped cream and pose the top half of each on top. Sprinkle with the remaining 1 tablespoon confectioners' sugar just before serving.

Pound cake is baked in large round pans and sold by the piece.

Quatre-Quarts | Pound Cake

Parisians who bake always seem to keep this pound cake in the house to serve with morning coffee, or with tea in the afternoon, or to accompany fresh berries of fruit compote for dinner.

Unsalted butter and all-purpose flour
  for preparing the cake pan
5 large eggs
1²⁄₃ cups sugar
Grated zest of 1 lemon
¹⁄₈ teaspoon salt

¹⁄₈ teaspoon ground mace
¹⁄₈ teaspoon ground cardamom
2 cups cake flour
¹⁄₂ pound (2 sticks) unsalted butter,
  at room temperature

1. Preheat the oven to 350°F. Butter and flour a 7-inch square or round cake pan and set aside.

2. In a large bowl, beat the eggs with a mixer on medium-high speed until they have nearly quadrupled in volume and are pale and thick. With the mixer on medium speed, add the sugar, lemon zest, salt, mace, and cardamom, then slowly add the flour. Add the butter and continue to mix until incorporated.

3. Pour the batter into the prepared cake pan. Place on the middle rack of the oven and bake for 50 minutes, or until a knife or toothpick inserted into the center of the cake comes out clean. Let the cake cool for 15 minutes before turning it out onto a wire rack.

4. Serve the cake plain, or accompany with crème fraîche, ice cream, or fruit macerated in Grand Marnier or other liqueur.

Index